Charles Wordsworth

On Shakespeare's Knowledge and Use of the Bible

Charles Wordsworth

On Shakespeare's Knowledge and Use of the Bible

ISBN/EAN: 9783337063146

Printed in Europe, USA, Canada, Australia, Japan

Cover: Foto ©Thomas Meinert / pixelio.de

More available books at **www.hansebooks.com**

SHAKSPEARE

AND

THE BIBLE.

'I commend my Soul into the hands of GOD, my Creator; hoping and assuredly believing, through the only merits of JESUS CHRIST, my Saviour, to be made partaker of life everlasting; and my Body to the earth, whereof that is made.'

SHAKSPEARE'S WILL.

ON

HAKSPEARE'S KNOWLEDGE

AND USE OF THE BIBLE.

BY

CHARLES WORDSWORTH, D.C.L.

BISHOP OF ST. ANDREWS.

'I will preach to thee; mark me!'—KING LEAR.

'Meliùs Chrysippo et Crantore.'—HORACE.

LONDON:

SMITH, ELDER, & CO., 65 CORNHILL.

1864.

TO

MY CHILDREN:

IN THE HOPE AND WITH THE AIM

THAT THEY MAY GROW UP READERS AND LOVERS

OF

SHAKSPEARE

AS

THE BOOK OF MAN;

BUT, STILL MORE, READERS AND LOVERS

OF

THE BIBLE

AS

THE WORD OF GOD.

PREFACE.

 am not aware that the attempt made in this small volume has been anticipated in any other. Even the notes of critics upon Shakspeare, superfluously full in pointing out his obligations, real or supposed, to secular authors, are singularly meagre in the references which they make to the Holy Scriptures. And yet how abundant is the room for such reference, and how much it may conduce to the mutual illustration of the two books, which as Christians and as Britons we should value most, will be seen, I trust, upon every page of the Second Part of the following dissertation.

With regard to the former and very much shorter Part, I must confess that it scarcely comes within the title and proper scope of my design; and that it will be found to contain little which can be new or interesting to older and more advanced readers; who may, therefore, if they think fit, pass it over: but to the young, for whom the volume is principally intended, I trust it may prove useful; and I was unwilling to miss the opportunity of giving *them* information which may help to improve their knowledge of their own language and at the same time enable them to understand better, and so to read with greater profit and pleasure, both their Bible and their Shakspeare—but especially the former.

In selecting the quotations which will be found in the following pages, and in arranging them systematically, no use has been made of any previous compilation: I have trusted solely to my own complete perusal and study of our great poet, with the particular objects which I have mentioned constantly in view, and with the additional motive of doing him a justice, which he has not yet fully received, ever present to my mind. On some accounts, indeed, I could have wished that my labours had been less independent; but such as they are, they are presented to the reader, in the hope that they may give him some portion of the pleasure which I have derived from them myself. In the meantime, I am fully conscious that the available material for both Parts of the work is far from being exhausted. As regards the latter Part, some handfuls at least, I doubt not, still remain to be gleaned in the same extensive field; while the former Part contains little more than a specimen of the ore which the same mine, if thoroughly worked, might be made to produce.

'The Bible and Shakspeare,' said one of the best and most esteemed prelates that ever sat upon the English bench—Dr. John Sharp, in the reign of Queen Anne—'The Bible and Shakspeare have made me Archbishop of York.' The Shakspeare of Greek Comedy—Aristophanes—is well known to have been the favourite author of the most celebrated preacher of the ancient church, S. John Chrysostom, some time patriarch of Constantinople. Under the shelter of high and venerated authorities such as these the present writer ventures to hope he may escape censure for allowing his name to appear upon the title-page of this volume. He had intended to put it forth anonymously, but his intention has been overruled by the publishers.

CONTENTS.

CHAPTER II.

Of Shakspeare's Religious Principles and Sentiments derived from the Bible 87

CHAPTER III.

Of the Poetry of Shakspeare as derived from the Bible 261

SHAKSPEARE'S KNOWLEDGE AND USE OF THE BIBLE.

GENERAL INTRODUCTION.

MUCH has been said and written on the learning of Shakspeare. How far the greatest genius of modern times was indebted to the storehouse of antiquity; whether or no he was altogether

> Untutored in the lore of Greece or Rome,

is a question which a hundred years ago was agitated among men of letters with intense interest. But neither in the course of that controversy, nor at any other time, has the enquiry, I believe, been raised to which I purpose in these pages to offer a reply; viz., how far Shakspeare was conversant with Holy Scripture, and whether or no he made use of his knowledge of the Bible to guide and assist him in the production of his immortal works. When I

say that this enquiry is a new one, I do not mean
that our poet's acquaintance with Scripture has altogether escaped the notice of every one of his numerous commentators ; for such is not the case :* and
had it been so, my undertaking might well be suspected of too great and too presumptuous a singu-
larity to warrant an expectation of its usefulness and
sobriety. All I would imply is that Shakspeare has
not yet received the credit, which I think I shall be
able to prove that he deserves, of having been, in a
more than ordinary degree, a diligent and a devout
reader of the Word of God; and that he has turned
this reading to far more and far better account than
any of his critics would seem to have suspected, or
at all events has yet attempted to point out.   His
marvellous knowledge of the Book of Nature is admitted on all hands : his knowledge of the Book of
Grace, though far less noticed, will be found, I believe, to have been scarcely less remarkable.   His
works have been called ' a secular Bible : ' my object is to show that while they are this, they are
also *something more*, being saturated with Divine
Wisdom, such as could have been derived only from
the very Bible itself.

And I enter upon my task with keener interest
and heartier zeal upon two accounts ; first, because

---

* For instance, I observe in Mr. Singer's edition of 1826 the
following note : — ' It has been remarked that Shakspeare was habi-
tually conversant with his Bible.'—Vol. v. p. 464.

I trust I shall be paying a duteous service to the memory of this great man, whom every Briton should delight to honour, by removing an imputation which has been (I am persuaded) hastily and inconsiderately cast upon him, as though he had, in some instances, designed to treat the Inspired Word with profaneness ; * and secondly, because, if it shall appear (as I doubt not it will) that a genius so incomparable was content to study, and rot unfrequently to draw his inspiration from the pages of Holy Scripture, submitting his reason to the mysterious doctrines which it reveals, and his conscience to the moral lessons which it prescribes ; it may be hoped that no one of my readers will consider it beneath him to follow an example, set by an authority so highly, so justly, and so universally esteemed.

'He was indeed *honest*,' says his friend Ben Jonson, 'and of an open and free nature.'† Upon such unquestionable testimony, it is pleasant to be permitted to think of our greatest poet, as one 'who in an *honest* and good heart, having heard the Word, kept it, and brought forth fruit with patience.' That he brought forth fruit—immortal fruit—to the glory of God and the benefit of mankind, no one can deny. Nor is there any conflicting record to prevent us from believing that the tenor of his life,

---

* See Mr. Boswell's Advertisement to the Variorum edition of Shakspeare, 1821, p. 8.

† *Ibid.* vol. i. p. 449.

especially in his later years, was in conformity with the confession of his death as exhibited in his will ;* unless indeed we are to admit two of his sonnets as evidence against himself, which if they prove him at one time to have yielded to the temptations with which he was beset, prove him also to have possessed afterwards the spirit of a true penitent. Of his personal history, all that is now known may be soon told. He was born in the year 1564, at Stratford-upon-Avon in Warwickshire, the eldest son of eight children, his father being a glover of that town ; and he died at his native place (whither he had retired in comfortable circumstances some years before) in 1616, when he was only in his fifty-third year. He married very young, before he was nineteen, a lady of the name of Hathaway, eight years older than himself, by whom he had two daughters and one son ; and who survived him seven years ; dying in 1623, at the age of sixty-seven. In that same year appeared the first edition of his collected plays, thirty-six in number, which are generally allowed to be genuine; though not more than fourteen or sixteen had been published in his lifetime, including *Titus Andronicus* and *Pericles, Prince of Tyre.* And there seems no reason to doubt that a great portion of what he wrote was composed, if not under the actual pressure of want, yet in a condition

---

* On the contrary, see two other contemporaneous testimonies to his ' honest ' character in Malone's Life, p. 280, *sq.*, and p. 284.

of life very unfavorable to carefulness and maturity of composition.

Whatever blemishes there may have been in the character of the first Scottish sovereign who sat upon the throne of England, it is only just to bear in mind that we owe to him, under the good Providence of God, that inestimable work, the translation* of the Bible which we all use; and moreover that to him we owe also the satisfaction which we must all feel when we learn that the best of uninspired writers was not without royal encouragement. Detract what we may from the merit of King James, on the score of pedantry, or of disingenuousness, the facts will remain, which, considering the subject I have now in hand, I rejoice to mention in his praise, and to interweave, as among the brightest ornaments of his crown—that he wrote to William Shakspeare a letter of commendation with his own hand,† and that he gave ' special command ' for the publication of the Scriptures in the revised and improved form, which Shakspeare and his contemporaries were the first to read.

Our great poet, then, and our translators of the Bible lived and flourished at the same time, and under the same reign. This is an interesting fact in the enquiry upon which we are about to enter, and suggests the propriety of dividing it into two

---

* First published in 1611.
† See Variorum Shakspeare, vol. i. p. 467, and vol. ii. p. 481.

parts. That is, we may not only seek to illustrate the subject-matter of the Bible by comparison with passages in Shakspeare which prove his knowledge and study of the Scriptures; but we may explain the language also by parallels which Shakspeare will afford us of the use of words and phrases (not indeed necessarily derived from the Bible, only or chiefly, but commonly current at that time) which have since undergone a change of meaning or become altogether obsolete. And upon this branch of the subject it will be natural to enter first.

PORCH OF TRINITY CHURCH, STRATFORD-ON-AVON.

PART I.

TRINITY CHURCH, STRATFORD-ON-AVON.

CHAPTER I.

Of noticeable Forms of Speech in the English Bible found also in Shakspeare.

N order to deal fairly with this former part of our investigation, it is necessary to remark, in the first instance, that, while the contents and general language of the Bible would be known to our poet from translations previously in use, in regard to particular words and modes of speech, it is probable that our translators of 1611 owed as much, or more, to Shakspeare than he owed to them. According to the chronological order of our poet's plays, as determined by Mr. Malone, only two of them were written after 1611; all the rest having been composed in the interval between that year and 1591. And the Bibles most commonly used during that period were either Parker's, called also the Bishops' Bible, of 1568, required to be read in churches; or various reprints of the Genevan Bible of 1560, with short marginal notes, and much used in private families (a translation which was due in

part to John Knox, while resident abroad); or the version by the Roman Catholics of the New Testament, published at Rheims in 1582, and of the whole Bible at Douay in 1609.

With this explanation, we may now proceed to the portion of our task which lies first before us, taking up whatever is noticeable in the use of the several parts of speech in their natural order.

1. To begin then with the use of *the Articles, definite and indefinite.*

In Acts xxii. 4, we read, as spoken by St. Paul, 'I persecuted this way unto *the death.*' There is no article in the original Greek, and yet in English it has been retained from the translation of Wickliff in 1380 to the present hour. The apostle does not mean any particular death, and therefore, as Bp. Lowth observed a century ago, in his *Short Introduction to English Grammar*, p. 31, the definite article is improperly used in our version of the text. The same inaccuracy occurs also in 2 Chron. xxxii. 24. 'In those days Hezekiah was sick *to the death,*' where there is no article in the Septuagint. And again in Revelation xii. 11. ' They loved not their lives unto *the death* ' (ἀχρὶ θανάτου), which has come down not from Wickliff, like the passage in the Acts, but from Tyndale, 1534. The expression which we meet with in S. Matt. xv. 4, and S. Mark vii. 10, and which is derived to us from Cranmer's Translation of 1539, ' He that curseth father or mother let him *die the death,*' is to be traced no doubt to the same origin, and involves a still further deviation from the sense of the original, which is literally 'let him die by death' (θανάτῳ τελευτάτω), and means, according to a Hebrew idiom, 'Let him *certainly* die.' And so we read in Levit. xx. 9, where the Septuagint has the same Greek words, 'he shall *surely* be put to death.' But now to turn to Shakspeare. He has several times used the expression 'to die the death;' e. g. in *Measure for Measure*, Act ii. Sc. 4 ; in *Cymbeline*, Act iv. Sc. 2, and again in *Midsummer Night's Dream*, Act i. Sc. 1, where in reply to Hermia's question what is to befall her in case she refuses to marry Demetrius, Theseus says :—

> Either to *die the death*, or to abjure
> For ever the society of man.

There can be little doubt that our poet took the phrase (as Steevens * observes) from the Bible ; but whether he attached the right meaning to it we cannot tell. Dr. Johnson, with less accuracy than might have been expected from him, remarks † that 'this seems to be a solemn phrase for *death inflicted by law.*' The simple form of expression, as first cited from the Acts, 'the death,' is to be found frequently in Chaucer, e. g.

> *The deth* he feeleth through his herte smite.
> *Cant. Tales*, v. 1222.

---

* Vol. ix. p. 92.   † *Ibid.*

Tyrwhitt has suggested that it seems to have been originally a mistaken translation of the French *la mort*. Shakspeare has it in *King Richard II*. Act iii. Sc. 1. ' This and much more condemns you to *the death*,' and again in *King Henry V*. Act iv. Sc. 1, ' Where they feared *the death*, they have borne life away.' Altogether the usage is a curious one. Chaucer, *Cant. Tales*, v. 1135, uses ' the peine ' in the same way.

2. The use of the *Indefinite Article* prefixed to plural substantives, especially nouns of number, is also one which admits of similar illustration.   In S. Luke ix. 28, we read, ' It came to pass about an eight days after these sayings.'   The questionable expression ' *an eight* days ' has been retained from Tyndale's translation in 1534.   In like manner we find in the Apocryphal Book, 1 Macc. iv. 15, ' There were slain of them upon *a three thousand* men.'   The same use of the indefinite article is to be met with more than once in Shakspeare.   Thus in *King Richard III*. Act iii. Sc. 7, Buckingham describes Lady Grey, afterwards married to King Edward IV., as

A care-crazed mother to *a many* sons.

See also *Merchant of Venice*, Act iii. Sc. 5.

3. To pass on from the article to the *Noun*.   I am not aware that our translators of the Bible afford any example of an anomaly, or, to speak more plainly, a false concord, not unfrequent in Shak-

speare,* whereby plural substantives are constructed as if singular, except in the single case of the word ' means,' which, partly perhaps on account of the biblical authority in its favour, is so employed to the present day. ' We certify the king,' write the adversaries of the Jews in the Book of Ezra iv. 16, 'that if this city be builded again . . . . by *this* means thou shalt have no portion on this side the river.' Johnson, under the word ' mean,' remarks, ' It is often used in the plural, and by some not very grammatically with an adjective singular, as " by *this* means." ' † Shakspeare seems to use the plural of this word indifferently both as singular and plural.

In like manner the two nouns of similar meaning, ' tidings' and ' news,' are used by our poet as of both numbers. Thus we find in him, ' It is *a* tidings,' and '*this* tidings,' as well as ' *these* tidings;' also, ' *This* news *is* mortal,' and ' *These* news *are* everywhere.' In the Bible we have ' these news,' 1 Kings i. title, and ' so *is* good news,' Prov. xxv. 25 ; but ' tidings' occurs only as plural, e. g. ' these glad tidings,' Luke i. 19.

4. The formation of our genitive case, originally by the addition of the syllable ' is,' as ' God*is*

---

* As ' our remedies . . . . lies ' in *Romeo and Juliet*, ii. 3 ; ' manners urges,' in *King Lear*, v. 3. See the critics upon *Cymbeline*, ii. 3.—Vol. viii. p. 71.

† See also *Lowth*, p. 34, note.

grace,' afterwards shortened into the letter 's' with an apostrophe, as ' God's grace,' has led to a corruption with which our printers seem most unwilling to part. I mean the transformation of ' is ' into ' his.' Thus in Gen. xvii. title, ' Abram *his* name ' and ' Sarah *her* name;' Deut x. title, 'Moses *his* suit;' S. Mark v. title, 'Jairus *his* daughter,' *Ibid.* x. title, 'Bartimæus *his* sight.' And it is a curious instance of the arbitrariness or incomplete accuracy which is apt to prevail in such matters, that while these three examples (and perhaps others) of the corruption in question are allowed still to remain in our Bible, two other examples which Bishop Lowth pointed out, viz. ' Asa *his* heart,' 1 Kings xv. 14, and ' Mordecai *his* matters,' Esth. iii. 4, have been set right. The same usage occurs at the end of the *Prayer for all conditions of men* in the Prayer Book. ' And this we beg for Jesus Christ *His* sake.' In the Variorum Shakspeare I have noticed six examples; all, except one, after words ending in *s*: three in *King Henry VI. 1st Part*, one in *King Henry V.*, and one in *Troilus and Cressida*. It is not a little remarkable that so great a master of the English language as Addison, and at a date so late as 1711, should have been under the impression that ' his ' in these cases is correct, and intended to represent the pronoun. See *Spectator*, No. 135. If this were so, how could we account for our genitives plural, as ' children's bread,' and genitives singular of females or feminine

names, as ' Persia's king ? ' See Lowth's *Grammar*,
p. 42, note ; who further observes that ' the direct
derivation of this case from the Saxon genitive is
sufficient of itself to decide the matter.' In one of
the three examples in *King Henry VI.*, Bowdler has
very improperly altered the text ' France *his* sword'
into ' France's sword,' not considering, probably,
that France is there to be understood not of the
country, but of the French king. If the alteration is
to be made in one instance, it should be made in all.

5. Proceeding to the *Pronouns*, I notice first the
elliptic use of the dative case of the pronouns of the
first person, ' me,' ' us,' instead of ' for me,' ' for us ;'
as in 2 Sam. xix. 26, ' I will saddle *me* an ass,'. and
in Josh. xxii. 26, ' Let us now prepare to build *us*
an altar.' The same is found also in the pronouns
of the second and third persons, as in Deut. x. 1,
' Make *thee* an ark,' and again in the same verse,
' Hew *thee* two tables of stone ;' in Josh. xxii. 16, ' Ye
have builded *you* an altar ;' in Kings xiii. 27, ' So
they saddled *him* the ass,' and Judges vi. 2, ' The
children of Israel made *them* the dens which are in
the mountains.' Examples of the first of these
usages are not unfrequent in Shakspeare.* Thus,
Shylock in the *Merchant of Venice* :—

> Go with me to a notary; seal *me* there
> Your single bond.   Act i. Sc. 3.

---

* It is also classical, as in *Horace* : —
Quid *mihi* Celsus agit ?

In *Othello*, Act i. Sc. 1 : —

Whip *me* such honest knaves.

And in *King Henry IV.*, Falstaff especially is fond of the usage.* Doubtless examples occur also in our poet of both the second and third personal pronouns similarly used; but I have marked down only these that follow, of the second person—none of the third.

In *King John*, Act iii. Sc. 4, Pandulf says :—

John lays *you* plots.

In *Hamlet*, Act v. Sc. 1, the grave-digger: —

He will last *you* some eight year or nine year,—

an idiom with which we are now quite familiar. The ambiguity to which such a manner of speaking may give rise, has been taken advantage of in the humorous scene between Petruchio and his servant Grumio at the door of Hortensio, in *Taming of the Shrew* :—

Petruchio. Here, sirrah Grumio; knock, I say.
Grumio. Knock, sir? Whom should I knock? Is there any man has *rebused* your worship?
Petruchio. Villain, I say, knock me here soundly.
Grumio. Knock you here, sir? Why, what am I, sir, that I should knock you here, sir?
Petruchio. Villain, I say, knock *me* at this gate,
And rap *me* well, or I'll knock your knave's pate. Act i. Sc. 2.

---

* Mr. Wise, in his elegant volume upon *Shakspeare and his Birthplace*, gives other instances, and speaks of it as an idiom still used in Warwickshire, p. 112, *sq.*

6. Formerly ' it,' the pronoun of the third person, besides borrowing the form ' thereof ' to supply the possessive case, was indebted for its declension to the pronouns of the second and third person, and instead of *its*, *his* and *hers* were used with reference to a thing * spoken of. Thus in Joshua iv. 18, ' The waters of Jordan returned unto their place, and flowed over all *his* banks, as they did before.' In S. Matthew xxvi. 52, ' Put up thy sword again into *his* place.' In Haggai ii. 3, ' ' Who is left among you that saw this house in *her* first glory ? ' These examples † are sufficient to prove that our poet was guilty of no vulgarity, as then considered, when he put into the mouth of Cæsar the following words addressed to Antony :—

> Let me lament
> That thou, my brother, my competitor,
> The arm of mine own body, and the heart
> Where mine *his* thoughts did kindle—
> *Antony and Cleopatra* Act v. Sc. 1.

---

* Since the above was written, I observe that Dean Alford, in his *Plea for the Queen's English*, ascribes this idiom to ' a reluctance to attribute personality to things without life.' For my own part, I should ascribe it to the very opposite reason, viz. a desire to personify *everything*; which desire prevails in the earlier and simpler stages of society and consequently of language. Compare the use of *who* for *which*; see below p. 18. The Dean informs us that ' *its* ' never occurs in the English version of the Bible, and that it is said only to occur three times in *Shakspeare*, and once in *Paradise Lost*. See *Good Words* for 1863, p. 192.

† See also Exod. xxxvii. 17; Acts xii. 10; Rev. xxii. 2, quoted by Dean Alford. Gen. i. 11; Ps. liv. 7, quoted in Mr. Booker's *Glossary*.

But it is curious that our translator of the Apocryphal Book of *Ecclesiasticus* should have so far differed at once from Shakspeare, and from himself,
as to make ' the heart' not masculine, but first feminine and then neuter, as he does in xxii. 19, 'He
that pricketh the heart maketh *it* to show *her*
knowledge.'

We find another example in the same play, where
Euphronius says to Cæsar :—

> Such as I am, I come from Antony:
> I was of late as petty to his ends,
> As is the morn dew on the myrtle leaf
> To *his* grand sea.   Act iii. Sc. 10.

The explanation of Steevens that by 'his' we
are to understand ' its,' is, I believe, the true one.

7. We know that the neuter of the relative
pronoun, *which*, was formerly used as masculine, or
feminine ; as in ' Our father *which* art in heaven,'
where we should now say 'who.'   Again, in Gen.
xviii. 27, 'Behold now, I have taken upon me to
speak unto the Lord, *which* am but dust and ashes.'
In Matt. xxvii. 55, 56, we have ' which ' for both
' who' and ' whom : '—' And many women were
there beholding afar off, *which* followed Jesus from
Galilee ministering unto him, among *which* was
Mary Magdalene,' &c.   Both usages are to be met
with in Shakspeare.   Thus in the *Tempest*, Act iii.
Sc. 1, Ferdinand says ' The mistress *which* I serve,'
and in *King Richard III.* Gloster, the future king,
to Prince Edward : —

Those uncles *which* you want, were dangerous.
Act iii. Sc. 1.

On the other hand we find in Shakspeare, though not, so far as I have noted, in our translation of the Bible, the use of ' who ' for ' which : ' as in the *Tempest*, Act i. Sc. 2 :—

A brave vessel,
Who had, no doubt, some noble creatures in her.

And again in the same play, Act iii. Sc. 3 :—

The elements
Of *whom* your swords are tempered.

There are two other peculiarities in the use of the relative pronoun, both of which may derive illustration from the comparison upon which we are engaged. I mean the redundant insertion before the relative, of the definite article, and also of the personal pronoun. Thus, ' *the* which,' Matt. xiii. 14, and ' in *the* which,' Acts xxvi. 6, may be compared with *Coriolanus*, Act i. Sc. 1, ' Fame, àt *the* which he aims ; ' and with *Antony and Cleopatra*, Act ii. Sc. 1 :—

To lend me arms and aid, when I required them,
The which you both denied.

And as examples of the other construction which I just now named, we have in Luke iv. 34, ' I know *thee* who thou art,' and in *King Lear*, Act i. Sc. 1, ' I know *you* what you are,' and again in *King Henry VI. 3rd Part*, Act ii. Sc. 6 :—

And he nor sees, nor hears *us* what we say.

The idiom is one supposed to be borrowed from the Greek. It is certainly frequent in the ancient Greek authors, especially the tragedians.

8. There is nothing which occurs to me as calling for remark in connexion with the grammar of *Adjectives* except the use of double comparatives and superlatives. Of the former Shakspeare would seem to have been specially fond. I have noted down more than thirty examples, and among them 'more better,' also 'worser' and 'more worse,' repeated several times. 'More richer,' 'more worthier,' 'more corrupter,' and 'more worse' are all to be found in *King Lear*, one of our poet's later and more finished compositions. Double superlatives, such as 'most best,' 'most unkindest,' he has used much less frequently, i. e. in not more, I believe, than eight instances. Both these anomalies also may be considered as of Greek extraction, or at least they both occur not unfrequently in the Greek drama.* But it is somewhat remarkable that our translators of the New Testament, from Tyndale downwards, have chosen to introduce the double superlative in Acts xxvi. 5, 'after the *most straitest* sect of our religion I lived a Pharisee,' though the original Greek is content with a single one. This is the only example of a double superlative which I have observed in the English Bible;† but the older

---

* See Bishop Monk's note on the *Hippolytus* of Euripides, v. 487.
† The word 'chiefest,' however, which is in principle equally anomalous, occurs several times in both the Old and New Testament.

version of the Psalms in the Prayer Book still retains the expression 'most highest' in more than a dozen places ; where, Bp. Lowth has well remarked, 'it acquires a singular propriety from the subject to which it is applied, viz. the Supreme Being, who is *higher than the highest.*' Of the double comparative no scriptural example occurs to me except in the use of the word 'lesser,' in Gen. i. 16 ; 'The *lesser* light to rule the night,' and in three other texts. Dr. Johnson tells us that the adjective 'little' has two comparatives, 'less' and 'lesser ; ' but I am rather inclined to agree with Bp. Lowth that it is a barbarism, and that *worser* sounds much more barbarous only because it has not been so frequently used. And may not this have arisen from the fact that our translators of the Bible have accepted the one, but rejected the other ? It is Lord Macaulay who* speaks of 'our noble translation of the Bible' as 'a book from the authority of which there is no appeal, where the question is about the force of an English word.'

9. The grammar of the *Verb* presents to us little or no occasion for remark, without descending to *minutiæ* which would be felt by the general reader to be irksome, if not out of place. The remaining parts of speech, *Adverbs, Prepositions,* and *Conjunctions,* I shall also dismiss without much notice.

The *adverb* 'when' was formerly often used

---

* *History of England,* ii. 486.

with the addition of 'as' or 'that.' Thus in Matt.
i. 18, we find, '*when as* His mother Mary was
espoused to Joseph,' &c. And in *King Henry IV.
2nd Part*, '*When that* your flock, assembled by the
bell,' &c. Act iv. Sc. 2.

In 1 Tim. v. 23, 'Use a little wine for thy
stomach's sake and thy *often* infirmities,' the *adverb*
'often' is employed to represent an adjective; as
adverbs, we know, constantly are in Greek, with
the help of the article. And upon the authority of
this passage Dr. Johnson, in his Dictionary, actually
gives it as an adjective with the meaning 'frequent.'
In like manner King Lear speaks of Cordelia as
'my *sometime* daughter,' Act i. Sc. 1. And in *King
Richard III.* the same construction enables us to understand a difficult line where the Queen Elizabeth,
widow of King Edward IV., says to Richard :—

> But that *still* use of grief makes wild grief tame,
> My tongue should to thy ears not name my boys.
>
> Act iv. Sc. 4.

'Still use,' i. e., as Steevens explains it, *constant*
use. In the same way Shakspeare uses the expression 'seldom pleasure' in his 52nd Sonnet :—

> So am I as the rich, whose blessed key
> Can bring him to his sweet up-locked treasure,
> *The which* he will not every hour survey
> For blunting the fine point* of *seldom pleasure.*

i.e. for fear of blunting &c.

---

* On the sentiments, see below, Part II. ch. ii.

The separation of the two parts of which the *preposition* 'toward' is composed, by placing between them the noun which the preposition governs, is a peculiarity with which we are familiar from more than one passage in the English Bible. Thus in 1 Sam. xix. 4, Jonathan, speaking to his father Saul respecting David, says, 'His works have been *to thee-ward* very good.' And ' *to God-ward*' for ' toward God' occurs three times, viz. Exod. xviii. 19, 2 Cor. iii. 4, 1 Thess. i. 8. The counterparts to this usage in Shakspeare, are the following :—

In *King Henry VI. 1st Part*, Act iii. Sc. 3 :—

> Hark! by the sound of drum you may perceive
> Their powers are marching *unto Paris-ward.*

In *Coriolanus*, Act i. Sc. 6 :—

> As merry as when our nuptial day was done,
> And tapers burned *to bed-ward.*

Compare also ' I go *wool-ward*,' in *Love's Labour's lost*, Act v. Sc. 2.

The use of the *preposition* ' against' with reference to *time* is now become almost obsolete, yet I am not aware that we have any other word which supplies its place, and the notion which it expressed is one of frequent recurrence. Thus we read in Gen. xliii. 25, concerning the sons of Jacob, 'They made ready the present *against* Joseph came at noon.' And in Exod. vii. 15, ' The Lord said unto Moses, Get thee unto Pharaoh, in the morning ;

lo ! he goeth out unto the water, and thou shalt stand by the river's brink *against* he come.'

In *Hamlet* it occurs three times :—

> Some say that ever '*gainst* that season comes,
> Wherein our Saviour's birth is celebrated,
> This bird of dawning singeth all night long.
> Act i. Sc. 1.

> But as we often see *against* some storm,
> A silence in the heavens—[i. e. just previous to].
> Act ii. Sc. 2.

> Yea, this solidity and compound mass
> With tristful visage, as *against* the doom,
> Is thought-sick at the act.   Act iii. Sc. 4.

But so far as I have noted, it is not to be found more than thrice in all the rest of Shakspeare, viz. in *Romeo and Juliet*, Act iv. Sc. 1, '*against* thou shalt awake ;' *Midsummer Night's Dream*, Act v. Sc. 1, '*against* your nuptial ;' and in *King Richard II.* :—

> They'll talk of state, for every one doth so,
> *Against* a change.   Act iii. Sc. 4.

The *conjunction* ' because ' is used in a remarkable manner, now quite obsolete, in Matt. xx. 31, 'The multitude rebuked them *because* they should hold their peace,' where the original means 'in order that.' There is an instance of the same quoted by Bp. Lowth from Bacon's 25th Essay ; but I have not discovered any parallel to it in Shakspeare.

10. I conclude this chapter by producing a few forms of speech which, either from their peculiarity,

or because they have now ceased to be used in the same manner, appear to deserve remark.

The letter 'a' prefixed to nouns, to adjectives, and to participles, as in the phrases to 'run *a-foot*,' to 'flee *a-pace*,' to 'be *a-hungered, a-thirst*,' to 'go *a-fishing*,' to 'lie *a-dying*,' all which are to be found in our English Bible, has given rise to much discussion and difference of opinion among our grammarians. Some of the same, and others like to these, we meet with also in Shakspeare, as 'approach *a-pace*;' 'they were *an-hungry*;' 'looked *a-squint*.' Bp. Lowth thinks that the 'a' in all such cases is the preposition 'on' a little disguised by familiar use and quick pronunciation. This is confirmed by the phrase in Acts xiii. 36, 'fell *on sleep*,' which comes down to us from Cranmer's translation, 1539, and instead of which in Acts vii. 60, that translation as well as our authorized version reads 'fell *asleep*.' Conversely, Shakspeare has in the *Tempest*, 'all *a-fire*,' for 'all on fire,' as we should now say. Forms like 'a-hungered,' may be considered as derived from verbs, after the same manner as to 'set at one' gave rise to the verb to 'atone.'* Thus, *to set on hunger* would become to *on-hunger*, and thence in the passive participle to be *on hungered, an hungered, a hungered*, and thence by corruption, *a hungry*.

'At unawares' is a remarkable phrase which both

---

* See below, ch. ii. p. 29.

Shakspeare and our translators of the Bible have used more than once. See Numbers xxxv. 11, 'The slayer . . . . which killeth any person *at unawares*,' but in verse 15 of the same chapter we read 'that killeth any person *unawares*,' without the 'at.' See also Ps. xxxv. 8, 'Let destruction come upon him *at unawares*,' and in the Apocrypha, 2 Macc. viii. 6. The examples in Shakspeare are three; two in *King Henry VI. 3rd Part* :—

> So we, well covered with the night's black mantle,
> *At unawares* may beat down Edward's guard.
> > Act iv. Sc. 2.
>
> Either betrayed by falsehood of his guard,
> Or by his foe surprised *at unawares.*   *Ibid.* Sc. 4.

And one in *Troilus and Cressida*, Act iii. Sc. 2.

The phrase 'and if,' in which *and* is redundant, occurs in 1 Cor. vii. 13, 'And the woman which hath a husband that believeth not, *and if* he be pleased to dwell with her, let her not leave him.' And again in verse 21 of the same chapter, 'But *and if* thou marry, thou hast not sinned.' So also Matt. xxiv. 48, 'But *and if* that evil servant shall say in his heart,' &c. In Shakspeare wherever the same phrase occurs the *and* is softened into *an*. Thus in *Othello* :—

> It is not lost, but what *an if* it were ?
> > Act iii. Sc. 4.

In *Two Gentlemen of Verona*, Act i. Sc. 1 :—

> Indeed a sheep doth very often stray,
> *An if* the shepherd be awhile away.

The phrase ' by and by,' as in S. Matt. xiii. 21, ' When tribulation or persecution ariseth because of the word, *by and by* he is offended ;' and again in S. Luke xxi. 9, ' The end is not *by and by*,' has gone through a considerable change since the beginning of the seventeenth century. In both those passages and in two others of the New Testament where it occurs, viz. S. Mark vi. 25, and S. Luke xvii. 7, it is used to represent a Greek word which signifies ' immediately.' And in Shakspeare it has sometimes the same meaning. Thus in *Romeo and Juliet*, Act iii. Sc. 4 :—

> It is so very late, that we
> May call it early *by and by*:—Good night.

And again in the same play, Act v. Sc. 3 :—

> Anon comes one with light to ope the tomb ;
> And *by and by* my master drew on him.

But occasionally our poet employs it more in accordance with the sense which it now bears ; as in *Hamlet*, Act v. Sc. 2 :—

> I dare not drink yet, madam ; *by and by*.

The classical reader may compare the different meanings of the Latin adverb ' maturè.'

CHAPTER II.

Of Noticeable Words in the English Bible found also in Shakspeare.

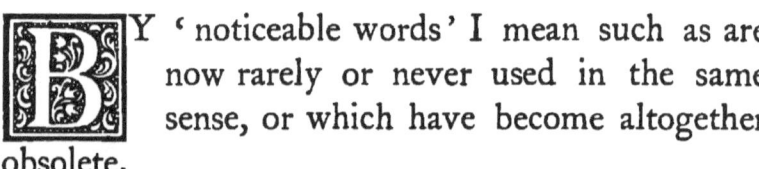Y 'noticeable words' I mean such as are now rarely or never used in the same sense, or which have become altogether obsolete.

The most convenient form into which the materials intended for this chapter can be cast will be that of a comparative glossary.

What follows forms but a portion of the author's own collection; and it is offered merely as a sample of what every reader of Shakspeare and the Bible may do for himself.

ABJECTS: once in Bible, and once in Shakspeare.

> Yea, the *abjects* gathered themselves together against me.
> > Ps. xxxv. 15.
> We are the Queen's *abjects*, and must obey.
> > *King Rich. III.* Act i. Sc. 1.

i. e. treated by her as *abjects*, or *vile persons*, rather than as *subjects* ought to be treated.

ADO ; once in Bible, frequent in Shakspeare.

> Why make ye this *ado*, and weep ? Mark v. 39.
> Make ye no more *ado*, but all embrace him.
> *King Hen. VIII.* Act v. Sc. 2.

It means *trouble, difficulty, bustle, tumult.*

ALLOW.

> That which I do, I *allow* not. Rom. vii. 15.
> Ye *allow* the deeds of your Fathers. Luke xi. 48.
> I like them all, and do *allow* them well.
> *King Hen. IV. 2nd Pt.* Act iii. Sc. 2.
> Praise us as we are tasted ; *allow* us, as we prove.
> *Troilus and Cressida,* Act iii. Sc. 2.

Thus used it means to *approve of.* In the present ordinary signification to *permit*, it is also found in Shakspeare, but not, I think, in the Bible.

AMAZE, AMAZEMENT.

> I do beseech your Majesty, make up ;
> Lest your retirement do *amaze* your friends.
> *King Hen. IV.* 1st *Pt.* Act v. Sc. 4.

i. e. *alarm* them, *confuse with terror.*

> I will make many people *amazed* at thee. Ezek. xxxii. 10.
> And are not afraid with any *amazement.* 1 Pet. iii. 6.

ATONE, ATONEMENT.

> `I would do much to *atone* them. *Othello*, Act iv. Sc. 1.

i. e. *reconcile* them, 'set them *at one* again,' as we read in Acts vii. 26. And we have the substantive *at onement*, in Bishop Hall's Satires, Book iii. S. vii. 69 :—

> Which never can be set *at onement* more.

Shakspeare uses both the verb and the substantive, and the former both as transitive and neuter.

> He and Aufidius can no more *atone.*   *Coriol.* Act iv. Sc. 6.

i. e. *be reconciled, agree.*   But in the Bible, though the substantive is used frequently, the verb does not occur at all.

BESTOW.

> ,There will I *bestow* all my fruits and my goods. Luke xii. 18.

i. e. *lay up, put away.*   See also 2 Kings v. 24; 2 Chron. ix. 25.

> We will *bestow* you in some better place.
> > *King Hen. VI.* 1st Pt. Act iii. Sc. 2.

BEWRAY=*discover, disclose.*

> Thy speech *bewrayeth* thee.   Matt. xxvi. 73.

See also Prov. xxvii. 16; xxix. 24.

> Should we be silent, and not speak, our raiment
> And state of bodies would *bewray* what life
> We have led since thy exile.   *Coriolanus,* Act v. Sc. 3.

From Isaiah xvi. 3, and from several places in Shakspeare, it appears that the use of this word was already fast becoming synonymous with that of the word *betray,* which has now superseded it.

BRAVERY : once only in the Bible.

> In that day the Lord will take away the *bravery* of their tink-
> ling ornaments about their feet.   Isaiah iii. 15.

i. e. *finery.*

> With scarfs and fans ,and double change of *bravery.*
> > *Taming of Shrew,* Act iv. Sc. 3.

It is remarkable that Shakspeare appears to use this substantive always in the above sense only ; though he uses the adjective *brave*, not only for *fine*, but much more often in its present signification, viz. for *courageous*; while in the Bible neither substantive nor adjective is used at all in the modern sense. The adverb *bravely*, for *finely*, *splendidly* (of dress), occurs in Judith x. 4.

BRING ON WAY=*escort*.

> Abraham went with them to *bring them on their way*.
> > Gen. xviii. 16.
> I pray you, *bring me on the way* a little.
> > *Othello*, Act iii. Sc. 4.

CARRIAGE, in the sense of *that which is carried, baggage, luggage*.

> We took up our *carriages*, and went up to Jerusalem.
> > Acts xxi. 15.

See also 1 Sam. xvii. 22, and margin there ; Isaiah i. 25 ; 1 Macc. ix. 31.

> Many *carriages* he hath despatched
> To the sea side. *King John*, Act v. Sc. 7.

Spenser uses the word in the same sense.

CASTAWAY=*a person lost*, or *abandoned by Providence*; once in the Bible, twice in Shakspeare.

> Lest that by any means when I have preached to others, I myself should be *a castaway*. 1 Cor. ix. 17.
> Why do you look on us, and shake your head,
> And call us—orphans, wretches, *castaways*?
> > *King Rich. III.* Act ii. Sc. 2.

CHOICE, adj. = *select, excellent.*

A *choice* young man, and a goodly.   1 Sam. ix. 2.
The *choice* and master spirits of this age.
Jul. Cæsar, Act iii. Sc. 1.

CHOICE, subst. = *the best of anything.*

In the *choice* of our sepulchres bury thy dead.
Gen. xxiii. 6.
Replete with *choice* of all delights.
King Henry VI. 1st *Pt.* Act v. Sc. 5.

CONVERSE, CONVERSATION.

The substantive, in the sense of *behaviour, manner of life, intercourse with,* is frequent in Scripture. See Ps. xxxvii. 14; Gal. i. 13; Phil. i. 27, &c. The verb occurs only in Baruch iii. 37, and in the title of Acts ii.   Neither word has in the Bible its present meaning of *discourse.*   In Shakspeare both meanings may, I think, be found; e. g.

All are banished till their *conversations*
Appear more wise and modest to the world.
Henry IV. 2nd *Pt.* Act v. Sc. 5.
Alas! who can *converse with* a dumb show?
Merch. of Ven. Act i. Sc. 2.

But the former, i. e. the old signification, is more common.

CUNNING, subst. *skill,* adject. *knowing, skilful.*

Let my right hand forget her *cunning.*   Ps. cxxxvii. 5.
In our sports my better *cunning* faints
Under his chance.   *Ant. and Cleop.* Act ii. Sc. 3.
Aholiab a *cunning* workman and embroiderer.
Exodus xxxviii. 23.
To *cunning* men
I will be very kind and liberal.
Taming of Shrew, Act i. Sc. 1.

DAYSPRING = *break of day, dawn.*

Hast thou commanded the morning since thy days; and caused the *dayspring* to know his place? Job xxxviii. 12.

See also Luke i. 78.

As flaws congealed in the *spring of day.*
King Henry IV. 2nd Part, Act iv. Sc. 4.

EAR = to *plough, till* the land.

He will set them to *ear* his ground. 1 Sam. viii. 12.

See also Is. xxx. 24; 'earing-time' in Exod. xxxiv. 21.

Let them go
To *ear* the land. *King Rich. II.* Act iii. Sc. 2.

See also Shakspeare's dedication of his poem *Venus and Adonis.*

FAVOUR = *countenance,* frequent in Shakspeare; in the Bible the adjective only is used, as *well-favoured, ill-favoured,* both which, and *hard-favoured,* occur also in Shakspeare.

I know your *favour* well,
Though you have now no sea-cap on your head.
Twelfth Night, Act iii. Sc. 3.
Rachel was beautiful and *well-favoured.* Gen. xxix. 17.
A shrewd *ill-favoured* wife. *Taming of Shrew,* Act i. Sc. 2.

The present meaning of the word is also found both in the Bible and in Shakspeare.

FEAR = to *frighten, terrify;* only once in Bible.

Though no terrible thing did *fear* them, &c. *Wisd.* xvii. 9.
We must not make a scare-crow of the law,
Setting it up to *fear* the birds of prey.
Meas. for Meas. Act ii. Sc. 1.

D

FULL, adv. = *very*.

Full well ye reject the commandment of God, that ye may keep your own tradition.   Mark vii. 9.

Prospero, master of a *full* poor cell.   *Tempest*, Act i. Sc. 2.

GOOD-MAN = *Master of the House, Paterfamilias*.

If the *good-man* of the house had known, &c.   Matth. xxiii. 43.

See also Prov. vii. 19.*

This story shall the *good-man* teach his son.
                    King Henry V. Act iv. Sc. 3.

HARD = *close, near*.

Naboth had a vineyard *hard* by the palace of Ahab.
                    1 Kings xxi. 1.

See also Acts xviii. 7. It occurs in several other places in the Old Testament; but in Ps. xxii. 11, and cvii. 8, where the Prayer Book version has ‘ *hard* at hand’ and ‘ *hard* at death’s door,’ the Bible has ‘ near ’ in both places.

Indeed, my lord, it followed *hard* upon.
                    Hamlet, Act i. Sc. 2.

HARNESS = *armour*.

Let not him that girdeth on his *harness* boast himself as he that putteth it off.   1 Kings xx. 2.

See also xxii. 34, and Prayer Book version of Ps. lxxviii. 10, where the Bible has ‘ being armed.’

Before the Sun rose he was *harnessed* light.
                    Troilus and Cressida, Act i. Sc. 2.

KNOW = *to acknowledge, approve, bless*.

The Lord *knoweth* the way of the righteous.   Ps. i. 6.

See also Exod. ii. 25, margin ; Hosea xiii. 5 ; Nahum i. 7 ; John x. 14, 27 ; 2 Tim. ii. 19. In the following passage Shakspeare seems to use the word in the same sense.

I know you are my eldest brother, and, in the gentle condition of blood, you should so *know* me.   *As you like it,* Act i. Sc. 1.

LEARN = to *teach.*

Lead me forth in thy truth and *learn* me.   Ps. xxv. 2.

Prayer Book version ; but in Bible ' teach me.' See also verse 8.

You must not *learn* me how to remember any extraordinary pleasure.   *As you like it,* Act i. Sc. 2.

LEASING = *lying.*

Thou shalt destroy them that speak *leasing.*
                              Ps. v. 6.   See also iv. 2.
                 In his praise
Have almost stamped the *leasing. Coriolanus,* Act v. Sc. 2.

i. e. made the lie current.

LET = to *hinder.*

Only he who now *letteth* will *let,* until he be taken out of the way.   2 Thess. ii. 7.

See also Exod. v. 4 ; Isaiah xliii. 13.

If nothing *lets* to make us happy. *Twelfth Night,* Act v. Sc. 1.

Shakspeare also uses the substantive *let=hindrance,* which does not occur in the Bible.

Therefore my kinsmen are no *let* to me.
                    Romeo and Juliet, Act ii. Sc. 2.
That I may know the *let,* why gentle peace
Should not expel these inconveniences.
                    , *King Henry V.* Act. v. Sc. 2.

LIKING = *good state of body, plumpness.*

> Their young ones are in good *liking*. Job xxxi. 4.
> I have an eye to make difference of men's *liking*.
> > *Merry Wives,* Act ii. Sc. 1.

We find the same word used also as an adjective.

> Why should he see your faces worse *liking?* Dan. i. 10.

See also the Prayer Book version of Ps. xcii. 13, 'fat and *well-liking* ;' in Bible, 'fat and flourishing.'

> *Well-liking* wits they have ; gross, gross ; fat, fat.
> > *Love's Labour's lost,* Act v. Sc. 2.

MAN-CHILD, MAID-CHILD, for *male* child, and *female* child; in the plural we have ' male children,' Josh. xvii. 2.

> If a woman have born a *man-child*. Levit. xii. 2.
> But if she bear a *maid-child*. *Ibid.* 5.
> I sprang not more in joy at first hearing he was a *man-child,* than now in first hearing he had proved himself a man.
> > *Coriolanus,* Act i. Sc. 3.
> > > She brought forth
> A *maid-child* called Marina. *Pericles,* Act v. Sc. 3.

NEPHEW = *grandson, descendant*; the Latin nepos.

> If any widow have children or *nephews*. 1 Tim. v. 4.

See also Judges xii. 14 ; Job xviii. 19 ; Isaiah xiv. 22.

> You'll have your *nephews* neigh to you. *Othello,* Act i. Sc. 1.

Shakspeare also uses NIECE for *grand-daughter*, in *King Richard III.*, Act iv. Sc. 1.

OR EVER = *before.*

> The lions brake all their bones in pieces *or ever* they came at the bottom of the den. Daniel vi. 24.

See also Prov. viii. 23 ; Eccles. xii. 6 ; Acts
xxiii. 15. Compare ' ere ever,' in Ecclus. xxiii. 20.

I drink the air before me, and return
Or *e'er* your pulse beat twice. *Tempest,* Act v. Sc. 1.

See also *Hamlet,* quoted below, Pt. II. ch. iii.
PATE = *head,* once in Bible, frequent in Shakspeare.

His mischief shall return upon his own head; and his violent
dealing shall come down upon his own *pate.* Ps. vii. 16.
*Enter, skirmishing, the Retainers of Gloster and Winchester, with
bloody pates.* *King Henry VI. 1st Part,* Act iii. Sc. 1.

See also *Taming of the Shrew,* quoted above, p. 16.
PLAY = to *fence, fight.*

Abner said to Joab, Let the young men now arise, and *play*
before us, 2 Sam. ii. 14.

Compare Bp. Andrewes' second sermon on Ash
Wednesday.

He sends to know if your pleasure hold to *play* with Laertes.
Hamlet, Act v. Sc. 2.

PORT = *gate* ; Latin, porta.

That I may shew all thy praises within the *ports* of the
daughter of Sion. Ps. ix. 14. Prayer Book version.

In the Bible ' gates.' The word does not
occur, I believe, at all in the Bible, either in this
sense (though ' porter '. does several times) or in
its more modern use for *harbour* ; Latin, portus.
Shakspeare uses it in both senses, even in the same
play :—

> Hark, the Duke's trumpets! I know not why he comes;—
> All *ports* I'll bar.   *King Lear*, Act ii. Sc. 1.
>   No *port* is free, no place
>   Does not attend my taking.   *Ibid.* 3.
>   Then is all safe! the anchor's in the *port*.
>   *Titus Andron.* Act iv. Sc. 4.

PREVENT = to (1) *come before*, (2) *go before*, in order to guide and *help*—not to hinder, as now used, (3) *anticipate* ; Latin, prævenio.

> 1. In the morning shall my prayer *prevent* thee.
>   Ps. lxxxviii. 13.
> 2. Let Thy tender mercies speedily *prevent* us.
>   Ps. lxxix. 8.   See also Ps. xxi. 3.
> 3. We which are alive shall not *prevent* them which are asleep.
>   1 Thess. iv. 15.   See also Ps. cxix. 148; Matth. xvii. 25.
> I would have staid till I had made you merry,
> If worthier friends had not *prevented* me.
>   *Merchant of Venice*, Act i. Sc. 1.

This seems to fall under the third meaning; and I am not sure that Shakspeare affords an example of any other; except the modern one, viz. to *hinder*, which is also found in the Bible. The instance, however, which Johnson quotes from Shakspeare, and interprets in the sense of to *hinder*, ought, I think, to be interpreted, in the sense of to *antici-pate*.

> I do find it cowardly and vile,
> For fear of what might fall, so to *prevent*
> The time of life.   *Julius Cæsar*, Act v. Sc. 1.

In the same play, iii. 1, the substantive PREVEN-TION is used with the same meaning :—

> Casca, be sudden; for we fear *prevention*.

PROPER = *good-looking, handsome, fair.*

Because they saw he was a *proper* child.   Heb. xi. 23.

The same Greek word, which is here used, is applied also to Moses, when a child, in Acts vii. 20, and is there translated ' fair.' Compare Exod. ii. 2, ' goodly child.'

> She finds, altho' I can not,
> Myself to be a marvellous *proper* man ;
> I'll be at charges for a looking glass.
> > *King Richard III.* Act i. Sc. 3.

QUICK = *alive, lively.*   QUICKEN = to *revive, animate.*

If the Lord make a new thing, and the earth open her mouth . . . . and they go down *quick* into the pit, Numb. xvi. 30. See verse 33, ' They went down alive into the pit.'   See also Ps. xxxv. 15, cxxiv. 3.   ' *Quick* and dead,' Acts x. 42 ; 2 Tim. iv. 1 ; 1 Pet. iv. 5.

> The word of God is *quick* and powerful.
> > Heb. iv. 12.   See also Isaiah xi. 3.

That which thou sowest is not *quickened,* except it die.
> > 1 Cor. xv. 36.

> Thou'rt *quick,*

But yet I'll bury thee.   *Timon of Athens,* Act iv. Sc. 3.

Now pile your dust upon the *quick* and dead.
> > *Hamlet,* Act v. Sc. 1.

The mistress which I serve *quickens* what's dead.
> > *Tempest,* Act iii. Sc. 1.

Shakspeare also uses the verb as neuter :—

These hairs which thou dost ravish from my chin, Will *quicken* and accuse thee.   *King Lear,* Act iii. Sc. 7.

ROAD = ' *raid,' inroad,* once in Bible.

Whither have ye made a *road* to-day ?   1 Sam. xxvii. 10.

This word does not occur in the Bible in the modern sense; but Shakspeare uses it (1) in the sense above named; (2) for *roadstead,* i. e. *a place for ships to anchor in;* and (3) in its present ordinary signification for *a public way.*

> 1. Against the Scot, who will make *road* upon us
> With all advantages.   *King Henry V.* Act i. Sc. 2.
> 2. Here I read for certain that my ships
> Are safely come to *road.*   *Merch. of Ven.* Act v. Sc. 1.
> 3. What wouldst thou have me . . . . enforce a thievish living
> On the common *road?*   *As you like it,* Act ii. Sc. 3.

In one place also, *Henry VIII.* iv. 2, ' with easy *roads* ' is used for easy *stages.*

ROOM = *place, seat at table.*

> When thou art bidden of any man to a wedding, sit not down in the highest *room.*   Luke xiv. 8.

> Grief fills the *room* up of my absent child,
> Lies in his bed, walks up and down with me.
>   *King John,* Act iii. Sc. 4.

RUNAGATE = *fugitive, rebel, apostate* ; French, renégat.

> God bringeth the prisoners out of captivity, but letteth the *runagates* continue in scarceness. *Prayer Book* version of Ps. lxviii. 6, where the Bible has ' the rebellious.'
>   I'll send to one in Mantua,
> Where that same banished *runagate* doth live.
>   *Romeo and Juliet,* Act iii. Sc. 5.

SORT = *class, order of persons.*

> Certain lewd fellows of the baser *sort.*   Acts xvii. 5.

> Assemble all the poor men of your *sort.*
>   *Julius Cæsar,* Act i. Sc. 1.

TABLE = *tablet.*

The *tables* were written on both their sides.
> Exod. xxxii. 15.   Comp. 2 Cor. iii. 3.

Therefore will he wipe his *tables* clean,
And keep no tell-tale to his memory.
> *Henry IV. 2nd Part,* Act iv. Sc. 1.

THOUGHT, used intensively for *care, anxiety, melancholy.*

Take no *thought* for your life, what ye shall eat.
> Matt. vi. 25.

Comp. Phil. iv. 6, where the same Greek word is rendered ' careful.'

If he love Cæsar, all that he can do
Is to himself; take *thought,* and die for Cæsar.
> *Jul. Cæsar,* Act ii. Sc. 1.

Compare *Antony and Cleopatra,* ' *think* and die.' Act iii. Sc. 2.

WIS, WIT, and WOT (originally the past tense of the former), to *know, perceive, think.*

They *wist* not what it was.   Exod. xvi. 15.
We do you to *wit* of the grace of God, &c.
> 2 Cor. viii. 1.   See also Exod. ii. 4.

My master *wotteth* not what is with me in the house.
> Gen. xxxix. 8.

What I shall choose, I *wot* not.   Phil. i. 22.
I *wis* your grandam had a worser match.
> *King Richard III.* Act i. Sc. 3.

Submission, Dauphin? 'tis a mere French word;
We English warriors *wot* not what it means.
> *King Henry VI. 1st Part,* Act iv. Sc. 7.

I conclude this chapter with a remark upon the

phrase *well stricken in years,* which we find in Luke
i. 7 : 'They had no child because that Elisabeth
was barren, and they both were now *well stricken in
years.'* In Tyndale's Translation, 1534, and Cranmer's, 1539, the words were 'well stricken in age ;'
which we find also in Gen. xviii. 11, and xxiv. 1.
Is it possible that our translator of St. Luke altered
the expression out of deference to the following
passage of Shakspeare ?

> We speak no treason, man ; we say the King
> Is wise and virtuous : and his noble Queen
> *Well struck in years.* *King Richard III.* Act i. Sc. 1.

Mr. Steevens, in his note upon the place (and there
is no other note upon it in the Variorum edition),
calls the phrase 'an odd, uncouth expression.' It
does not appear to have occurred to him that it is
used several times in the English Bible (see besides the passage in St. Luke, and the other texts
referred to above, Josh. xiii. 1, xxiii. 1, and 1 Kings
i. 1); still less that our poet might have *chosen* it
in the above passage because the Queen spoken of
was also an *Elizabeth,* wife of King Edward IV.

PART II.

GRAMMAR SCHOOL AND GUILD CHAPEL, STRATFORD-ON-AVON.

INTRODUCTION.

HERE are three ways by which we may estimate the extent of Shakspeare's knowledge and use of Holy Scripture. The first is the obvious references to the facts and characters of the Bible which his plays contain ; the second, the tone and colouring which pervade his moral and religious principles and sentiments ; and the third, the poetical thoughts or imagery which he appears to have borrowed more or less directly from the Scriptures. I shall begin with the first, that is, the historical references, as affording the clearest and most direct proofs of our poet's study of the Bible, which it is my purpose to establish ; because, if we are satisfied that the point in question is demonstrated by these, we shall be more ready to admit the same conclusion when we come to deal with the two other branches of the evidence, which, from their own nature, must necessarily be of a less definite and exact, and consequently less convincing character.

But before proceeding with the task thus prescribed, it is due to the character of our great poet that I should point out how much misconception respecting Shakspeare's treatment of Holy Scripture has prevailed among his critics, even of the highest rank. Let me produce one notable example, derived from the play of *Antony and Cleopatra,* Act iii. Sc. 11..

After the ignominious flight, in which Antony had followed Cleopatra from the coast of Actium back to Alexandria, Octavius Cæsar, the conqueror, sends a messenger to endeavour to detach the queen from her paramour. This messenger is received favourably by Cleopatra in a private interview, and just as he is kissing her hand, previous to his departure, Antony comes in, and in the highest strain of indignation, embittered by the consciousness of his downfall and disgrace, upbraids her as follows :—

> *Antony.* To let a fellow that will take rewards,
> And say, *God quit you !* be familiar with
> My playfellow, your hand ; this kingly seal,
> And plighter of high hearts !   O that I were
> *Upon the hill of Basan, to outroar*
> *The horned herd,* for I have savage cause :
> And to proclaim it civilly, were like
> A halter'd neck, which does the hangman thank
> For being yare * about him.

This passage gives striking evidence of our poet's familiarity with the Old Testament ; see

---

* i. e. adroit.

Ps. xxii. 12, lxviii. 15 ; Ezek. xxxix. 18 ; Amos iv. 1.
But is there anything to give offence even to the
most pious mind, in the way in which he has applied
his knowledge of these passages ? And yet not
only has Mr. Bowdler omitted the reference to
the 'hill of Basan' as indecorous, but critics, including Johnson himself, have concurred in con-
demning it as matter for regret, nay even for
' pity and indignation ! '

I confess I am not surprised that the editor of
the ' Variorum edition,' Mr. James Boswell, though
he professes in general to have scrupulously retained all the critical remarks of his predecessors,
yet made an exception, by venturing, as he says, ' in
a very few instances,' to expunge a note in which
Shakspeare had been, in his opinion, ' most per-
versely and injuriously charged with an irreverent
allusion to Scripture.' * I am sorry he did not carry
the process of expunction so far as to delete the note
·of Johnson just referred to.† Nor can I omit to
add that, while I desire to express my thankfulness
to Mr. Bowdler for the manner in which he has
executed his praiseworthy undertaking in many respects, I very much regret the undue sensitiveness
which has led him sometimes to alter, and sometimes
to omit, passages perfectly inoffensive, for no other

---

* Vol. i. Advertisement, p. 8.

† See also another note of Johnson, to the same effect, given in
that edition, vol. xi. p. 455.

reason that I can discover, except the allusion they contain to the language of Scripture.

The following example affords an instance both of alteration and of omission. In the *Second Part of King Henry VI.* Queen Margaret says to the king : —

> What, dost thou turn away, and hide thy face ?
> I am no loathsome leper, look on me.
> What, art thou, *like the adder*, waxen deaf?
> Be poisonous too, and kill thy forlorn queen.
>
> Act iii. Sc. 2.

These three last lines are *omitted* by Mr. Bowdler. And why ?   Because we read about ' lepers,' and still more, because we read about ' deaf adders ' in the Bible.   See Psalm lviii. 4, 5 : ' Their poison is like the poison of a serpent ; they are like the *deaf adder* that stoppeth her ear ; they will not hearken to the voice of charmers, charming never so wisely.' This beautiful image appears to have struck the imagination of our poet, and not without reason.   He therefore makes use of it again, and with singular propriety, in *Troilus and Cressida*; where Hector says to Paris and Troilus :—

> Pleasure and revenge
> Have ears *more deaf than adders*, to the voice
> Of any true decision.   *Act iii. Sc. 2.

This Mr. Bowdler has *altered* into

> Have ears for ever deaf unto the voice, &c.,

whereby the notion of truth *charming wisely, but in*

vain, is altogether lost, and a most flat line substituted for a most vigorous one. And why ? Because
Mr. B. appears to have been haunted by an exagge-
rated and mistaken fancy, that whatever is calculated
to remind the reader of a Scriptural image, however
beautiful and however appropriate, must necessarily
be profane ! What, I wonder, would Mr. B. have
done if he had undertaken to edit, not only the
plays, but also the sonnets of Shakspeare ; in the
cxii. of which we read as follows :—

> In so profound abysm I throw all care
> Of others' voices, that *my adder's sense*
> To critic and to flatterer *stopped* are—

where, by a curious instance of the figure, called in
Greek σχῆμα πρὸς τὸ σημαινόμενον, ' are ' seems as
if put to agree with *ears*, implied in ' adder's sense.'

I now pass on to the evidence of which I proposed to treat in the first instance.

E

CHAPTER I.

Of the Allusions in Shakspeare to the Historical Facts and Characters of the Bible.

IN this chapter I have to show the extent of Shakspeare's knowledge of the contents of the Bible in its historical aspect ; how fully and how accurately the general tenor of the facts recorded in the sacred narrative was present to his mind.

We may begin then from the very first chapter of the Book of Genesis. There can be no doubt that the Mosaic record of the creation of the sun and moon, on the fourth day, when ' God made two great lights ; the greater light to rule the day, and the lesser light to rule the night,' gave occasion to those words of Caliban in the *Tempest*, where he describes how Prospero, on his first coming to the island, had been wont to treat him kindly ; and as trying to educate him, would often teach him

How
To name *the bigger light*, and how *the less*,
That burn by day and night.   Act i. Sc. 2.

We know what followed only too soon after the
Creation ;—and although whatever comes from the
mouth of Falstaff may provoke a smile, yet we must
all feel that there is the greatest occasion in reality
for deep seriousness, when we hear him say to Prince
Henry :—

Dost thou hear, Hal ? Thou knowest *in the state of innocency
Adam fell*, and what should poor Jack Falstaff do in the days of
villainy ? *King Henry IV.* 1*st Part,* Act iii. Sc. 3.

It is the same Prince Henry, of whom afterwards,
when he became king, the Archbishop of Canterbury thus testified :—

The breath no sooner left his father's body,
But that his wildness, mortified in him,
Seemed to die too : yea, at that very moment,
Consideration like an angel came
And whipp'd *the offending Adam* out of him ;
Leaving his body as a paradise,
To envelop and contain celestial spirits.
  King Henry V. Act i. Sc. 1.

And he himself, as king, spake thus of the vile
conspirator Lord Scroop :—

I will weep for thee ;
For this revolt of thine methinks is like
Another *fall of man.* *Ibid.* Act ii. Sc. 1.

Yet once again, in *Much Ado about Nothing*, we
meet with a reference to the same chapters of
Genesis, in a passage which the fastidiousness of
Mr. Bowdler has not allowed him to retain, but
which surely need not excite any feeling of irreve-

rence towards the sacred record. ʿI would not marry her,ʾ says Benedick of the Lady Beatrice, ʿthough she were endowed with *all that Adam had left him before he transgressed.*ʾ (Act ii. Sc. 1.) Nor need we, I think, be offended at the dialogue between the two clowns in *Hamlet*, where allusion is made to the same primeval history :—

1st Clown. Come, my spade. There is no ancient gentlemen but gardeners, ditchers and grave-makers : they hold by Adam's profession.

2nd Clown. Was he a gentleman ?

1st Clown. He was the first that ever bore arms.

2nd Clown. Why, he had none.

1st Clown. What, art a heathen ? How dost thou understand scripture ? The scripture says, *Adam digged.* Could he dig without arms?   Act v. Sc. 1.

And as Adam digged, so he would be exposed to the inclemency of the weather ; which has been also the lot of the greater portion of his posterity; thus alluded to in *As you like it* : Scene, Forest of Arden :—

Duke Sen. Now, my co-mates and brothers in exile,
Hath not old custom made this life more sweet
Than that of painted pomp ? Are not these woods
More free from peril than the envious court ?
Here feel we but * the *penalty of Adam,*

---

* The emendation of Theobald for ʿnot,ʾ which Boswell objects to, and pronounces the old reading to be right. I wonder that neither of them has remarked how much the conjecture of the former is confirmed by the song which follows in Act ii. Sc. 5 :—

ʿHere shall we see
No enemy
But winter and rough weather.ʾ

The season's difference; as, the icy fang
And churlish chiding of the winter's wind.   Act ii. Sc. 1.

2. The history of Cain and Abel is of such a
character that it would naturally suggest materials
of thought to a tragic poet. Accordingly, the references which Shakspeare has made to it are frequent
and striking.   First, in *King Richard II.* :—

> *Bolingbroke.* Further I say, and further will maintain,
> That he* did plot the Duke of Gloster's death;
> And, consequently, like a traitor coward,
> Sluiced out his innocent soul through streams of blood :
> Which blood, *like sacrificing Abel's, cries*
> *Even from the tongueless caverns of the earth*
> To me for justice, and rough chastisement.   Act i. Sc. 1.

It is needless to observe how accurately, and at
the same time how reverently, this language represents both the letter and the spirit of the Bible
narrative. And so, too, where the King says in
Hamlet :—

> O, my offence is rank, it smells to heaven ;
> It hath *the primal eldest curse upon't,*
> *A brother's murder !*   Act iii. Sc. 3.

There is a still more recondite reference to the
same tragical history in the *First Part of King
Henry VI.,* a passage which Bowdler has thought
it necessary to expunge, where the poet with much
propriety puts into the mouth of the Bishop of
Winchester, in addressing Humphrey, Duke of
Gloster, these bold and wrathful lines :—

---

* Mowbray, Duke of Norfolk.

Nay, stand thou back, I will not budge a foot:
This be Damascus : be thou *cursed Cain,*
To slay thy brother Abel, if thou wilt.   Act i. Sc. 3.

It had been recorded by Sir John Mandeville,
who travelled in the East in the fourteenth century,
that 'in that place where Damascus was founded,
Cain slew his brother Abel.' It is also said that the
name Damascus means 'a sack of blood,' or 'a
cup of blood.' But our poet has turned the same
history to a still more striking account, in the
Second Part of King Henry IV., where the Earl of
Northumberland, as an enemy to the King, thus
speaks, throwing upon the ground the cap which he
had worn in sickness :—

Hence, thou sickly quoif;
Thou art a guard too wanton for the head,
Which princes, flushed with conquest, aim to hit.
Now bind my brows with iron ; and approach
The ragged'st hour that time and spite dare bring,
To frown upon the enraged Northumberland !
Let heaven kiss earth ! Now let not nature's hand
Keep the wild flood confined ! Let order die !
And let this world no longer be a stage,
To feed contention in a lingering act ;
But let *one spirit of the first-born Cain*
Reign in all bosoms, that, each heart being set
On bloody courses, the rude scene may end,
And darkness be the burier of the dead.   Act i. Sc. 1.

A magnificent speech, in which the classical reader
may fancy that he sees the utmost merit of two great,
but most opposite Roman poets—Lucretius and
Lucan—combined in one.

Another passage remains, which I shall not hesitate to produce, though, more than any of the foregoing, it requires to be read with allowance for the speaker, for the scene, and for the circumstances in which it was spoken. It is from the grave scene of *Hamlet*. The clown is engaged in digging, and having thrown up a scull, Hamlet thus speaks : —

That scull had a tongue in it, and could sing once. How the knave jowls * it to the ground, as if it were *Cain's jaw-bone, that did the first murder.*   Act v. Sc. 1.

3. To the next great event in the history of the world—the Universal Deluge—there is less reference in our poet's works than might perhaps have been expected. Indeed, so far as I have noted, it is only alluded to once, and then very briefly; viz. in *Twelfth Night*, Act iii. Sc. 2. Fabian, the servant of Olivia, says to Sir Andrew Ague-cheek—' I will prove it legitimate, Sir, upon the oaths of Judgment and Reason; ' to which Sir Toby Belch adds, with as much deep truth as wit—' And they (i. e. Judgment and Reason) have been grand jurymen since before *Noah was a sailor.*' Our poet therefore knew the sacred history; and he also knew not only that of the three sons of Noah ' was the whole earth overspread,' but that the natives of Europe were descended from Japhet. This appears in the

---

* i. e. dashes it violently.

Second Part of King Henry IV., where Poins, proceeding to read Falstaff's letter to Prince Henry, begins thus :—

> *Poins* [reads]. ' John Falstaff, *knight.*'—Every man must know that as oft as he has occasion to name himself. Even like those that are kin to the king; for they never prick their finger, but they say ' *There is some of the king's blood spilt :*' ' *How comes that?*' says he, that takes upon him not to conceive : the answer is as ready as a borrower's cap. ' *I am the king's poor cousin, Sir.*'
>
> *P. Henry.* Nay, they will be kin to us, or they *will fetch it from Japhet :*—   Act ii. Sc. 2.

that is, even if they go up so high as to Japhet to trace the descent.

4. The history of Job has the misfortune to appear only in connexion with Sir John Falstaff, first in the *Merry Wives of Windsor*, where the following dialogue takes place in his presence :—

> *Mrs. Page.* Why, Sir John, do you think, though we would have thrust virtue out of our hearts by the head and shoulders, and have given ourselves without scruple to hell, that ever the devil could have made you our delight?
>
> *Ford.* What, a hodge pudding? a bag of flax?
>
> *Mrs. Page.* A puff'd man?
>
> *Page.* Old, cold, wither'd, and of intolerable entrails?
>
> *Ford.* And one that is *as slanderous as Satan*?
>
> *Page.* And *as poor as Job*?
>
> *Ford.* And as *wicked* as his wife?   Act v. Sc. 5.

Our poet's reference to Satan in the foregoing passage would seem to show that he remembered not only the history of Job, but the manner also in which it comes to be introduced.

To one portion of this complex accusation Falstaff has the grace to plead guilty, when in the *Second Part of King Henry IV.* he is brought up for trial before the Chief Justice, and, as making a shift to escape, counterfeits deafness.

Chief Justice. You hear not what I say to you.

Falstaff. Very well, my lord, very well: rather, an't please you, it is the disease of not listening, the malady of not marking, that I am troubled withal.

Chief Justice. To punish you by the heels,* would amend the attention of your ears; and I care not, if I do become your physician.

Falstaff. I am *as poor as Job*, my lord; but not so *patient*: your lordship may minister the potion of imprisonment to me, in respect of poverty; but how I should be your patient to follow your prescription, the wise may make some dram of a scruple, or indeed a scruple itself.   Act i. Sc. 2.

5. The use which our poet has made of the history of Jacob and Laban in the *Merchant of Venice*, appeared, I conclude, objectionable to Mr. Bowdler; for he has omitted the entire passage, amounting to thirty-two lines:—but to me it appears so far otherwise, that I venture to cite almost the whole of it, as a remarkable instance of the tact with which Shakspeare could apply with perfect accuracy a passage of Scripture open to misconception, and yet divest its application of all dangerous tendency. Shylock, the rich Jew, is speaking to Antonio, the

---

* i. e. to put you in the stocks.

merchant of Venice, who proposed to borrow of
him a large sum of money :—

Shylock. Well, then, your bond : and let me see—but hear you ;
Methought you said you neither lend, nor borrow,
Upon advantage.
Ant.   I do never use it.
Shyl. When Jacob grazed his uncle Laban's sheep,
This Jacob from our holy Abraham was
(As his wise mother wrought in his behalf)
The third possessor—aye, he was the third.
Ant. And what of him ?   Did he take interest ?
Shyl. No, not take interest ; not, as you would say,
Directly interest :   mark what Jacob did.
When Laban and himself were compromised,
That all the eanlings * which were streak'd and pied,
Should fall as Jacob's share, ...
The skilful shepherd peeled *me* † certain wands,
And stuck them up before the fulsome ewes,
Who, then conceiving, did in eaning time
Fall ‡ party-coloured lambs, and those were Jacob's.
This was a way to thrive, and he was blest ;
And thrift is blessing, if men steal it not.
Ant. This was a venture, Sir, that Jacob served for ;
A thing not in his power to bring to pass,
But sway'd and fashion'd by the hand of heaven.
Was this inserted to make interest good ?
Or is your gold and silver, ewes and rams ?
.   .   .   .   .   .
The devil can cite Scripture to his purpose.
An evil soul, producing holy witness,
Is like a villain with a smiling cheek ;
A goodly apple rotten to the heart ;
O, what a goodly outside *falsehood* hath !   Act i. Sc. 2.

---

* Young lambs just dropt, or *eaned.*
† See above, Pt. I. ch. i. p. 15.
‡ i. e. let fall, give birth to.

All this, I say—even to the beautiful and instructive lines with which the passage concludes—Mr.
Bowdler has omitted ; and so has deprived his
reader of the opportunity of observing Shakspeare's
knowledge of the Bible not only in the case of the
narrative to which I am now mainly referring, but
also in two other instances.   In the line

> The devil can quote Scripture to his purpose,

there is evidently an allusion to the history of
our Lord's temptation, as recorded in Matt. iv. and
Luke iv.   And the same allusion occurs again in
King Richard III., where the wicked Gloster (as he
still was) is speaking of the treason and other crimes
which he had committed, and not only disguised,
but laid to the charge of others, who, he pretended, had by those same crimes wronged and
displeased him :—

> But then I sigh, and with a piece of Scripture,
> Tell them that God bids us do good for evil:
> And then I clothe my naked villainy
> With old odd ends, *stolen forth of Holy Writ*,
> And seem a saint, when *most I play the devil*.
>
> Act i. Sc. 3.

i. e. by so quoting and misapplying Scripture.
The other instance in which a close knowledge
of the Bible may be traced is in the use of the word
' falsehood ' in the last line for ' knavery,' or ' dis-
honesty.'*

---

* See below, Ch. ii. Sect. 12.

It was not likely that the touching language of the same patriarch, Jacob, when at a later period of his life he refused to allow his son Benjamin to be carried down into Egypt, would be thrown away upon our great dramatist. I allude to Gen. xlii. 38 (compare xliv. 29, 31):—

And he said, My son shall not go down with you; for his brother is dead, and he is left alone: if mischief befall him by the way in which ye go, then shall ye bring down my gray hairs with sorrow to the grave.

Let us see how this pathetic passage has been turned to account in the *Second Part of King Henry VI.*, where Humphrey, Duke of Gloster, after the condemnation of his Duchess Eleanor for treason, thus speaks:—

Mine eyes are full of tears, my heart of grief,
Ah! Humphrey, this dishonour in thine age
Will *bring thy head with sorrow to the ground.*

And if we could entertain any doubt as to the source from whence this line has been derived, the doubt would be removed by what immediately follows. The duke adds, addressing the king:—

I beseech your majesty give me leave to go:
Sorrow *would* solace, and mine age *would* ease.

(i. e. 'would have,' 'requires,' as Johnson explains it.) To which the king replies:—

Stay, Humphrey, Duke of Gloster: ere thou go
Give up thy staff: Henry will to himself
Protector be: and God shall be my hope,
My *stay,* my *guide,* and *lantern to my feet*

And *go in peace*, Humphrey ; no less beloved
Than when thou *wert* protector to thy king.
Act ii. Sc. 3.

Here ' wert ' in the indicative mood, though
supported by other high authorities, is ungram-
matical, for ' wast.'* But let that pass. Upon the
words, ' lantern to my feet,' Steevens has a note in
these words : ' This image, I think, is from our
Liturgy : *" a lantern to my feet and a light to my
paths."'* If by ' Liturgy ' is meant the Psalter, or
Version of the Psalms contained in the Prayer Book,
this is correct; and a reference should have been made
to Ps. cxix. 105. But it is a sufficient proof of the
little attention that has been paid to the branch of
Shakspearian criticism upon which we are engaged
that this loose and inaccurate note should have been
allowed to stand; and that both Steevens and Malone,
ready as they were to encumber their poet's page,
and to disagree, should, on this occasion, have found
nothing more to say ; though other expressions in
the same speech, such as ' my stay, my guide,' and
again, ' go in peace,' might also have received illustration from Holy Scripture. See 2 Sam. xxii. 19.
Ps. xviii. 18, ' They prevented me in the day of my
calamity, but the Lord was *my stay*.' Ps. xlviii. 14,
' This God is our God for ever and ever : He will
be *our Guide*, even unto death.' Exod. iv. 18,
' Jethro said to Moses, *Go in peace*.' 2 Sam. xv. 9,

---

* See Lowth's *Grammar*, p. 72.

'The king (David) said to Absalom, *Go in peace* ;' and the same phrase occurs frequently elsewhere in the Bible.

6. We find further evidence of our poet's familiarity with the Book of Genesis in a reference to the former of Pharaoh's two dreams which Joseph interpreted ; see Gen. xli., and compare *King Henry IV. 1st Part*, where Falstaff says to Prince Henry :—

> If to be old and merry be a sin, then many an old host that I know is lost : if to be fat be to be hated, then *Pharaoh's lean kine* are to be loved.   Act ii. Sc. 2.

From that passage we are carried on, first to *Twelfth Night*, where the clown says to Malvolio :—

> There is no darkness but ignorance, in which thou art more puzzled than *the Egyptians in their fog*.   Act iv. Sc. 2.

and then to *As you like it*, Act ii. Sc. 5, where Jaques says :—

> I'll go sleep if I can ; if I cannot, I'll rail against all *the first-born of Egypt*.

Upon these last words we find the two following notes in the Variorum edition, one by Johnson, the other by Steevens :—

> 'The first-born of Egypt,' a proverbial expression for high-born persons.   JOHNSON.

> The phrase is Scriptural as well as proverbial. So in Exodus xii. 29 : ' And the Lord smote all the first-born of Egypt.'
>   STEEVENS.

This is rather a curious way of stating the matter, and one feels somewhat at a loss to determine
whether of the two pieces of criticism, though very
different in kind, is the less satisfactory. The play
in which the passage occurs turns upon two incidents,
in both of which an *eldest* brother is mainly concerned, in the one as suffering, and in the other as
doing injury. And the reflection, therefore, naturally
presents itself to the moralising Jaques, that to be
a *first-born son* is a piece of good fortune not to be
coveted now, any more than it was in the days of
Pharaoh, when *all the first-born of Egypt* were cut
off, but rather to be ' railed at.' In Act i. Sc. 1,
Orlando says to Oliver, ' The courtesy of nations allows you my better in that you are the *first born.*' If
it be objected that Jaques was not yet aware of what
had happened to Orlando, still, I think the poet
might have put the sentiment into the mouth of
such an one as Jaques, to be as a kind of waking
dream, half experimental in regard to what he
already knew, half prophetical of what he would
soon discover ; but, at all events, the reference to
' the old Duke,' who had been ' banished by his
younger brother, the new Duke,' will hold good.
See Act i. Sc. 1. And he ' rails at ' him, not only
as showing sympathy, after his quaint manner, with
the old Duke's banishment, but as reflecting upon
his own folly in becoming voluntarily a partaker
of the banishment, and thereby forfeiting all his

' lands and revenues' to the usurper; as he had sung *just before* in the verse, which (he says) ' I made yesterday in despite of my invention :'—

> If it do come to pass
> That any man turn ass,
> *Leaving his wealth and ease,*
> *A stubborn will to please,*
> Here shall he see
> Gross fools as he,
> An if* he will come *to me.*

7. In *King Lear*, when the eyes of Gloster had been put out by Cornwall, the servants who were present thus philosophize upon the savage cruelty which he and Regan had shown :—

> 1*st Serv.* I'll never care what wickedness I do
> If this man comes to good.
> 2*nd Serv.*   If she live long,
> And, *in the end, meet the old course of death,*
> Women will all turn monsters.   Act iii. Sc. 4.

To ' meet the old course of death ' is the same idea which we find in the mouth of Moses, with reference to the fate of the rebels Korah and his company.

> If these men die *the common death of all men,* or if they be visited after the visitation of all men, then the Lord hath not sent me.   Numb. xvi. 29.

A further reference to an incident in the early history of the Israelites is to be met with in *King Henry V.*, where the King asks :

> May I with right and conscience make this claim ?*

---

* Sée above, Pt. I. ch. i. p. 26.

viz. the claim to the kingdom of France, in virtue of his actual, though irregular, succession to Edward IV., whose mother Isabella was daughter to King Philip IV. of France—a claim alleged to have been barred by the operation of the Salic law. The Archbishop of Canterbury answers :—

> The sin upon my head, dread sovereign!
> For in the *Book of Numbers* it is writ,
> *When the son dies, let the inheritance*
> *Descend unto the daughter.* Act i. Sc. 2.

The 'Variorum edition' affords neither note nor reference. Our poet alludes to the divine answer given to the plea of the daughters of Zelophehad, as recorded in Numbers xxvii. 1–8, and again in Joshua xvii. 3, 4.

8. I am not sure that our poet is justified in putting a sword into the hand of Deborah, as he does in *King Henry VI. 1st Part*; where Charles, the Dauphin of France, says to the Maid of Orleans : —

> Stay, stay thy hands ; thou art an Amazon,
> And fightest with *the sword of Deborah.* Act i. Sc. 2.

All that we know from the sacred narrative is, that she consented to accompany Barak in the successful expedition against Sisera. See Judges iv. 9.

The same play of *King Henry VI. 3rd Part*, contains a reference to another portion of the same Book of Judges, viz. xi. 30–40.

Clarence.   Why, trow'st thou, Warwick,
That Clarence is so harsh, so blunt, unnatural,
To bend the fatal instruments of war
Against his brother, and his lawful king?
Perhaps, thou wilt object my holy oath:
To keep that oath, were more impiety
Than *Jephthah's when he sacrificed his daughter.*

Act v. Sc. 1.

This last line Mr. Bowdler has thought it necessary to omit. That Jephthah was one 'who obtained
a good report through faith,' we know from the
New Testament, Heb. xi. 32, 39; but I see no
sufficient cause to conceal the sacred narrative to
which our poet refers, still less to condemn the use
which he has made of it. We may conjecture that
he had heard read in church the Homily 'against
swearing and perjury,' the second part of which
contains what follows :—

And Jephthah, when God had given to him victory of the
children of Ammon, promised (of a foolish devotion) unto God,
to offer for a sacrifice unto Him, that person which of his own
house should first meet with him after his return home. By
force of which fond and unadvised oath, he did slay his own and
only daughter, which came out of his house with mirth and joy
to welcome him home. Thus the promise which he made most
foolishly to God, against God's everlasting will, and the law of
nature, most cruelly he performed: so committing against God
a double offence. Therefore, whosoever maketh any promise,
binding himself thereunto by an oath, let him foresee that the
thing which he promiseth be good and honest and not against
the commandment of God; and that it be in his own power to
perform it justly; and such good promise must all men keep
evermore assuredly. But if a man at any time shall, either of

ignorance or of malice, swear to do anything which is either against the law of Almighty God, or not in his power to perform, let him take it for an unlawful and ungodly oath.

Godly and wholesome doctrine, which Shakspeare has taken occasion to insist upon in several other passages. Thus in the *Second Part* of the same play, Act v. Sc. 1 :—

> *K. Henry.* Hast thou not sworn allegiance unto me ?
> *Salisbury.* I have.
> *K. Hen.* Canst thou dispense with Heaven for such an oath ?
> *Salis.* It is great sin, to swear unto a sin ;
> But *greater sin to keep a sinful oath.*
> Who can be bound by any solemn vow
> To do a murderous deed, to rob a man,
> To reave the orphan of his patrimony,
> To wring the widow from her custom'd right,
> And have no other reason for this wrong,
> But that he was bound by a solemn oath ?

So in *Troilus and Cressida,* Act v. Sc. 3 :—

> *Hector.* Begone, I say : the gods have heard me swear.
> *Cassandra.* The gods are deaf to hot and peevish vows ;
> They are polluted offerings, more abhorr'd
> Than spotted livers in the sacrifice.
> *Androm.* O ! be persuaded : do not count it holy
> To hurt by being just : it is as lawful,
> For * we would give much, to use violent thefts,
> And rob in the behalf of charity.
> *Cassand.* It is the purpose that makes strong the vow ;
> But *vows to ev'ry purpose must not hold.*

And once more, in *King John,* where Cardinal

---

* Because, in order to.

F 2

Pandulph, the Pope's legate, says to Philip, King of France :—

> O! let thy vow
> First made to Heaven, first be to Heaven performed;
> What since thou swor'st, is sworn against thyself,
> And may not be performed by thyself;
> For that which thou hast sworn to do amiss
> Is [more *] *amiss when it is truly done*;
> And being not done where doing tends to ill,
> The truth † is then most done not doing it.
>
> .   .   .   .   .   .
>
> It is religion that doth make vows kept,
> But thou hast sworn against religion.
>
> .   .   .   .   .   .
>
> [So] thou dost swear only to be forsworn,
> And *most forsworn to keep what thou dost swear.*
>
> Act iii. Sc. 1.

To return to Jephthah, whose history is again noticed by our poet in *Hamlet*, Act ii. Sc. 2 :—

Hamlet. O Jephthah, Judge of Israel—what a treasure had'st thou!
Polonius. What treasure had he, my lord?
Hamlet. Why—*one fair daughter, and no more,*
    The which he loved passing well.

9. We are now arrived at the history of David. His encounter with Goliath—' the staff of whose spear,' we are told, ' was like a weaver's beam ' (1 Sam. xvii. 7), is taken advantage of in the *Merry Wives of Windsor*, where Falstaff declares :—

In the shape of man, master Brook, I fear not *Goliath with a weaver's beam*; because I know also *life is a shuttle.*

Act v. Sc. 1.

---

* So I would propose to read for ' not.'
† See below, Ch. ii. sect. 12.

The comparison in these last words is taken from Job vii. 6, ' My days are swifter than a weaver's shuttle, and are spent without hope.' Both references are a proof of Shakspeare's close acquaintance with Holy Scripture.

It is reasonable therefore to suppose that, in *Cymbeline*, the manner of Cloten's death, which Guiderius thus describes—

> With his own sword,
> Which he did wave against my throat, I have ta'en
> His head from him — Act iv. Sc. 2.

was derived from the same history. See 1 Sam. xvii. 51.

And again, the circumstances of the death of Saul, when having lost his army, and his sons among the slain, he and his armour-bearer killed themselves, may be compared with the scenes between Antony and Eros, in *Antony and Cleopatra*, Act v. Sc. 12 ; and between Cassius and Pindarus, and again between Brutus and Clitus first, then Volumnius, and lastly Strato, in *Julius Cæsar*, Act v. Sc. 3 and 5.

The scene in *King Richard III.*, where Hastings is made to condemn himself, in answer to the question of Gloster —

> I pray you all, tell me what they deserve
> That do conspire my death ? Act iii. Sc. 3.

admits of similar comparison with the scene between

David and the prophet Nathan, recorded in 2 Sam.
xii. 5–7.

The devices by which Absalom 'stole the hearts
of the men of Israel' from his father's government,
as we read in 2 Sam. xv. 1–6, have been well trans-
ferred by our poet to the artful usurper, Bolingbroke, in the *First Part of King Henry IV.*, where
he himself confesses :—

> And then I *stole* all courtesy from heaven,
> And dressed myself *in such humility*,
> That I did *pluck allegiance from men's hearts*,
> Loud shouts and salutations from their mouths,
> Even in the presence of the crowned king.
>
> Act iii. Sc. 2.

And still more at length in a later passage of the
same play, where Hotspur describes the treasonable
practices of the same usurper :—

> He presently—as greatness knows itself—
> Steps me * a little higher than his vow
> Made to my father, while his blood was poor;
> And now, forsooth, takes on him to reform
> Some certain edicts, and some strait decrees,
> That lie too heavy on the commonwealth :
> Cries out upon abuses, seems to weep
> Over his country's wrongs ; and, by this face,
> This seeming brow of justice, did he win
> The hearts of all that he did angle for.   Act iv. Sc. 3.

Compare with this the narrative of Scripture before referred to :—

---

* See Pt. I. ch. i. p. 15.

And Absalom rose up early, and stood beside the way of the gate; and it was so that when any man that had a controversy came to the king for judgment, then Absalom called unto him . . . . and said unto him, See thy matters are good and right; but there is no one deputed of the king to hear thee. Absalom said moreover, O! that I were made judge in the land, that every man which hath any suit or cause might come unto me, and I would do him justice! And it was so that when any man came nigh to him to do him obeisance, he put forth his hand, and took him, and kissed him. And on this manner did Absalom to all Israel that came to the king for judgment : so Absalom stole the hearts of the men of Israel.

The affecting language in which David mourned for the death of his rebellious son :—

O my son Absalom, my son, my son Absalom! would God I had died for thee, O Absalom, my son, my son!

2 Sam. xviii. 33.

am I wrong in supposing that this pathetic language may be traced in *Titus Andronicus?* where the boy, son to Lucius, exclaims :—

O! grandsire, grandsire! even with all my heart
Would I were dead so you did live again!   Act v. Sc. 3.

though it cannot be doubted, I suppose, that such display of affection is more true to nature when it is found, as in Scripture, in a descending line from the father to the son, than in ascent from the boy to the grandfather.

Once more; the description of Absalom's personal beauty is in these words :—

From the sole of his foot even to the crown of his head there was no blemish in him.   2 Sam. xiv. 25.

The description of Benedick's social attractions in
Much Ado about Nothing is, that

> *From the crown of his head to the sole of his foot* he is all mirth.
>   Act iii. Sc. 2.

10. In the concluding scene of *King Henry VIII.*,
in which our poet exerts himself to do honour first
to Queen Elizabeth, and then to King James, he
shows his knowledge of the Bible in a remarkable
manner by the speech which he puts most appropriately into the mouth of Archbishop Cranmer;
beginning with a reference to the visit of the Queen
of Sheba to King Solomon; see 1 Kings x., 2 Chron.
ix., and Matt. xii. 42.

> This royal infant (heaven still move about her!),
> Tho' in her cradle, yet now promises
> Upon this land a thousand thousand blessings,
> Which time shall bring to ripeness : she shall be
> A pattern to all princes living with her,
> And all that shall succeed.   *Sheba was never*
> *More covetous of wisdom*, and fair virtue,
> Than this pure soul shall be . . . .
> She shall be loved and fear'd : her own shall bless her ;
> Her foes shake like a field of beaten corn,
> And hang their heads with sorrow : good grows with her.
> *In her days, every man shall eat with safety*
> *Under his own vine*, what he plants ; and sing
> The merry songs of peace to all his neighbours.
> *God shall be truly known.*

And then, speaking of her successor, in the same
prophetic strain :—

> Wherever the bright sun of heaven shall shine,
> His honor and the greatness of his name

Shall be, and make new nations : he shall flourish,
And, *like a mountain cedar,* reach his branches
To all the plains about him. Our children's children
Shall see this, and bless heaven.   Act v. Sc. 4.

It is of King Solomon's reign that we read ' Judah
and Israel dwelt safely, every man under his vine
and under his fig tree,' 1 Kings iv. 25. See also
Micah iv. 4; Zech. iii. 10.

11. To deny sleep to God, as the Psalmist does—

Behold, He that keepeth Israel shall neither slumber nor sleep—
                                        Ps. cxxi. 4.

is an image which beautifully expresses the vigilance
of God's providential care ; for we know of no
created being in the world that sleepeth not. And
the taunt, therefore, of Elijah against the priests of
Baal, when he mocked them, and said :—

Cry aloud, for he is a god; either he is talking, or he is pur-
suing, or he is in a journey, or peradventure *he sleepeth,* and *must
be awaked—*   1 Kings xviii. 27.

is just and natural. It is by an adoption of the same
image that, in *Pericles Prince of Tyre,* Cleon says to
his wife Dionyza :—

          Our tongues sound deep our woes
      Into the air : our eyes do weep, till lungs
      Fetch breath that may proclaim them louder ; that,
      If *Heaven slumber,* while their creatures want,
      They may *awake their helps* to comfort them :—
                                        Act i. Sc. 4.

where the old copy reads ' helpers.'
When Jezebel had been thrown out of the window,

and so killed, by the command of Jehu, he first trod her under foot, but afterwards, 'when he came in,' and had eat and drunk, he said :—

> Go see now this cursed woman, and *bury her : for she is a king's daughter.*   2 Kings ix. 34.

This command not improbably suggested to Shakspeare the speech which he has put into the mouth of Belarius, in *Cymbeline*, when Guiderius had come in with the head of Cloten, whom he had encountered and killed in self-defence :—

> Great griefs, I see, medicine the less : for Cloten
> Is quite forgot. *He was a queen's son*, boys :
> And, though he came our enemy, remember,
> He was paid for that. Tho' mean and mighty rotting
> Together, have one dust : yet reverence
> (That angel of the world) doth make distinction
> Of place 'tween high and low. Our foe was princely ;
> And tho' you took his life, as being our foe,
> Yet *bury him as a prince.*   Act iv. Sc. 2.

12. When references to the facts of Sacred History are put into the mouth of a clown, we must expect to have occasion to remember the Horatian maxim,

> Ridentem dicere verum
> Quid vetat ?

But are all such references necessarily to be condemned as profane ? In *All's well that ends well* the following dialogue occurs between Lafeu and the Clown, respecting Helena, whom they supposed to be dead :—

Lafeu. ' Twas a good lady, 'twas a good lady : we may pick a thousand salads, ere we light on such another herb.

Clown. Indeed, Sir, she was the sweet-marjoram of the salad, or, rather, the herb of grace.*

Lafeu. They are not salad-herbs, you knave; they are nose-herbs.

Clown. I am no great *Nebuchadnezzar,* Sir; I have not much *skill in grass.*   Act iv. Sc. 5.

Mr. Bowdler thought it necessary to omit the former clause of this last speech—' I am no great Nebuchadnezzar '—out of respect, no doubt, to the Scripture narrative to which allusion is made. See Daniel iv. 25. Upon a point like this there may be a difference of opinion; but if we suppose—and for my own part, I do suppose—that the fact of Nebuchadnezzar's punishment was accepted by our poet in all simplicity of faith, and that no sinister intention whatever is implied by him in the allusion to it, we can scarcely, I think, find ground for censure, and shall be inclined to conclude that if the levity of a clown obtains through his wit a ready acceptance in other instances, it may at least be excused in this.†

It is perhaps to the reign of Nebuchadnezzar that we are to assign *the History of Susannah,* which we find in the Apocrypha. But however this may be, there can be no doubt that Shakspeare had that story in view, and the detection by Daniel of the wickedness of the two elders, in that well-known

---

* Rue. See *Hamlet,* Act iv. Sc. 5.

† See *Supplementary Note* at end of the volume.

passage of the *Merchant of Venice*, where Shylock is
made to exclaim :—

> *A Daniel* come to judgment! yea, *a Daniel!*
> O wise young judge, how I do honour thee!
>
> Act iv. Sc. 1.

Daniel, according to the history, v. 45, was 'a
young youth' when he convicted the elders 'of
false witness by their own mouth,' v. 61. And
'from that day forth was Daniel held in great
reputation in the sight of the people,' v. 64. His
detection also of the imposture of the priests of
Bel, as we read in the Apocryphal *History of the
Destruction of Bel and the Dragon*, may have contributed to suggest the propriety of the same
allusion.

13. We pass on now into the New Testament.
The character of Herod, as a violent and blood-
thirsty prince, might have been, and no doubt was,
well known to our poet from the Ancient Mysteries. And it is probably to his experience of
Herod, as acted in a mystery, that in the advice
given by Hamlet to the players, 'not to tear a
passion to tatters,' &c., we owe the expression, '*It
out-herods Herod*; pray you avoid it,' Act iii. Sc. 2.
But we need not doubt that Shakspeare had in his
mind's eye the Scriptural account of the murder of
the Innocents, and of the affliction of their discon-
solate mothers, represented by 'Rachel weeping
for her children,' Matt. ii. 16–18, when, in *King*

Henry V., he made the king, speaking before the gates of Harfleur, to summon it to surrender in these terms :—

Therefore, you men of Harfleur,
Take pity of your town, and of your people:
.   .   .   .
If not, why in a moment look to see,
.   .   .   .
Your naked infants spitted upon pikes,
Whiles the mad mothers with their howls confused
Do break the clouds, *as did the wives of Jewry
At Herod's bloody-hunting slaughtermen.*
                                    Act iii. Sc. 2.

Our poet's allusions to occurrences in our Lord's ministry, while they leave no doubt of the attention which he had paid to the Gospel narrative, would seem also, I think, to indicate something more of reverence and reserve as felt to be due to that portion of the sacred volume. When in *King Lear*, Edgar, as poor Tom, is met by Gloster and the old man upon the heath, he says to them :—

Poor Tom hath been scared out of his good wits. Bless the good man from the foul fiend ! *Five fiends* have been in poor Tom at once.   Act iv. Sc. 1.

We should rather have expected ' seven fiends ; ' but I am willing to believe that Shakspeare preferred to avoid so close a reference to the case of Mary Magdalene, Luke viii. 2, and to the teaching of our Lord in Matthew xii. 45. There is the same kind of occult allusion, somewhat awkwardly introduced, to the discourse which followed upon Christ's healing the man born blind (which St. John relates,

ix. 41), in *King Henry VI. 2nd Part.*   A pretended miracle of the same kind had been wrought at S. Alban's shrine, and when the man, Simpcox, is brought to the king, the latter is made to say :—

> Great is his comfort in this earthly vale;
> Altho' *by his sight his sin be multiplied.*   Act ii. Sc. 1.

The same king, in another part of the same play, has these words with reference to the rebels led on by Jack Cade :—

> O! graceless men! *they know not what they do.*
>   Act iv. Sc. 4.

I need not remind the reader WHEN, and by WHOM, the same words were originally spoken with reference to a rebellion which has no parallel.

There is a noble speech put into the mouth of the Bishop of Carlisle, in *King Richard II.*, where that prelate protests against the usurpation of Bolingbroke, and prophesies of its evil consequences : —

> I speak to subjects, and a subject speaks—
> My lord of Hereford here, whom you call king,
> Is a foul traitor to proud Hereford's king :
> And if you crown him, let me prophesy,
> Disorder, horror, fear, and mutiny,
> Shall here inhabit, and this land be called
> The *field of Golgotha, and dead men's sculls.*
> O! if you rear *this house against this house,*
> It will the woefullest *division* prove
> That ever fell upon this cursed earth.   Act iv. Sc. 2.

Besides the Scriptural reference in the name Gol-

gotha (which occurs again in *Macbeth*, Act i. Sc. 2),
there is perhaps in these last lines a further allusion
to the domestic ' divisions ' which were prophesied
to follow after the Crucifixion of Christ ; see Mark
xiii. 8, 12 ; Luke xii. 52. Compare also Matt.
xii. 25.

In *King Henry VIII.*, Archbishop Cranmer is
thus warned by his sovereign of the conspiracy which
had been formed to effect his overthrow :—

> Your enemies are many and not small.
> .   .   .   .   At what ease
> Might corrupt minds procure knaves as corrupt
> To swear against you ! *Such things have been done.*
> You are potently opposed : and with a malice
> Of as great size.   Ween * you of better luck,
> I mean, *in perjured witness, than* YOUR MASTER,
> Whose minister you are, *whiles here He lived*
> *Upon this naughty earth* ?   Act v. Sc. 1.

See Mark xiv. 55, also Matt. x. 25 ; John xv. 20.

Mr. Bowdler has omitted two passages in which
reference is made by our poet to the traitor Judas,
without sufficient reason, as it seems to me, for the
omission in either case.† I will therefore transcribe
them both. The former is in *King Richard II.*,
where the king says:—

---

* Think, imagine, expect.

† There is a third reference to Judas, also omitted by Mr. B., and
perhaps with better reason, in *King Richard II.* Act iii. Sc. 2, where
the three traitors, Bagot, Bushy, and Green, are described as ' Three
Judases, each one thrice worse than Judas ! '

Alack, why am I sent for to a king,
Before I have shook off the regal thoughts
Wherewith I reign'd ?   .   .   .
Give sorrow leave a while to tutor me
To this submission.   Yet I well remember
The favours * of these men.   Were they not mine ?
Did they not sometime cry ' All hail !' to me ?
As Judas did to Christ: but *He, in Twelve,*
Found truth in all but one ; I, in twelve thousand, none.

                                        Act iv. Sc. 1.

Compare Matt. xxvi. 48. The other passage is in the *Third Part of King Henry VI.*, and the revolting comparison is more justly appropriated to himself by the wicked Gloster. The king (Edward IV.) says to his brothers :—

K. Edw. Clarence and Gloster, love my lovely queen ;
And kiss your princely nephew, brothers both.
Clar. The duty that I owe unto your majesty,
I seal upon the lips of this sweet babe.
K. Edw. Thanks, noble Clarence; worthy brother, thanks.
Glo. And, that I love the tree from whence thou sprangst,
Witness the loving kiss I give the fruit :—

                                        [*Then aside.*

To say the truth, so *Judas kissed his master* ;
And *cried ' All hail !' when as he meant all harm.*

                                        Act v. Sc. 7.

There are two passages in *Antony and Cleopatra* which remind us of the reconciliation of Herod and Pilate, effected, as it would seem, by their common action in the death of Christ.   See Luke xxiii. 12.

---

* Countenances.   See Pt. I. ch. ii.

But soon that war had end, and the time's state
Made friends of them, jointing their force 'gainst Cæsar.
                                                    Act 1. Sc. 2.
                    I know not, Menas,
How lesser enmities may give way to greater.
Were't not that we stand up against them all,
'Twere pregnant they would square between themselves ;
For they have entertained cause enough
To draw their swords : but how the fear of us
May cement their divisions, and bind up
The petty difference, we yet not know.   Act ii. Sc. 1.

Pilate's washing his hands, as recorded in Matt.
xxvii. 24, is referred to by Shakspeare in two instances, one of which is omitted by Mr. Bowdler,
while the other is retained.

When King Richard II. is pressed by Bolingbroke
and York to resign the crown, and Northumberland
presents the paper containing the crimes alleged
against him as the ground for his abdication, he thus
upbraids them :—

Nay, all of you, that *stand and look upon me,*
Whilst that my wretchedness doth bait myself,—
Tho' some of you, *with Pilate, wash your hands,*
Showing an outward pity ; yet *you Pilates*
Have here *delivered me to my sour cross,*
And water cannot wash away your sin.   Act iv. Sc. 1.

In place of the two intermediate lines, Mr.
Bowdler has this one :—

Tho' some of you are showing outward pity.

In *King Richard III.,* after the murder of Clarence,
one of the assassins exclaims :—

G

A bloody deed, and desperately despatched !
How fain, *like Pilate, would I wash my hands*
Of this most grievous guilty murder done.

Act i. Sc. 4.

The fine passage, at the opening of *Hamlet,* which Shakspeare has put into the mouth of Horatio, owes probably quite as much to S. Matthew or S. Mark as it does to Plutarch, or to Ovid ; though the critics have traced it only to the two latter.

In the most high and palmy state of Rome,
A little ere the mightiest Julius fell,
The graves stood tenantless, and the sheeted dead
Did squeak and gibber in the Roman streets.
Stars shone with trains of fire ; dews of blood fell ;
Disaster veiled the sun ; and the moist star
Upon whose influence Neptune's empire stands,
Was sick almost to doomsday with eclipse.

Act i. Sc. 1.

14. The references made by our poet to the history of the Acts are few and not of much moment; yet they indicate somewhat curiously, if I am not mistaken, the minuteness of his attention to the sacred record.

In the *First Part of King Henry VI.,* among other compliments paid by Charles Dauphin of France to Joan of Arc, she is pronounced superior to ' Saint Philip's daughters,' Act i. Sc. 2, that is the ' four daughters, virgins that did prophecy ' of Philip the Evangelist, who are mentioned in Acts xxi. 9.

In the *Comedy of Errors*,* the scene of which is laid at *Ephesus*, Pinch the *Schoolmaster* is represented also as a *conjuror*.† It will be remembered that Ephesus was the place where S. Paul 'disputed daily in the school of one Tyrannus,' and where 'many of them also that used *curious arts* brought their books together and burned them before all men.' See Acts xix. 9, 19. But previously to this burning of the books we read in the same narrative, v. 13 :—

Then certain of the vagabond Jews, exorcists, took upon them to call over them which had evil spirits the name of the Lord Jesus, saying 'We *adjure* thee by Jesus whom Paul preacheth.'

Compare with this the speech of Pinch in Act iv. Sc. 4.

I charge thee, Satan, housed within this man,
To yield possession to my holy prayers,
And to thy state of darkness hie thee straight;
I *conjure thee* by all the saints in heaven.

To this I may add that in *Pericles, Prince of Tyre*, a servant at Ephesus, which was not far from Colossæ, has the name of Philemon.

In *King Richard III.* we read these words of Gloster, addressed first to Hastings, and then to the officers in attendance :—

---

* One is inclined to suspect that the name *Antipholus* among the characters of this play is a mistake (on the part of author or printer) for *Amphibolus*; i. e. ἀμφίβολος, *ambiguous, doubtful.*

† On the union of the occupations of schoolmaster and conjuror, see Drake's *Shakspeare and his Times*, vol. i. p. 95.

> Thou art a traitor—
> Off with his head! Now, *by Saint Paul I swear,*
> *I will not dine* until I see it done.   Act iii. Sc. 4.

What are we to understand by this adjuration of
S. Paul? Is there an allusion in it to what we read
in Acts xxiii. 12?

> Certain of the Jews banded together, and *bound themselves under
> a curse,* saying that they would *neither eat nor drink* till they had
> killed Paul.

And was there some confusion in our poet's re-
collection of the circumstances, or remembering
them aright, did he still make use of the name of
the apostle on their account? It must be stated,
however, that the same wicked king is made to use
the same oath on other occasions; for instance, in the
scene before the Battle of Bosworth :—

> *By the Apostle Paul,* shadows to-night
> Have struck more terror to the soul of Richard
> Than can the substance of ten thousand soldiers,
> Arm'd in proof, and led by shallow Richmond.
> Act v. Sc. 3.

Why this oath should have been assigned no less
than five times to King Richard III., but to no one
else, in this play, and yet should not be found so
much as once in any other, I am unable to explain;
nor am I aware that the fact has been noticed by
any of the critics.

We know how S. Paul has ' protested ' of himself with reference to his daily life of mortification,
of hardship and self-denial :—

> I die daily.   1 Cor. xv. 31.

The same character is given in *Macbeth*, by Macduff, to the mother of Malcolm, whom he is addressing :—

> Thy royal father
> Was a most sainted king : the queen, that bore thee,
> Oftener upon her knees than on her feet,
> *Died every day she lived.*   Act iv. Sc. 3.

Moreover, we know how the same great apostle has protested also, that neither in his own teaching, nor in the promises of God, through Christ, is there any uncertainty, any vacillation, any saying of both ' yea and nay.' 2 Cor. i. 17–20. And so King Lear, complaining of the treatment he had received from his unnatural daughter :—

> To say *ay*, and *no*, to every thing I said ! *Ay and no too was no good divinity.*   Act iv. Sc. 6.

Once more : Prospero says to Miranda, in the *Tempest :*—

> The direful spectacle of the wreck which touch'd
> The very virtue of compassion in thee,
> I have with such provision in mine art
> So safely ordered, that there is no soul—
> No, *not so much perdition as an hair,*
> Betid to any creature in the vessel
> Which thou heard'st cry, which thou saw'st sink.
>   Act i. Sc 2.

And Ariel afterwards reports, ' Not a hair perished.' In a note upon this passage, it has been suggested, with good reason, by Mr. Holt White, that Shakspeare may have had in his mind the hortatory speech of S. Paul to the ship's company, where he assures them that, though they were to suffer ship-wreck :

There shall not an hair fall from the head of any of you.

Acts xxvii. 34.

CHAPTER II.

Of Shakspeare's Religious Principles and Sentiments derived from the Bible.

E are now to enter upon that which is the most important, and, I trust, will be found the most interesting part of our undertaking. We are to show how scriptural, and consequently how true and just, are the conceptions which Shakspeare entertained of the being and attributes of God, of His general and particular Providence, of His revelation to man, of our duty towards Him and toward each other, of human life and of human death, of time and of eternity— in a word, of every subject which it most concerns us as rational and responsible beings to conceive aright.

SECT. 1. *Of the Being and Nature of God.*

To begin, then, with the titles and attributes of God. Among the names by which He is revealed to us in Scripture, are these: The Lord of Hosts, the King Immortal, the King of Kings.

In the *First Part of King Henry VI.* the Bishop of Winchester, Cardinal Beaufort, thus speaks of the deceased King Henry V. in the presence of his corpse, lying in state :—

> He was a king, blessed of the KING OF KINGS,
> The battles of the LORD OF HOSTS he fought.
>
> Act i. Sc. 1.

And, in the *Second Part of King Henry IV.*, Prince Henry to his father lying on his death-bed :—

> There is your crown :
> And HE that wears the crown IMMORTALLY
> Long guard it yours !   Act iv. Sc. 4.

Among the attributes of God, we have been taught by revelation that He knows* all things; that He sees all things, even our most secret thoughts; that He neither slumbers, nor sleeps; and that His ways are not as our ways.

Truly, therefore, is it said by Helena to the King of France :—

> It is not so with HIM THAT ALL THINGS KNOWS,
> As 'tis with us that square our guess by shows;
> But most it is presumption in us, when
> The help of Heaven we count the act of men.
>
> *All's well that ends well.*   Act ii. Sc. 1.

Justly, too, does Hermione express her confidence when falsely accused :—

---

* On the divine omniscience.   See below, Ch. iii.

If powers divine
Behold our human actions, *as they do*,
I doubt not then but innocence shall make
False accusation blush, and tyranny
Tremble at patience. *Winter's Tale*, Act iii. Sc. 2.

Nor was it without reason that Laèrtes, seeing and hearing proofs of the madness of his sister Ophelia, appealed to the divine compassion :—

Do you see this, O GOD ? *Hamlet*, Act iv. Sc. 5.

Nor, again, that Queen Elizabeth, wife of King Edward IV., after the murder of her children, the two young Princes in the Tower, should thus expostulate :—

Wilt thou, O GOD, fly from such gentle lambs,
And throw them in the entrails of the wolf?
When *did'st Thou sleep*, when such a deed was done ?
K. Richard III. Act iv. Sc. 4.

Nor, once more, that Queen Katharine should protest against the two cardinals who had lent themselves to accomplish her divorce from King Henry VIII. :— .

Ye have angels' faces, but *Heaven knows your hearts*.
K. Henry VIII. Act iii. Sc. 1.

It may be that the striking description of Divine Providence, which we read in *Troilus and Cressida*, is pitched too high for heathen characters (a subject of which I shall have occasion to speak presently), but if admissible there at all, it could not be better placed than it is in the mouth of Ulysses :—

The providence that's in a watchful state,
Finds bottom in the uncomprehensive deeps ;
Keeps place with thought, and almost, *like the gods,*
Does *thoughts unveil* in their dumb cradles.*

Act iii. Sc. 3.

In a note upon this passage, Dr. Henley asks, 'Is there not here some allusion to the sublime description of the Divine Omnipresence in the 139th Psalm ?' However this question may be answered, there will be no doubt in other passages that our poet's views of the providence, goodness, and justice of God were drawn directly from Holy Scripture. Thus, where Hamlet says—

There is a special providence in the fall of a sparrow—

Act v. Sc. 2.

we cannot doubt of the poet's allusion to our Lord's words :—

Are not two sparrows sold for a farthing ?   And one of them shall not fall on the ground without your Father.   Matt. x. 29.

Or again, where good old Adam, in *As you like it,* says to Orlando :—

I have five hundred crowns,
The thrifty hire I saved under your father,

.   .   .   .

Take that : and HE *that doth the ravens feed,*
Yea, *providently caters for the sparrow,*
Be comfort to my age !   Act ii. Sc. 3.

We cannot doubt that our poet had in mind both the Psalmist and the Evangelist ; the Psalmist, who writes of GOD, that

---

* To be pronounced, probably, as a trisyllable.

He feedeth the young ravens that call upon Him.

Ps. cxlvii. 9.

and the Evangelist, who records our Lord's words :

Behold the fowls of the air ; for they sow not, neither do they reap, nor gather into barns, yet your Heavenly Father feedeth them. Matt. vi. 26.

From such an image it was an easy step for one with Shakspeare's imagination to moralize as he does in the following lines, spoken by King Henry VI. to the Duke of Suffolk :—

But what a point, my lord, your falcon made,
And what a pitch she flew above the rest!
To see how *God in all his creatures works*!
Yea, man and birds are fain * of climbing high.

K. Henry VI. 2nd Part. Act ii. Sc. 1.

And equally easy was it for a mind of Shakspeare's versatility to make a wicked man apply conversely the doctrine of God's goodness in His general providence, as does King Richard III.—the doctrine, I mean, which we read also in the Sermon on the Mount, that our Heavenly Father

maketh His sun to rise on the evil and on the good, and sendeth rain on the just and on the unjust. Matt. v. 45.

K. Rich. Give me a calendar.
Who saw the sun to day ?
Ratcliff. Not I, my lord.
K. Rich. Then he disdains to shine ; for, by the book,
He should have brav'd the east an hour ago :
A black day will it be to somebody.—
Ratcliff,—

---

* Fond.

Rate. My lord?
K. Rich. The sun will not be seen to-day;
The sky doth frown and lour upon our army.
I would these dewy tears were from the ground.
Not shine to-day! Why, what is that to me,
More than to Richmond? for *the self-same Heaven*
That frowns on me, looks sadly upon him.
K. Richard III. Act v. Sc. 3.

But this assertion of the general providence and common goodness of God, as we find them asserted in Scripture, does not prevent our poet from appealing confidently to the Divine Justice, as an unerring arbiter and maintainer of the right. It is in the spirit in which Laban said to Jacob,

See, God is witness betwixt me and thee—Gen. xxxi. 50.

that Malcolm says to Macduff:—

God above

Deal between thee and me.   *Macbeth,* Act iv. Sc. 3.

And the double lesson which is taught in the following passage, viz. that kings are not to be deposed by their subjects, and that, acting rightly, we may depend upon the Divine protection, is in both respects plainly Scriptural, and therefore true; though in neither case so as to forbid qualification, or exclude exception.

K. Rich. Not all the water in the rough rude sea
Can wash the balm from an anointed king:
The breath of worldly men cannot depose
The deputy elected by the Lord.
For every man that Bolingbroke hath pressed
To lift shrewd steel against our golden crown,

God for his Richard hath in heavenly pay
A glorious angel ; then, if angels fight,
Weak men must fall ; for *Heaven still guards the right.*
K. Richard II. Act iii. Sc. 2.

Both sentiments are repeated in the same play—
the former thus :—

K. Rich.   Show us the hand of God
That hath dismiss'd us from our stewardship ;
For well we know, no hand of blood and bone
Can gripe the sacred handle of our sceptre,
Unless he do profane, steal, or usurp.   *Ibid.* Sc. 3.

And again :—

Gaunt.   Let Heaven revenge; for I may never lift
An angry arm against His minister.   *Ibid.* Act i. Sc. 2.

which reminds us directly of David's forbearance
towards Saul, 1 Sam. xxiv. 6 ; xxvi. 4.

The latter sentiment is very significantly indicated
in an earlier part of the same scene, where the following dialogue occurs between York and Bolingbroke :—

Boling. Mistake not, uncle, further than you should ;
York.   *Take not,* good cousin, further than you should,
Lest you mistake : *the Heavens are o'er your head.*
Boling. I know it, uncle ; and oppose not myself
Against their will.

We know with how little truth these last words
were spoken. And yet the same Duke of York
did not fail still to trace, with reverence and submission, the hand of Providence in the ursurpation that
ensued :

> Heaven hath a hand in these events,
> To whose high will we bound our calm contents.
>> *Ibid.* Act v. Sc. 2.

It was not so meekly that the spirit of Old John of Gaunt was content to show itself, though exhibiting the same faith in the overruling Providence, but looking also to the just judgment of God :—

> Put we our quarrel to the will of Heaven ;
> Who when He sees the hours ripe on earth,
> Will rain hot vengeance on offenders' heads.
>> *Ibid.* Act i. Sc. 2.

And with equal beauty and propriety Queen Katharine utters the same sentiment in *King Henry VIII.*, addressing the two Cardinals :—

> Is this your Christian counsel ? out upon ye !
> *Heaven is above all yet* :* there sits a Judge
> That no king can corrupt.   Act iii. Sc. 1.

And He is the judge ' to whom judgment belongeth,' because He alone is ' set in the throne, judging right,' and discerning all things, as the religious King Henry VI. piously confesses :—

> O THOU, *that judgest all things, stay my thoughts* ;
> If my suspect be false, forgive me, GOD :
> For judgment only doth belong to THEE.
>> *King Henry VI. 2nd Part,* Act iii. Sc. 2.

---

* A corresponding sentiment is put by Sophocles with great effect into the mouth of the Chorus addressing Electra :

> Θάρσει μοι, Θάρσει, τέκνον·
> ἔστι μέγας ἐν οὐρανῷ
> Ζεὺς, ὃς ἐφορᾷ πάντα καὶ κρατύνει.
>> Soph. *Elect.* 173–6.

When the Duke öf Albany, in *King Lear*, hears from a messenger that the Duke of Cornwall was ' dead, slain by his servant,' he exclaims :—

> This shows You are above,
> You justicers, that these our nether crimes
> So speedily can venge !   Act iv. Sc. 2.

On the other hand, the tender mercy and loving kindness of the Divine Being, more especially towards those who need them most, are exhibited by our poet, again and again, in passages which represent the teaching of Scripture no less faithfully. For example ; He who

> is a Father of the fatherless, and defendeth the cause of the widow,   Ps. lxviii. 5.

is thus described in *King Richard II.* :—

> *Duchess.* Where then, alas! may I complain myself?
> *Gaunt.*   To Heaven—*the Widow's Champion and Defence.*
>   Act. i. Sc. 2.

And He who ' giveth sight to the blind,' and ' light to him that is in misery,' thus, in *King Henry VI.* *2nd Part* :—

> *K. Henry.* Now God be praised, that to believing souls,
> Gives light in darkness, comfort in despair.   Act ii. Sc. 1.

But, of all others, the well-known speech of Portia, · in the *Merchant of Venice*, exhibits the Divine attributes of mercy and forgiveness most clearly, and with the plainest reference to Holy Scripture :—

> *Portia* (to Antonio). Do you confess the bond ?
> *Anton.*   I do.

Port. Then must the Jew be merciful.

Shylock. On what compulsion must I ? tell me that.

Port. The quality of mercy is not strained :
It droppeth, as the gentle rain from heaven
Upon the place beneath : it is twice blessed ;
It blesseth him that gives, and him that takes :
'Tis mightiest in the mightiest ; it becomes
The throned monarch better than his crown :
His sceptre shows the force of temporal power,
The attribute to awe and majesty,
Wherein doth sit the dread and fear of kings ;
But mercy is above this scepter'd sway,
It is enthroned in the hearts of kings ;
It is an attribute to God himself ;
And earthly power doth then show likest God's,
When mercy seasons justice.   Therefore, Jew,
Tho' justice be thy plea, consider this,—
That, in the course of justice, none of us
Should see salvation : we do pray for mercy ;
And that same prayer doth teach us all to render
The deeds of mercy.   I have spoke thus much,
To mitigate the justice of thy plea ;
Which if thou follow, this strict court of Venice
Must needs give sentence 'gainst the merchant there.

    Shylock.   My deeds upon my head ! I crave the law,
The penalty and forfeit of my bond.   Act iv. Sc. 1.

In this last answer of Shylock, our poet has adopted
with great propriety a form of speech— ' my deeds
upon my head '—which reminds us, as Dr. Henley
has pointed out, of the imprecation of the Jews,
addressed to Pilate—

His blood be on us, and on our children.   Matt. xxvii. 25.

On the other hand, the concluding part of Portia's
speech called forth from Sir W. Blackstone the

remark that to 'refer the Jew to the Christian doctrine of salvation, and the Lord's Prayer, is a little out of character.' The learned judge was probably not aware that the Lord's Prayer was not composed by our Lord as containing anything which would be new and strange to His disciples, but as putting together, in a short form, all that was most valuable in the Jewish liturgies already known to them. See Lightfoot, vol. ii. p. 159, and p. 439, and Grotius on S. Matthew, vi. 9; who also refers to Ecclesiasticus xxviii. 2-4 :—

Forgive thy neighbour the hurt that he hath done unto thee, so shall thy sins also be forgiven when thou prayest. One man beareth hatred against another, and doth he seek pardon from the Lord? He sheweth no mercy to a man which is like himself, and doth he ask forgiveness of his own sins?

The critics, therefore, who, like Burkitt, except the particular clause which Portia refers to, viz. ' as we forgive them that trespass against us,' from the foregoing representation in regard to the origin of the several petitions of the *Lord's Prayer*, have, in all probability, made that single exception without sufficient reason. Besides, it is to be borne in mind that many of the Jews, though they did not accept Christ as their Messiah, yet they did accept Him as 'a teacher come from God.' And certainly it is not correct to suppose that the Christian *Doctrine* of salvation is not also the doctrine of salvation to the faithful Jew.

Upon the opening lines of the same speech of

H

Portia, Mr. Douce has pointed out the resemblance to Ecclesiasticus xxxv. 20 :—

> Mercy is seasonable in the time of affliction, as *clouds of rain* in the time of drought.

And the argument drawn by Portia from the need which we all have for the mercy of God is repeated by our poet in the *Second Part of King Henry VI.*, where Lord Say says to the rebels, who are carrying him off to execution :—

> Ah, countrymen ! if when you make your prayers,
> God should be so obdurate as yourselves,
> How would it fare with your departed souls ?
>
> Act iv. Sc. 8.

I have been loath to question the propriety of an observation made by so sound a thinker and so well-informed a writer as Judge Blackstone ; and now I ought not to quit this portion of my subject without drawing attention to a remark of one whose authority upon matters of this kind is still higher. I mean Dr. Johnson. In a note upon the last scene of *King Lear* he complains that ' our author, *by negligence,* gives his Heathens the sentiments and practices of Christianity.' And Mr. Singer has repeated the remark in his edition of 1826. But I am inclined to doubt whether it is altogether well-founded.* The lines which appeared to give occasion for it are these :—

> The gods are just, and of our pleasant vices
> Make instruments to scourge us.   Act v. Sc. 3.

---

* See *Supplementary Note* at end of the volume.

Now, we meet with the same sentiment in the Apocryphal Book of *Wisdom* :—

For the foolish devices of their wickedness wherewith being deceived they worshipped serpents void of reason and wild beasts, Thou didst send a multitude of wild beasts upon them for vengeance, that they might know that *wherewithal a man sinneth, by the same also shall he be punished.* xi. 16.

And though I cannot now remember any passage of a profane author* that comes *fully* up to the same sentiment, or nearer to it than what we read in Æschylus (Agam.† v. 170, *sq.*) and Juvenal (Sat. i. 142, *sqq.*), yet I have little doubt that such a passage may be found. But with regard to the remark itself, the truth, I believe, is that Shakspeare does, for the most part, make a difference between his Heathen and his Christian characters. For instance, in the very play upon which Johnson's remark is made, *King Lear*, we find the following sentiment, which I very much doubt whether our poet would have allowed any but a Heathen character to utter :—

As flies to wanton boys, are we to the gods ;—
They kill us for their sport :

lines which Mr. Bowdler has *omitted*, instead of

---

* We have it in St. Chrysostom upon the third Psalm, with a play upon the words, which must be lost in a translation. ὅϑεν ἡ πηγὴ τῆς ἁμαρτίας, ἐκεῖϑεν ἡ πληγὴ τῆς τιμωρίας.—Vol. v. p. 3.

† Compare the sentiment in *K. Lear*, Act ii. Sc. 4.
            ' To wilful men,
    The injuries that they themselves procure
    Must be their schoolmasters.'

suggesting in a note that they are spoken by one
who was not a Christian. Again, I am inclined to
think, that in *Coriolanus*, it is *purposely* left a doubtful point whether mercy was an attribute of the
Deity or no. I allude to the following dialogue
between Menenius and Sicinius, respecting Coriolanus, towards the close of the play :

> *Menenius.* What he bids be done, is finished with his bidding.
> *He wants nothing of a god but eternity and a heaven to throne in.*
> *Sicinius.* Yes, *mercy*, if you report him truly.
> *Menenius.* I *paint him in the character.** Mark what mercy
> his mother shall bring from him. There is *no more mercy in him*
> *than there is milk in a male tiger.* ˙Act v. Sc. 4.

At the same time I must admit that in *Titus Andronicus*, of which the characters are Heathen also,
mercy is undoubtedly recognized as a divine attribute, where Tamora, Queen of the Goths, says to
Titus :—

> Wilt thou draw near the nature of the gods?
> Draw near them, then, in being merciful. Act ii. Sc. 2.

In regard to this passage, however, it may be
observed, *first*, that the play in which it occurs is
generally allowed not to be Shakspeare's; *secondly*,
that the date of the action belongs to a period
almost as many centuries *after*, as Coriolanus was
before, the commencement of the Christian era; and,
thirdly, that in the interval are to be found, even
in heathen authors, passages which fall little, if at

---

* That is, to the life, as he is.

all, short of the same sentiment. Take, for example, what Cicero had said in addressing Cæsar on
behalf of Ligarius—a passage partly quoted by
Mr. Whalley :—

Nihil est tam populare quam bonitas; nulla de virtutibus tuis
plurimis nec admirabilior nec gratior *misericordiâ* est. Homines
enim *ad Deos nullâ re propius accedunt* quam salutem hominibus
dando.—*Orat. pro Ligario,* c. 12.

There is, however, one play of Shakspeare to
which it must, I think, be admitted, the remark of
Johnson is justly applicable, at least in some degree.
I allude to *Cymbeline,* where Jupiter is made to
say :—

Whom best I love,* I cross.   Act v. Sc. 4.

And again, in the 1st Scene of the same Act, where
Posthumus exclaims :—

Gods ! if you
Should have ta'en vengeance on my faults, I never
Had lived to put on † this : so had you saved
The noble Imogen to repent, and struck
Me wretch, more worth your vengeance. But, alack !
You snatch some hence for little faults ; *that's love,
To have them fall no more* ; you some permit
To second ills with ills, each elder worse.

Compare Isaiah lvii. 1,

Merciful men are taken away, none considering that the
righteous is taken away from the evil to come.

---

* There is also a passage in *Othello,* too painful to be quoted,
where it has been remarked that reference is made to the doctrine of
Scripture. 'Whom the Lord *loveth,* He *chasteneth.'*—See Act v.
Sc. 2.
    † i. e. to incite, instigate.

Upon the whole, then, while I cannot deny altogether the justice of Dr. Johnson's censure, still I would remark that to draw any *very broad* lines of distinction in the case referred to would have been impossible without giving certain and perhaps just cause for offence ; and therefore to bring an accusation of ' negligence ' for not doing so, may not unfairly be regarded as somewhat captious and unreasonable:

SECT. 2. *Of the Holy Angels, and of the Fallen.*

A devout invocation for the ministering help of the Holy Angels is not to be confounded with the impiety of addressing them in prayer. The one is encouraged, the other is forbidden in Holy Scripture. Such invocations abound in *Hamlet*, and though the story of that play refers to a period long before the Reformation, and though, on that account, Shakspeare would seem to have intended to represent the characters as tinged, to some extent, with the errors of Romanism,* yet I am not sure that upon

---

* Thus the Ghost of Hamlet's father speaks of his being
      ' Confined to fast in fires,
   Till the foul crimes, done in my days of nature,
   Are burnt and purged away ;'   Act i. Sc. 5.
that is, the doctrine of purgatory ; and again, of being
   ' Cut off even in the blossoms of my sin,
   Unhousel'd, disappointed, *unanel'd* ; '
that is, without the sacrament of extreme unction. And Hamlet, in

the point now before us he has transgressed the limits which a sound theology would impose. For instance, there is nothing to object to in the exclamation of Hamlet, at the sight of the Ghost—

Angels and ministers of grace, defend us !   Act i. Sc. 4.

for,

Are they not all ministering spirits, sent forth to minister for them that shall be heirs of salvation ?   Heb. i. 14.

And again, when the Ghost reappears in Act iii. Sc. 4 :

Save me, and hover o'er me with your wings,
You heavenly guards !

Nor is the exclamation of the guilty king, when struggling to repent, and to betake himself to prayer, less appropriate :—

Help, Angels, make assay !
Bow, stubborn knees ! and, heart with strings of steel,
Be soft as sinews of the new-born babe !
All may be well.   Act iii. Sc. 3.

And how pious and touching is the farewell of Horatio when Hamlet dies :—

Now cracks a noble heart : Good night, sweet prince ;
And *flights of angels sing thee to thy rest !* Act v. Sc. 2.

The singing of angels, and their loving attendance upon the good at all times, but especially in their last moments, have furnished our poet with beautiful

---

addressing the players, Act ii. Sc. 2, swears ' By 'r Lady ! ' and again in Act iii. Sc. 4. ' By the rood.'   Of which oaths Mr. Bowdler omits the former, but not the latter.   On the other hand, however, also in the last-named scene, Hamlet says to the Queen :—

' Confess yourself *to Heaven.*'

and affecting imagery on two other occasions. The former in the *Merchant of Venice*, in the moonlight scene where Lorenzo says to Jessica :—

> Look how the floor of heaven
> Is thick inlaid with patines of bright gold ;
> There's not the smallest orb, which thou behold'st,
> But in his motion *like an angel sings*,
> Still quiring to the young-eyed cherubims.   Act v. Sc. 1.

The latter, in *King Henry VIII.*, where the Duke of Norfolk, speaking of Cardinal Wolsey in reference to the good Queen Katharine, thus testifies to her duty and affection for her unworthy husband :—

> He counsels a divorce—a loss of her,
> That, like a jewel, has hung twenty years
> About his neck, yet never lost her lustre ;
> Of her that loves him with that excellence,
> That *angels** love good men with* ; even of her,
> That, when the greatest stroke of fortune falls,
> Will bless the king.   Act ii. Sc. 2.

It is an opinion held by tradition in the Church, rather than directly derived from Scripture, that pride, or ambition, was the sin which led to the fall of Satan, and his associate angels.   To this opinion our poet has referred in the well-known dying speech of Cardinal Wolsey to his servant Cromwell, afterwards the celebrated Earl of Essex :—

> Cromwell, I charge thee, fling away ambition ;
> By that sin *fell the angels* ; how can man, then,
> The image of his Maker, hope to win by 't ?
>   Act iii. Sc. 2.

---

* Angels are represented as ' *weeping* ' over the pride and follies of men in *Measure for Measure*, Act ii. Sc. 2.

In a previous part of the same scene, Wolsey had soliloquised to the same effect, using the same comparison, with the addition of the fearful consideration that such a fall is without hope :—

> O ! how wretched
> Is that poor man, that hangs on princes' favours !
> There is, betwixt that smile we would aspire to,
> That sweet aspect of princes, and their* ruin,
> More pangs and fears than wars or woman have :
> And when he falls, *he falls like Lucifer,*
> Never to hope again.

The simile in this last passage is evidently formed upon Isaiah xiv. 12,

> How art thou fallen from heaven, O Lucifer, Son of the morning;

where the well-known Oriental figure † of speech, in which the overthrow of kingdoms is represented by the falling or eclipse of the Heavenly Bodies, is applied prophetically to the downfall of the King of Babylon.   But there is no Scriptural authority for giving the name of Lucifer, or Morning Star, to Satan.   The misapplication of the name, however, if it is to ·be considered such, did not originate with our poet.   On the contrary, we find that in very early times ‡ the Prophet Isaiah was understood to speak in that place of the evil spirit; and long before Shakspeare the name Lucifer had been, in consequence, popularly so applied.   Mr. Malone quotes

---

* i. e. Their displeasure, producing overthrow.
† See *Lowth* on Isaiah xiii. 10.
‡ e. g. By Tertullian.—See *Advers. Marcion.* Lib. v. pp. 475, 482.

very appositely from Churchyard's Legend of Cardinal Wolsey (published in Higgin's *Mirrour for
Magistrates,* 1527)—

> Your fault not half so great as was my pride;
> For which offence fell Lucifer * from the skies.

In a scene which shows that our poet possessed a
remarkable insight into the Scotch character, and
designed to exhibit it, more especially in Malcolm,
the son of the murdered king, we read :—

> Angels are bright still, *tho' the brightest fell.*
> *Macbeth,* Act iv. Sc. 3.

And then became most deformed. So our poet
speaks of ' the fiend ' in *King Lear,* Act iv. Sc. 2; of
' the common enemy of man,' in *Macbeth,* Act iii.
Sc. 1, and in *Twelfth Night,* Act iii. Sc. 4. And
he follows up the idea in *King Henry V.* :—

> What is it then to me, if impious war,
> *Arrayed in flames,* like to the *prince of fiends,*
> Do, with his *smirch'd complexion,* all fell feats
> Enlink'd to waste and desolation ?   Act iii. Sc. 3.

Again, he is described, in the language of Scripture,
as the ' Prince of Darkness,' in *King Lear,* Act iii.
Sc. 3, and in *All's well,* &c., Act iv. Sc. 5 ; also, in
the latter place, as ' the Prince of the World ;' and
by implication, as ' the Father of Lies,' in *King
Henry IV.* 1*st Part,* where Hotspur says to Glendower :—

> And I can teach thee, coz, to shame *the devil,*
> By *telling truth.*   Act iii. Sc. 1.

---

* See also *Christian Year,* 3rd Sunday in Lent.

And as a ' slanderer,' or false accuser, in the *Merry Wives of Windsor*, Act v. Sc. 5.
The passage of St. Peter,

> Be sober, be vigilant : because your adversary the devil, as a roaring lion, walketh about, seeking whom he may devour ;
> 1 Pet. v. 8.

was plainly in our poet's mind, in *King Henry V.*, where the king says to the traitor Lord Scroop ;

> If that same dæmon, that hath gull'd thee thus,
> Should *with his lion gait walk the whole world*,
> He might return to vasty Tartar * back
> And tell *the legions*,† I can never win
> A soul so easy as that Englishman's.   Act ii. Sc. 2.

The power which we learn from S. Paul that Satan possesses of ' transforming himself into an angel of light,' 2 Cor. xi. 14, is ascribed to him in *Hamlet*.

> The devil hath power
> To assume a pleasing shape.   Act ii. Sc. 2.‡

And again, with the addition that such deceitful disguises are most used when the worst temptations are to be practised, in *Othello* :—

> When devils will their blackest sins put on,
> They do suggest at first with heavenly shows.
> Act ii. Sc. 3.

---

* i. e. Tartarus.
† See Mark v. 9. and comp. *Twelfth Night*, Act iii. Sc. 4.
‡ See also the doubtful passage in Act iii. Sc. 4, ' That monster custom,' &c.

SECT. 3. *Of God's Goodness in Creation, and in the Redemption of Man.*

How comprehensive is the view which our poet has taken of the goodness of creation in all its stages, from the composition of the simplest herb up to the crowning work of all—the soul of man! And how natural the transition from the rising of day out of night, of light out of darkness, to the reproduction of all things out of the earth, to which they fall and sink as into a grave! How just, also, and how Scriptural, the representation, that though all things were made 'very good' by their Creator, His creature, man, has the power of perverting them to evil, and will abuse that power, or will keep it in subjection, according as he follows the guiding of his own free but corrupted will, which brought death into the world, or obeys the dictates of conscience and of the spirit of grace! I allude to the scene in *Romeo and Juliet*, before Friar Laurence's cell, where the friar, entering with a basket, thus soliloquizes :—

> The grey-eyed morn smiles on the frowning night,
> Checking the Eastern clouds with streaks of light;
> And flecked * darkness *like a drunkard reels*,
> From forth day's path, and Titan's fiery wheels :—

Was our poet indebted here to that bold figure of the the prophet Isaiah, ' The earth shall reel

---

* Spotted, streaked.

to and fro like a drunkard, and shall be removed like a cottage?'—xxiv. 20.

> Now ere the sun advance his burning eye,
> The day to cheer, and night's dank dew to dry,
> I must fill up this osier cage of ours
> With baleful weeds and precious-juiced flowers.—
> The earth, that's nature's mother, is her tomb;
> What is her burying-grave, that is her womb;
> And from her womb children of divers kinds
> We, sucking on her natural bosom find;
> Many for many virtues excellent,
> *None but for some,* and yet all different.
> O! mickle is the powerful grace that lies
> In herbs, plants, stones, and their true qualities;
> *For nought so vile that on the earth doth live,*
> *But to the earth* some special good doth give.*
> Nor aught so good, but strained from that fair use,
> Revolts from true birth, stumbling on abuse :
> Virtue itself turns vice, being misapplied;
> And vice sometimes by action dignified :—

i. e. by the manner, or circumstances in which it is done. We must remember that a Franciscan Friar is speaking; but our poet might have had in mind cases like that of Jacob deceiving his father, or Jael killing Sisera :—

> Within the infant mind of this small flower,
> Poison hath residence, and medicine power;
> For this, being smelt, with that part † cheers each part,
> Being tasted, slugs all senses with the heart.
> Two such opposed foes encamp them still
> In man as well as herbs—*grace and rude will* :

---

* i. e. To the inhabitants of the earth.

† i. e. The sense that smells.

And where the worser is predominant,
Full soon the canker death eats up that plant.

Act ii. Sc. 3.

What a depth of theological truth lies in this last couplet! It is the teaching of S. Paul—'If ye live after the flesh,' the φρόνημα σαρκὸς—the *rude will*—'ye shall die,' Rom. viii. 13; and of S. James, 'when lust hath conceived it bringeth forth sin, and sin, when it is finished, bringeth forth death.' i. 15.

But to continue the subject more immediately before us. There are times when the sight of all this goodness and beauty of creation, and even the contemplation of man himself, so 'fearfully and wonderfully made,' has no sufficient power to remove the weight which presses upon the mind; and in such a mood was Hamlet, when he testified at once to the excellency of what we see above us, and around us, and still more of what we ourselves are, and at the same time to the inability of all to give his spirit the relief it sought:—

Indeed it goes so heavily with my disposition, that this goodly frame, the earth, seems to me a steril promontory; this most excellent canopy, the air, look you, this brave* o'erhanging firmament, this majestreal roof fretted with golden fire, why, it appears no other to me than a foul and pestilent congregation of vapours. What a piece of work is man!† How noble in reason! How infinite in faculty! In form and moving how express and admirable! In action how like an angel! In apprehension how

---

* Fine.   See above, Pt. I. ch. ii.
† Comp. Act. iii. Sc. 2.

like a God! The beauty of the world! The paragon of animals! And yet to me what is this quintessence of dust? Man delights not me; no, nor woman neither.   Act ii. Sc. 2.

And why was this? It was from the knowledge of sin, which had marred all. There had been

A foul defacer of God's handiwork,*

as Queen Margaret calls the wicked King Richard III. in the play so named, Act iv. Sc. 4. And Hamlet knew full well that not only the commission of crime, but the unprofitable employment of our existence, is a contravention of the purpose for which we were created. Hear what he says in a later scene :—

What is a man,
If his chief good, and market † of his time
Be but to sleep, and feed? A beast, no more.
Sure, HE that made us with such large ‡ discourse—
Looking before, and after—gave us not
That capability and god-like reason,
To fust § in us unused.   Act iv. Sc. 4

Our poet's meaning in the use of the word ' discourse' in this passage may be seen by an expression which occurs before, viz. in Act i. Sc. 2 :—

O! heaven! a beast that wants *discourse of reason*
Would have mourned longer.

And I know of no better explanation of the word in this sense than that which may be gathered from Cicero *de Officiis*, lib. i. c. 4 :—

---

* A line omitted by Mr. Bowdler, most needlessly.
† Profit.   ‡ Latitude of comprehension.   § Grow mouldy.

Homo autem, quod *rationis* est particeps (*per quam* consequentia cernit, causas rerum videt, earumque progressus et quasi antecessiones non ignorat, similitudines comparat, rebusque præsentibus adjungit atque adnectit futuras), facile totius vitæ *cursum* videt, ad eamque degendam præparat res necessarias.

But did our poet think that 'discourse of reason,' however 'large,' could avail to remove the depression which arises, but too often, from a sense of unprofitableness, and from a knowledge of sin, both in ourselves and others? No! We have the witness of his last will and testament to the contrary. From that we learn where his hope was fixed. There we read :—

First, I commend my soul into the hands of God, my Creator; hoping and assuredly believing, *through the only merits of Jesus Christ my Saviour*, to be made partaker of life everlasting.

It is in accordance with this Christian hope, this assured belief, that Clarence is made to say to the man who had been sent to murder him in the Tower :—

I charge you, as you hope to have *redemption*,
By Christ's dear blood, shed for our grievous sins,
That you depart, and lay no hands on me..
     King Richard III. Act i. Sc. 4.

And again, our blessed Lord is spoken of, in *King Richard II.* as

The *world's ransom*, blessed Mary's Son.
       Act iv. Sc. 1.

And again, in *King Henry VI. 2nd Part*, as

That dread king that took our state upon Him
To *free us from His Father's wrathful curse*.

And in *King Henry IV.* 1st *Part,* Palestine is described as

> Those holy fields,
> Over whose acres walked *those blessed feet,*
> *Which, fourteen hundred years ago, were nailed*
> *For our advantage on the bitter cross.* Act i. Sc. 1.

It is remarkable, too, how fully our poet recognized the glorious truth, which too many, alas! have endeavoured to obscure ; that Redemption is no partial gift ; that as the disease, which it was mercifully designed to cure, is universal, so the application of the remedy is universal also : according to the teaching of 'S. Paul, that

> As by the offence of one judgment came upon all men to condemnation—and so death passed upon all men, for that all have sinned ;—even so by the righteousness of one the free gift came upon all men unto justification of life. Rom. v. 18 and 12.

The universality of the disease is indicated in *Measure for Measure,* where the virtuous Isabella thus speaks to Angelo, the wicked Lord Deputy, in the Duke's absence :—

> Alas! Alas!
> Why, *all the souls that* * *are,* were forfeit once ;
> And HE that might the vantage best have took,
> *Found out the remedy.* How would you be,
> If He, which is the top of judgment, should
> But judge you as you are ? O think on that;
> And mercy then will breathe within your lips,
> *Like man new made.* Act ii. Sc. 2.

---

* The common reading is ' were,' which is interpreted to refer to Adam and Eve ; but I agree with Warburton in substituting ' are.' To confine the meaning to Adam and Eve, appears to me to render what follows *illogical.*

I

The critics—Warburton, Johnson, Malone, and Holt White—have severally offered different explanations of these last words ; but I am inclined to think they have all missed the poet's meaning. ' Like man new made,' means, I believe, *like man redeemed, like the redemption of man ;* and the words are to be understood as put, *per epexegesin,* in reference to the entire clause in the preceding line ; thus, Isabella says in effect :—

' Your merciful act will be like the mercy shown in the redemption of the world, whereby mankind, lost and condemned to death (as her brother Claudio was), are restored to life.' And so the universality of the remedy will also be implied in those words, as it is plainly stated in these which follow, from *King Henry VI. 2nd Part* :—

> Now, by the death of HIM that *died for all* !
>
> Act i. Sc. 1.

This all-important subject—the extent of evil, and its cure—will receive further elucidation in the next and subsequent sections.

SECT. 4. *Of Human Life, and of ' The World.'*

It was worthy of the position which Wolsey had held in church and state, that his voice should be made the instrument, at the close of his career, to recommend, in a few words, all the great points of

the highest Christian morality, however he had
fallen short in his own practice of them. I refer to
the speech in which he gave his final charge to
Cromwell :—

> Love thyself last. *Cherish those hearts that hate* thee.*
> Corruption wins not more than honesty.
> Still in thy right hand carry gentle peace,
> To silence envious tongues. Be just, and fear not.
> Let all the ends thou aimest at be thy country's,
> Thy God's, and Truth's : then if thou fall'st, O Cromwell,
> Thou fall'st a blessed martyr.
> > *King Henry VIII.* Act iii. Sc. 2.

Here we have duty to God, to our neighbour,
to our country ; renunciation of self ; love of enemies ; the practical study of truth, of justice, of
integrity, of peaceableness ; all these strung together like so many pearls upon one string, in a
manner that may remind us of S. Paul's delineation
of charity, or of the summaries of moral duty, which
we read in the 12th chapter of the Epistle to the
Romans, and in the concluding chapter of the 1st
Epistle to the Thessalonians.

Nor was it less worthy of the highest officer in
a king's household, the Lord Chamberlain Polonius,
that in sending forth his son into the world he
should thus give him lessons for life ; lessons which
again may remind us of those given to their respec-

---

* Warburton proposed to read ' wait,' for reasons which rightly,
I think, appeared unsatisfactory to Steevens.

tive sons, under circumstances more or less similar,
by King James, by Sir Walter Raleigh, by Lord
Burleigh, by the Earl of Strafford,* and to his
nephew, afterwards Lord Camelford, by the Earl of
Chatham :—

> There—my blessing † with you ;—
>   [*Laying his hand upon Laertes' head.*]
> And these few precepts in thy memory
> Look thou character.   Give thy thoughts no tongue,
> Nor any unproportioned thought his act.
> Be thou familiar, but by no means vulgar.
> The friends thou hast, and their adoption tried,
> Grapple them to thy soul with hooks of steel.
>
>   .   .   .   .   .   .
>
> Give every man thine ear, but few thy voice.
> Take each man's ‡ censure, but reserve thy judgment.
>
>   .   .   .   .   .
>   §
> Neither a borrower, nor a lender be :
> For loan oft loses both itself and friend ;
> And borrowing dulls the edge of husbandry.
> This above all : TO THINE OWN SELF BE TRUE ;
> And it must follow, as the night the day,
> Thou canst not then be false to any man.
> Farewell ;—my blessing season this in thee !
>   *Hamlet*, Act i. Sc. 3.

In the foregoing injunction respecting hearing
and speaking, especially when taken in connection
with one which I have not quoted, viz.

> Beware of entrance to a quarrel—

---

* See K. James' works, and a collection entitled *Practical Wisdom,
or the Manual of Life*, published in 1824.

† See below, *Sect.* 8.   ‡ Opinion.

§ In one of the lines here omitted our poet probably had in view
Ecclesiasticus xix. 30, quoted by Mr. Todd.

we may fancy that we hear an echo to the precepts of S. James :—

> Let every man be swift to hear, slow to speak, slow to wrath.
>
> James i. 19.

And it would be easy to produce Scriptural parallels to other parts of the same passage, especially from the Book of Proverbs; but in so doing I should be losing sight of the object which I have now more immediately in hand. The design of this section is not to enter into the details, of which human life and Christian duty are made up, but to prepare the way for entering upon such details in the sections that are to follow. A general view has been taken of the subject proposed; and now, before we proceed further into particulars, it will be necessary to notice some abstruser points which lie at the root of all moral action for us Christians; such as the corruption of nature, already touched upon in the last section; the need of grace; and the theory of the formation of moral habits : and then to say something of ' the world,' and of life, as it is seen at different stages and in several conditions; and of the duty of preserving the gift which God has given us.

How beautiful is the description, in *Winter's Tale*, given by Polixenes, of the innocent boyhood of himself and Leontes, which, with poetical exaggeration, he represents to have been free

from all other taint, save only that of original
sin :—

> We were as twinn'd lambs, that did frisk i' the sun,
> And bleat the one at the other : what we changed,
> Was innocence for innocence; we knew not
> The doctrine * of ill-doing, nor dream'd
> That any did : had we pursued that life,
> And our weak spirits ne'er been higher rear'd
> With stronger blood, we should have answer'd Heaven
> Boldly, *Not guilty : the imposition clear'd,*
> *Hereditary ours.*   Act i. Sc. 2.

That is, provided the guilt imposed upon us by
descent from Adam had not made us sinners. And
the effect of this taint is such, and so universal,
especially upon the thoughts of the heart, that
Solomon enquires—

> *Who* can say, I have made my heart clean, I am pure from my
> sin ?   Prov. xx. 9.

In like manner, Iago asks—

> Where's that palace, whereinto foul things
> Sometimes intrude not? Who has a breast so pure,
> But some uncleanly apprehensions,
> Keep leets † and law-days, and in sessions sit,
> With meditations lawful ?   *Othello,* Act iii. Sc. 3.

This is the source from which offences spring ;
and the saying of William's to King Henry—

> All offences, my liege, come from the heart—
>   *K. Henry V.* Act iv. Sc. 8.

is no other than the teaching of our Lord himself,
in the Gospels. See Matt. xv. 18 ; Mark vii. 21.

---

* To be read as a trisyllable.   † Meetings in court.

And the heart being thus universally corrupt, we are at no loss to account for the universality of actual sin. Bearing upon this point, there is a re-markable passage in *Hamlet*, which has caused no little stir among the commentators. It is in the dialogue between Hamlet and Polonius in Act ii. Sc. 2 :—

> *Ham.* I would you were so honest a man.
> *Pol.* Honest, my lord ?
> *Ham.* Ay, sir ; to be honest, as this world goes, is to be one man picked out of ten thousand.
> *Pol.* That's very true, my lord.
> *Ham.* For if the sun breed maggots in a dead dog, being a god, kissing carrion—

The sense is there broken off; but with the help of Warburton's emendation* of the text—an emenda-tion which Johnson commends so highly as to say of it, that ' it almost sets the critic on a level with the author '—we can scarcely doubt that the poet's meaning was (as Warburton explains it) to vindi-cate the Providence of God from the false conclu-sions to which the prevalence of evil in the world might appear to give rise, and to represent the Deity as no more responsible for the corruption in man's heart than the sun is responsible for the maggots bred in a dead dog.† In a latter part of

---

* The only difficulty in accepting it arises from the illative particle ' For.' And I am inclined to think we should read ' Nor ;' and then the inference would be *Nor is God to blame for this, any more than the sun*, &c.

† See the parallel passage in *Measure for Measure*, Act ii. Sc. 2.

the same scene there is another dialogue between Hamlet and Polonius, in which the truest Christian philosophy, in reference to the same point, is again embodied. Hamlet has told Polonius to ' see the players well bestowed,'· or, in other words, ' well used ' :—

> *Pol.* My lord, I will use them according to their desert.
> *Ham.* Much better, man ! use every man after his desert, and who shall 'scape whipping ? *Use them after your own honor and dignity.* The less they deserve, the more merit is in your bounty.

And once more, in Act iii. Sc. 1, Hamlet says to Ophelia :—

> I am myself indifferent honest : but yet I could accuse me of such things that it were better my mother had not borne* me.
> . . . . . What should such fellows as I do crawling between earth and heaven ! *We are arrant knaves all* : Believe none of us.

And if Hamlet could speak after this fashion, how much more Timon the misanthrope !

> All is oblique :
> There's nothing level in our cursed natures,
> But direct villainy. *Timon of Athens*, Act iv. Sc. 3.

A statement painfully strong, and yet not stronger, nor so strong, coming from a heathen, as that of S. Paul, in the third chapter of his Epistle to the Romans, or of the Psalmist whom he there quotes. A more temperate, and therefore, more exact representation of human frailty, as arising partly from

---

* See Matt. xxvi. 24.

natural corruption and partly from our own wilfulness, occurs in *Troilus and Cressida* ; but, though
put also into the mouth of a heathen, it could
scarcely have been written by one who was not
familiar with Holy Scripture :

> *Something may be done* that we *will* not;
> And *sometimes we are devils to ourselves,*
> When we will tempt the frailty of our powers,
> Presuming on their changeful potency.   Act iv. Sc. 4.

The reader will be reminded of James i. 19; and
of Rom. vii. 15–23 ; a passage which was evidently
present to our poet's thoughts on another occasion,
viz., in *Hamlet,* where the sentiment, ' It is no more
I that do it, but sin that dwelleth in me,' is trans-
ferred by Hamlet to his assumed madness, Act v.
Sc. 2.   How just, and like S. Paul again, are the
reflections which pass between the two lords, in
All's well, &c., respecting the origin, the course,
and the result of wicked actions :

> 1*st Lord.* Now Heaven delay our rebellion : *as we are in our-
> selves, how weak are we* !
> 2*nd Lord. Merely our own traitors.* And as in the common
> course of all treasons, we still see them reveal themselves, till they
> attain to their abhorred ends ; so he, that in this action contrives
> against his own nobility, in his proper stream o'erflows* himself.
> Act iv. Sc. 3.

Our poet is still in the same vein, and gives the
same testimony, in *Measure for Measure* :—

---

* Johnson interprets this to mean ' betrays his own secrets in his
own talk.'

> Our natures do pursue,
> (Like rats that ravin down their proper bane),
> A thirsty evil, and when we drink, we die. Act i. Sc. 3.

Men are destroyed, when they suffer themselves to be enticed by unlawful pleasure, as rats are killed by the poison which is set for them to drink.

And, as the Church of England testifies, in her Ninth Article : ' This infection of nature doth remain, yea, in them that are regenerated ;' a truth which our poet, a faithful son of the Church of England, thus represents :—

> Virtue cannot so inoculate our old stock, but we shall relish of it, i. e. *of the old stock.* *Hamlet,* Act iii. Sc. 1.

But if Shakspeare's views of the corruption of human nature were thus clear, and formed upon the teaching of Holy Scripture, so also was his perception of the method of its recovery, through Divine grace. This has been already shown in part, and will be seen more fully in the next section, when we come to speak of the doctrine of repentance. In the mean time, that we are not able of ourselves, and in our own strength alone, to subdue the evil which is so natural to us, we may gather sufficiently from *Love's Labour's lost*, where Biron declares that

> Every man with his affects* is born,
> Not by might mastered, but *by special grace.*
> Act i. Sc. 1.

Shakspeare, no doubt, had learnt his Catechism

---

* Affections and lusts.

well, and would remember the words— ' My good child, know this, that thou art not able to do these things of thyself, nor to walk in the commandments of God, and to serve Him, without His *special grace.*' And not only so ; not even Aristotle, or Bishop Butler himself, has taught the theory and practise of the formation of moral habits more accurately than our poet has done, where Hamlet, seeking to disengage the Queen, his mother, from all inter-course with her wicked and incestuous husband, thus addresses her :—

> Refrain to-night,
> And that shall lend a kind of easiness,
> To the next abstinence : the next more easy : '
> For use almost can change the stamp of nature,
> And either curb the devil, or throw him out
> With wondrous potency. 　　. *Hamlet*, Act iii. Sc. 4.

But our poet would remind us further, that, if a virtuous habit is to be formed, the good purpose which is to lead to it must not be trifled with :—

> For
> Purpose is but the slave to memory ;
> Of violent birth, but poor validity. 　　*Ibid.* Sc. 2.

And, therefore, he justly argues :—

> That we would do,
> We should do, when we would ; for this *would* changes,
> And hath abatements, and delays as many,
> As there are tongues, are hands, are instruments.
> 　　*Ibid.* Act iv. Sc. 7.

Before we quit this subject, I cannot refrain

from noticing how little the mind of Shakspeare appears to have have been infected by the Calvinistic and Puritanical leven which had already begun, in his time, to exercise a strong and spreading influence among his countrymen. It is true he does not shrink—because neither does the Scripture itself shrink—from hinting, more than once, at the mysterious subject of God's decrees. Thus, in Hamlet:

> Our indiscretion sometimes serves us well,
> When our deep plots do fail:* and that should teach us,
> *There's a Divinity that shapes our ends,*
> *Rough-hew them how we will.*   Act v. Sc. 2.

And, apparently, with direct reference to the words of S. Paul, in the Epistle to the Romans, Chap. ix. v. 15, 18 :—

> The words of Heaven—*on whom it will, it will,*
> (i. e. have mercy)
> *On whom it will not, so ;* yet still 'tis just.

At the same time he takes care to explode the pernicious doctrine of fatalism, and the still more monstrous delusions of judicial astrology, which, as Warburton has observed, were also prevalent, when Shakspeare wrote :—

> This is the excellent foppery of the world, that when we are sick in fortune (often the surfeit of our behaviour) we make guilty of our disasters, the sun, the moon, and the stars, *as if we were villains by necessity* ; fools by heavenly compulsion ; . . .

---

* This reading is doubtful : all early authority is in favour of 'pall.'

and all that we are evil in by a divine thrusting on : an admirable
evasion of . . man, to lay his . . disposition to the charge of a star !
K. Lear, Act i. Sc. 2.

Shakspeare divides ' the world ' into that which
is ' familiar to us,' and that which is ' unknown.'
King Henry, Act vii. Sc. 7. And of that which is
familiar to us he, more than once, draws a picture,
the colouring of which, however unattractive, must
be allowed to be faithfully and severely scriptural :

O God ! O God !
How weary, stale, flat and unprofitable,
Seem to me all the uses of this world !
Fye on't ! O fye ! 'tis an unweeded garden,
That grows to seed ; things rank and gross in nature,
Possess it merely.*　　　　　　　*Hamlet*, Act i. Sc. 2.

And again,

Vain pomp, and glory of this world, I hate ye.
K. Henry VIII. Act iii. Sc. 2.

Compare the teaching of the Apostle S. James,
iv. 4, and of S. John, 1st Epistle, ii. 15. But,
if we would see the whole mechanism of ' the
world,' its pride, its emptiness, its parasitism,
its false estimate of men and things, its impatient
jostlings for distinction, its forgetfulness of all but
what presently strikes the eye, I know of nothing
to compare with the dialogue between Achilles and
Ulysses, in *Troilus and Cressida*, Act iii. Sc. 3.
It is too long to quote ; nor is there much in it

---

* i. e. Entirely, absolutely.

which admits of direct comparison with Scripture ; but the reader who is not acquainted with it will be amply rewarded, if he study it at his leisure.

In passing on to speak of *the varied fortune* and *fleeting character* of the several stages and different conditions of human life, I may first make one re-mark upon the mode of reckoning time. In Mark xiii. 35, 'the cock crowing' is used to specify the time of early morning, which Shakspeare denotes more than once in the same manner, distinguishing also the 'first' and the 'second cock ;' while, in *King Richard III.* Act v. Sc. 3, the close of the evening has the name of 'cock shut time,' from a net so called, which was used in the evening twilight to catch woodcocks.

> The *web* of our life is of a mingled *yarn*, good and bad to-gether.

So writes our poet in *All's well*, &c. Act iv. Sc. 3 ; and the metaphor which he uses has now be-come so familiar that we scarcely care to trace it to any source ; though, if we did, we should probably find none more ancient than Isaiah xxxviii. 12. 'My life* is cut off, as by the weaver.' The same may be said of the images which represent life 'vain as a shadow that declineth,' and transitory 'as a tale that is told ;' both of frequent occurrence in

---

* I have adopted Bishop Lowth's translation.

Holy Scripture, and both adopted by our poet in *Macbeth*, and elsewhere :—

> Life's but a walking *shadow* :—
> .   .   .   .   it is *a tale*,
> Told by an idiot.   Act v. Sc. 5.

We find also the comparison, ' life is a shuttle,' in *Merry Wives of Windsor*, Act v. Sc. 2, which requires Job vii. 6, to interpret it, ' My days are *swifter* than a weaver's shuttle.'

Such, then, being our life, so uncertain, so tran-sitory, to ' fear always,'* to ' watch and pray always,' are Divine precepts, which need nothing to recom-mend them to a thoughtful mind. Even a heathen poet like Horace saw reason more than enough for unceasing caution and watchfulness :—

> Quod quisque vitet, nunquam homini satis
> Cautum est in horas : —

And it is *Hecate*, who, in addressing the three witches, is made by Shakspeare to declare :—

> You all know *security*
> Is mortals' chiefest enemy.   *Macbeth*, Act iii. Sc. 5.

The well-known passage, in which ' the world' is described by Shakspeare as ' a stage,' was doubtless derived from no other source than imagination acting upon his own experience as a player ; but the elaborate and melancholy, not to say painful, picture of life, which we read in *Measure for*

---

* See Prov. xxviii. 14 ; xxiii. 17.

Measure, is no less certainly indebted to the Bible for more than one touch of its colouring. The Duke, disguised as a friar, visits Claudio in prison, when condemned to death, and thus addresses him :—

> Reason thus with life,—
> If I do lose thee, I do lose a thing
> That none but fools would keep : *a breath thou art,*
> Servile to all the skiey influences,
> That doth * this habitation, where thou keep'st,
> Hourly afflict.   .   .   .   .
> .   .   .   Happy thou art not:
> For what thou hast not, still thou striv'st to get;
> And what thou hast, forget'st.   Thou art not certain ;
> For thy complexion shifts to strange effects,
> After the moon.   If thou art rich, thou art poor ;
> For, like an ass, whose back with ingots bows,
> Thou bear'st thy heavy riches but a journey,
> And death unloads thee.   .   .   .
> .   .   † Thou hast nor youth nor age ;
> But as it were, an after dinner's sleep,
> Dreaming on both.   Act iii. Sc. 1.

Malone has remarked upon this passage that 'an ass bearing ingots' is an eastern image, and was probably derived from the Scriptures.   See Isaiah xxx. 6. But however gloomy the view which our poet might sometimes take of human life, he does not allow us

---

* Thus I venture to read, instead of 'dost,' (which Hanmer changed into 'do ') in preference to Porson's suggestion of putting the line above in a parenthesis.   I take 'doth ' to be the plural form, which anciently was in common use; as in ' Manners *makyth* man.' Compare Wisdom v. 8, 'What good *hath* riches, with our vaunting, brought us ?' though 'riches ' is there perhaps used as singular, from Fr. *richesse.*

† In the lines here omitted there is an evident reference to 2 Sam. xvi. 11.   'My son which came forth of my bowels, seeketh my life.'

to hesitate respecting the duty imposed upon every man that lives, to do all he can to preserve the precious gift which God has given him.

> The single and peculiar life is bound,
> With all the strength and armour of the mind,
> To keep itself from 'noyance.   *Hamlet*, Act iii. Sc. 3.

And there is nothing in which he is more emphatic than in representing the act of suicide as a direct violation of the Divine law; first, in that same play—

> O! that the Everlasting had not fix'd
> His canon 'gainst self-slaughter;—   Act i. Sc. 2.

Again in *Cymbeline* :—

> Against self-slaughter
> There is a prohibition so divine,
> That cravens my weak hand.   Act iii. Sc. 4.

I am not aware that such a prohibition is to be found * in Holy Scripture ; and in the latter of these plays any reference to Revelation would have been out of place.   The 'canon,' therefore, to which our poet refers must be one of natural religion ; and this is confirmed by a similar sentiment being attributed to Gloster in *King Lear*, and to Brutus in *Julius Cæsar*,† though, in the latter case, with something of subsequent appearance of contradiction in word, and still more of inconsistency in deed.   That such an one as Cleopatra is represented should first call in question the law, and then pronounce it noble to

---

* Unless it be in the Sixth Commandment.   † See below, Sect. 13.

disobey it, is in perfect harmony with her bold bad character :—

> Is it sin
> To rush into the secret house of death,
> Ere death dare come to us ? . .
> . . . What's brave, what's noble,
> Let's do it after the high Roman fashion,
> And make death proud to take us.
>
> *Ant. and Cleop.* Act iv. Sc. 13.

and again :—

> It is great
> To do that thing that ends all other deeds,
> Which shackles accidents and bolts up change.
>
> *Ibid.* Act v. Sc. 2.

I must not omit to add that great and various as are the merits of *Romeo and Juliet*, the pleasure and admiration excited by that play, and the interest felt in the hero and heroine, are all marred in some degree by the suicide which they both commit,* being Christians, and shortly after they had been united in holy matrimony.

SECT. 5. *Of Sin and Repentance.*

We have already spoken of the cause of sin, and of its existence, both original and actual, as universal. It follows to trace it in its operation, and then to speak of its necessary corrective—so far

---

* I am surprised that this should have been overlooked by so acute and sound a critic as Schlegel, who speaks of them as ' still appearing enviable ' in their deaths.

as the correction of it lies within our own power and agency, viz. repentance.

The subtlety of the Tempter, and the craft with which he adapts his temptations, so that he may bring evil out of good, and that virtue itself may be made to minister to sin, for the overthrow of those who could not otherwise be assailed, is very forcibly expressed in *Measure for Measure* :—

> O ! cunning enemy, that to catch a saint,
> With saints doth bait thy hook ! most dangerous
> Is that temptation, that doth goad us on
> To sin in loving virtue.   Act ii. Sc. 3.

It was thus that the beloved apostle was tempted to worship the angel, who had shown him, in the Revelation, the things which he had seen and heard (xxii. 8) ; and countless multitudes of Christians have since been tempted only too successfully to worship the Virgin Mary and other saints, because they remembered not the injunction given on that occasion to St. John, ' See thou do it not !' In like manner we are warned of the danger of entering upon evil courses from the insecurity which attends them, from the distraction and instability which they introduce into the 'counsels of the heart,' and from the inevitable tendency which the doing of one wrong action has to beget another :—

> Alack ! when once our grace we have forgot,
> Nothing goes right ; we would, and we would not.
>   *Measure for Measure*, Act iv. Sc. 4.

And so the wicked King Richard exclaims :—

> I am in
> So far in blood, that *sin will pluck on sin.*
> *King Rich. III.* Act iv. Sc. 2.

And the virtuous Pericles, Prince of Tyre, testifies to the same effect :—

> One sin I know another doth provoke ;
> Murder's as near to lust as flame to smoke.
> Act i. Sc. 1.

It is remarkable that the same holds good of that which is more or less directly the consequence of sin, viz. *sorrow*, which, according to the proverb, *never comes single*.

> One sorrow never comes, but brings an heir,
> That may succeed, as his inheritor.   *Ibid.* Sc. 4.

The course by which sin makes us feel, first naked, like Adam and Eve after their fall, then suspicious, then cowardly, is traced by our poet with remarkable accuracy and Scriptural truth ; and on the other hand, he has not failed to catch the image by which S. Paul speaks of 'the armour of God'— 'the armour of righteousness on the right hand and on the left'—as the defence of all who walk uprightly.

> There is no terror, Cassius, in your threats,
> For I am *armed* so strong *in honesty*,
> That they pass by me as the idle wind,
> Which I respect not.
> *Julius Cæsar*, Act iv. Sc. 3.

What stronger *breastplate*, than *a heart untainted*?
Thrice is he armed that hath his quarrel just;
And he but *naked*, tho' locked up in steel,
Whose *conscience with injustice is corrupted*.
King Hen. VI. 2nd Part, Act iii. Sc. 2.

Suspicion always haunts *the guilty mind*,
The thief doth fear each bush an officer.
King Hen. VI. 3rd Part, Act v. Sc. 6.

The poetical image in this last line will remind the classical reader of Juvenal, Sat. x. 21 :—

˜Motæ ad lunam trepidabis arundinis umbram:—

while the reader of the Bible will recall the fears and suspicions of Herod Antipas, the murderer of John the Baptist, in illustration of the general sentiment.

That ' the righteous is bold as a lion,' that he ' will not be afraid of any evil tidings,' and, on the other hand, that the ungodly are ' brought into great fear even where no fear is,' and that they ' flee when no man pursueth'—these, and such like truths of Holy Scripture, are set forth again and again, in the pages of Shakspeare, with a vividness proportioned to their moral weight. Thus in *King Henry VI. 2nd Part*:—

The trust I have is in mine innocence,
And therefore am I bold and resolute. Act iv. Sc. 4.

And again in *King Lear* :—

Where I could not be honest,
I never yet was valiant.   Act v. Sc. 1.

And again we are taught, if we would be truly

valiant, 'not to fear them that kill the body,' provided that the heart be kept sound and upright.

> He's truly valiant that can *wisely* suffer
> The worst that man can breathe, and make his wrongs
> His outsides; wear them like his garment, carelessly;
> And ne'er prefer his injuries to his heart
> To bring *it* into danger. *Timon of Athens*, Act iii. Sc. 5.

that is, by suffering it to be provoked to uncharitableness or to revenge. At the same time, there are
few who *can* show courageousness like that of S. Paul,
because there are few who exercise themselves
as he did, ' to have always a conscience void of
offence toward God and toward men,' Acts xxiv.
16. ' Thus,' as Hamlet truly testifies :—

> *Conscience does make cowards of us all;*
> And thus the native hue of resolution
> Is sicklied o'er with the pale cast of thought;
> And enterprises of great pith and moment,
> With this regard, their currents turn awry,
> And lose the name of action ;—   Act iii. Sc. 1.

a testimony which the guilty queen his mother soon
after confirms, speaking from her own experience:

> To my sick soul, as *sin's true nature is,*
> Each toy * seems prologue to some great amiss ;†
> So full of artless jealousy is guilt,
> It spills itself in fearing to be spilt.   Act iv. Sc. 5.

And the wicked King Richard III. still more
forcibly :—

---

* Trifle.   † Disaster.

O! coward conscience, how dost thou afflict me!

.   .   .   .   .   .

My conscience hath a thousand several tongues,
And every tongue brings in a several tale,
And every tale condemns me for a villain.   Act v. Sc. 3.

The dialogue between the two murderers, whom
the same wicked king employed to assassinate his
brother, the Duke of Clarence, in the Tower, is an
extraordinary instance of our poet's deep acquaintance
with the most secret workings of the human heart
—such as I know not where to look for in any
other, unless it be in the author of the Book of Proverbs, King Solomon.   The 'bloody deed' was not
yet committed :—

1*st Murd.* What, if thy conscience come to thee again ?
2*nd. Murd.* I'll not meddle with it, it is a dangerous thing ;
it makes a man a coward; a man cannot steal, but it accuseth him ;
a man cannot swear, but it checks him ; a man cannot lie with
his neighbour's wife, but it detects him.   Act i. Sc. 4.

I have not thought it necessary to follow Mr.
Bowdler in omitting this last clause, which shows,
by the bye, how much our poet's mind was tinctured
with the phraseology of Scripture.   The phraseology
indeed would be of small account, if the imitation
of Scriptural language were not accompanied, as it
most evidently is, by an honest desire to give effect
to the moral lessons which the Bible contains.   But
the truth is, that not even the Bible itself represents more vividly than our poet has done, not only
in single passages but in whole plays, the evil

consequences of sin, or shows more plainly how the wicked are confounded by the works of their own hands—that sooner or later our *sin will find us out*, and that it will also most assuredly, sooner or later, be *found out itself*. How are the evils of ambition made to be seen and read of all men in *King Richard III.* and in *Macbeth* ; the evils of jealousy in *Othello* ; the evils of arrogance and self-will in *Coriolanus* !

Of single passages tending to the same general effect it may suffice to produce what follows. In *King Richard II.* Act ii. Sc. 1 :—

> · *York.* What will ensue hereof, there's none can tell ;
> But by bad courses may be understood,
> That their events can never fall out good.

In *King Henry VI. 2nd Part*, Act ii. Sc. 1 :—

> *King Henry.* O God, what mischief work the wicked ones ;
> Heaping confusion on their own heads thereby !

In the *Tempest*, Act iii. Sc. 3 :—

> *Gonzalo.* All three of them are desperate ; their great guilt,
> *Like poison given to work a great time after,*
> Now 'gins to bite the spirits.

In *Hamlet*, Act i. Sc. 2 :—

> *Hamlet.*   Foul deeds will rise
> Though all the earth o'erwhelm them, to men's eyes.

From the disease we naturally pass to the remedy ; and as we have no other source from whence to learn with certainty the true nature of

repentance, except the Bible ; so it may be said,
without exaggeration, that no professed divine ever
understood the doctrine of repentance better, or has
expounded it more clearly than Shakspeare.

He takes care to let us know that our repentance,
in order to be real must proceed from sorrow felt
not because we are to be punished for our sin, but
because by it we have offended ONE whom it concerned us most of all to please ; that, in order to be
acceptable, it must be accompanied by confession and
amendment—amendment which will lead us to make
reparation to the utmost of our power, for what we
have done amiss ; and that, after all, its efficacy con-
sists not in any power of its own, but solely in the
covenanted mercy and promises of God, through
Christ. Thus, in *Measure for Measure*, the duke,
disguised as a friar, instructs Juliet in the prison,
upon the first of these points, as follows :—

> *Duke.* Repent you, fair one, of the sin you carry ?
> *Juliet.* I do, and bear the shame most patiently.
> *Duke.* I'll teach you how you shall arraign your conscience,
> And try your penitence, if it be sound,
> Or hollowly put on.

He then proceeds to warn her :—

> Lest you do repent,
> As that the sin hath brought you to this shame,
> Which sorrow is always *toward ourselves, not Heaven* ;
> Showing we'd not spare* Heaven, *as we love it*,
> But as we stand *in fear*—

* i. e. Spare to offend heaven.

> *Juliet.* I do repent me, *as it is an evil,*
> And take the shame *with joy.*   Act ii. Sc. 3.

There is a difficult passage in *Cymbeline*, which must, I imagine, look for its true interpretation to the views which our poet has elsewhere expressed upon the subject of this great duty. It is towards the conclusion of the play, where Posthumus, in prison, thus soliloquizes :—

> My conscience ! thou art fettered
> More than my shanks and wrists : you good gods, give me
> The penitent instrument, to pick that bolt,
> Then, free for ever !

that is, he wishes for death, as the only way to everlasting freedom, provided he might die with a quiet conscience :—

> Is't enough I am sorry ?
> So children temporal fathers do appease ;
> Gods are more full of mercy.   Must *I repent ?*

And, as involved in the notion of repentance, must I take my punishment as Juliet did hers, ' with joy ;' and, moreover, must I make satisfaction ?—

> I cannot do it better than in gyves,
> *Desired, more than constrained* ; to *satisfy,*
> (If of my freedom 'tis the main part) take
> No stricter render of me than *my all*:—

that is, take my life—if such satisfaction be the *main part,* be the chief point, or principal condition of *freedom* from future punishment.   So Steevens explains it ; and, I think, rightly.

The speech concludes with a recurrence to the view of a man being able to make *satisfaction* for himself, in a sense (as I believe) *purposely unchristian*, Posthumus being a heathen :—

> And so, great Powers,
> If you will *take this audit*, take this life,
> And *cancel* these cold bonds.   Act v. Sc. 4.

This is the very notion, on the part of the heathen, which the Scriptures of the Old Testament so frequently protest against. See Job ix. 32. Micah vi. 7. At the same time, I have admitted that *Cymbeline* is the play to which the remark of Johnson, discussed above, in Sect. 1, may be applied perhaps with least injustice.

In the *Tempest*, where the characters also are *not Christian*, Ariel, after reminding Alonso, Sebastian, and Antonio of the crime of which they had been guilty in ' supplanting Prospero '—

> For which foul deed,
> *The Powers delaying, not forgetting*, have
> Incens'd the seas, and shores, yea, all the creatures,
> Against your peace :   .

goes on to warn them, and Alonso more especially, of the necessity of repentance in general terms :—

> Thee of thy son, Alonso,
> They have bereft ; and do pronounce by me,
> Lingering perdition (worse than any death
> Can be at once) shall step by step attend
> You and your ways ; whose wrath to guard you from,
> Which here, in this most desolate isle, else falls
> Upon your head, is nothing but *heart's sorrow*
> And *a clear life ensuing*.   Act iii. Sc. 3.

Let us now see how our poet teaches that repentance cannot be effectual—in other words, that
there can be no forgiveness—without confession, and
without amendment, testified by 'restitution and
satisfaction (to man), according to the uttermost of
our power, for all injuries and wrongs' that we have
done. The former, confession, is indirectly prescribed in *King Lear*, Act i. Sc. 1 :—

> Who *cover faults*, at last shame them derides.

That is, as we read in the Book of Proverbs,
xxviii. 13 :—

> He that *covereth his sins* shall not prosper; but he that *con-
> fesseth*, and *forsaketh them*, shall have mercy.

In regard to the latter, viz. amendment and
satisfaction, nothing could be fuller, or better for
the purpose, than the well-known speech of the
king, in *Hamlet* :—

> What if this cursed hand
> Were thicker than itself with brother's blood?
> Is there not rain enough in the sweet heavens
> To *wash it white as * snow*? Whereto serves mercy,
> But to confront the visage of offence?
> And what's in *Prayer*, but this two-fold force,—
> To be forestalled, ere we come to fall,
> Or pardoned, being down? Then I'll look up;
> My fault is past. But, O! what form of prayer
> Can serve my turn? Forgive me my foul murder!—
> *That cannot be; since I am still possessed
> Of those effects for which I did the murder,*

---

* See Ps. li. 7; Isaiah i. 18.

My *crown*, *mine own ambition, and my queen.*
May one be pardoned, and *retain the offence?*
In the corrupted currents of this world,
Offence's gilded hand may shove by justice ;
And oft 'tis seen, the wicked prize itself
Buys out the law. But 'tis not so above :
There is no shuffling; there the action lies
In *his* * true nature ; and we ourselves compelled,
Even to the teeth and forehead of our faults,
To give in evidence. What then ? what rests ?
Try what *Repentance* can : What can it not ?
Yet what can it, when one *can not repent ?*—

that is, as Johnson has very properly explained it,
What can repentance do for a man that cannot be
penitent, for a man who has only *part* of penitence—
distress of conscience—without *the other part*, resolution of amendment ?

Shakspeare has been equally explicit in teaching
the further lesson, that we must be 'ready to forgive others who have offended us, as we would
have forgiveness of our offences at God's hand '—
a lesson with which we are familiar from the lips of
our Blessed Lord himself. I allude to the speech
of Portia, in the *Merchant of Venice*, which has
been already† noticed :—

We do pray for mercy,
And that same prayer doth teach us all to render
The deeds of mercy. Act iv. Sc. 1.

And so it follows, or ought to follow, as we read
in the *Two Gentlemen of Verona* :—

---

* See above, p. 17.   † See above, p. 95.

> Who by repentance is not satisfied
> *Is not of heaven, nor earth ; for these are pleased;*
> *By penitence the Eternal's wrath's appeased.* Act v. Sc. 4.

Not, however, *for its own sake.* This is beautifully set forth, though not without a tincture of Romish doctrine, which was appropriate and necessary under the circumstances of the person and of the time, in a speech of the pious King Henry V. before the battle of Agincourt :—

> O God of battles! steel my soldiers' hearts!
> Possess them not with fear! Take from them now
> The sense of reckoning if the opposed numbers
> Pluck their hearts from them! Not to-day, O Lord,
> O not to-day, think not upon the fault
> My father made in compassing the crown!
> I Richard's body have interred new ;
> And on it have bestow'd more contrite tears
> Than from it issued forced drops of blood.
> Five hundred poor I have in yearly pay,   ·
> Who twice a day their wither'd hands hold up
> Toward heaven, to pardon blood; and I have built
> Two chantries, where the sad and solemn priests
> Still sing for Richard's soul. More will I do :
> *Tho' all that I can do is nothing worth ;*
> Since that my penitence comes after all,
> *Imploring pardon.* *King Hen. V.* Act iv. Sc. 1.

These last lines have given rise to much discussion and difference of opinion among the critics. I am inclined to accept Dr. Johnson's explanation, as correctly representing what Shakspeare (who, in his affection for this good king, was willing to divest his Romanism of an unscriptual tendency, as far as possible) meant to convey. ' *I do all this,* says the

King, *though all that I can do is nothing worth*, is so far from an adequate expiation of the crime, that *Penitence comes after all imploring pardon*, both for the crime and the expiation.'

It is in the spirit of a true penitent that at the commencement of the same scene, the king had spoken of the purifying effect of hardships and distresses—borne after 'example' of holy men who have gone before us, or are still alive—and had desired opportunity for solitary meditation :—

'Tis good for men to *love their present pains,*
Upon example ; so the spirit is eas'd :
And, when the mind is quickened, out of doubt,
The organs, tho' defunct and dead before,
Break up their drowsy grave, and newly move
With casted slough, and fresh legerity.

.   .   .   .   .   .
.   .   .   .   .   .

I and my bosom must debate awhile,
And then I would *no other company*.

It only remains to point out how fully our poet recognised that while repentance may come too late, or may be unreal, judicial blindness and infatuation are the sure portion of the impenitent. It is King Lear who exclaims :—

Woe, that too late repents.   Act i. Sc. 4.

i. e. woe is to him that does so.

And it is scarcely necessary to say that it is Falstaff who makes merriment in teaching a lesson, which is however a very solemn one—and no less needful than solemn—viz. that we are too apt to make our repentance an easy thing, if not a matter of renewed self-indulgence. The passage to be quoted is in the dialogue with the Chief Justice, *King Henry IV. 2nd Part*, Act i. Sc. 2 :—

> For the box o' the ear the prince gave you—he gave it like a rude prince, and you took it like a sensible lord. I have checked him for it; and the young lion *repents* : marry, not *in sackcloth and ashes* ; but in new silk and *old sack*.

It is also a sensualist, but a sensualist of a very different class, who thus moralizes upon the consequences of a vicious and impenitent course. The words are in every way worthy of *Mark Antony* :—

> When we in our viciousness grow hard,
> (O ! misery on't !) the wise gods seel * our eyes ;
> In our own filth drop our clear judgments; make us
> *Adore our errors* ; laugh at us, while we *strut*
> *To our confusion.*   *Ant. and Cleop.* Act iii. Sc. 9.

Sentiments as awful as they are just; and which will not appear either too irreverent for a Christian man to write, when we remember how often in the Psalms, and in the Book of Proverbs, God is said ' to laugh,' and ' to mock ' at the calamities of those who have despised His laws ; or too profound for a Heathen man to utter, when we compare the deep sayings of Persius respecting the confirmed and reprobate votaries of vicious self-indulgence, in his 3rd Satire :—

---

* i. e. Close : a term of falconry, not to be confounded with *seal*.

Sed *stupet* hic vitio, et fibris increvit * opimum
Pingue ; *caret culpâ* ; nescit quid perdat, et alto
Demersus, summâ rursum non bullit in undâ.

Nothing can exceed the irony which represents a man as *faultless,* only because he has rendered himself *senseless,* and incapable of judging between right and wrong.

SECT. 6. *Of Faith and Thankfulness towards God.*

' Put not your trust in princes, nor in àny child of man,' is a Scriptural precept which Shakspeare has not been slow to echo, nor has he failed to do full justice to the contrast with which the Scriptures so often accompany that precept, viz. the duty and the satisfaction of placing our trust in. God. The devoted, but not over-honest nurse in *Romeo and Juliet* can tell her mistress—

> There's no trust,
> No faith, no honesty in men ; all perjured,
> All forsworn, all nought, all dissemblers.
> Act iii. Sc. 2.

And the Duke of Bedford can ask, in *King Henry VI. 1st Part* :—

> What is the trust or strength of foolish men ?
> Act iii. Sc. 1.

And yet we are senseless enough, as the Lord Hastings tells us, in *King Richard III.,* to make

---

* Comp. Habakkuk ii. 6.

L

more account of man's favour, which is so worthless, than of the favour of God, which is above all
price :—

> O ! momentary grace of mortal men,
> Which we more hunt for than the grace of God!
> Who builds his hope in air, of your fair looks,
> Lives like a drunken sailor on a mast,
> Ready with every nod to tumble down
> Into the fatal bowels of the deep.　　Act iii. Sc. 4.

As Cardinal Wolsey ' tumbled down ' from the
eminence to which he had been raised, and thereby
was led, all too late, to exclaim :—

> O ! Cromwell, Cromwell,
> Had I but served my God with half the zeal
> I served my king, He would not in mine age
> Have left me naked to mine enemies.　　Act iii. Sc. 2.

And so the good King Henry V. felt the blessedness of being able to place his confidence where
alone it ought to be placed, when he said to the
Duke of Gloster :—

> We are in God's hands, brother, not in theirs.
> 　　　　　*King Henry V.* Act iii. Sc. 5.

And he felt it sinful to boast of anything he could
do by his own power :—

> Forgive me, God,
> That I do brag thus ! this your air of France
> Hath blown that vice in me ; I must repent,
> Go, therefore, tell thy master—

he is speaking to Montjoy, the French herald—

> Here I am ;
> My ransom is this frail and worthless trunk ;

My army but a weak and sickly guard :
Yet, God* before, tell him we will come on,
Though France himself, and such another neighbour,
Stand in our way.   Act iii. Sc. 6.

And how different was the result! Nor was the
grateful piety of the father less conspicuous in the
son, whose prayer it is :—

O ! Lord, that lends me life,
Lend me a heart replete with thankfulness !
                    King Henry VI. 2nd Pt. Act i. Sc. 1.

There are two occasions—one extraordinary, the
other of ordinary occurrence—in regard to which our
poet desired, it would seem, more especially to recommend this great duty of thankfulness towards
God. The extraordinary occasion is when a victory
has been gained. It is delightful to observe in what
an amiable light the character of King Henry V.
has been placed in this respect. Not even David
himself has exhibited more fervent gratitude to the
Divine Author of his victories than our pious sovereign, after the defeat of the French in the battle of
Agincourt. Thus, when Montjoy, the French
herald, first announced to the king—' The day is
yours '—his first exclamation is a *Non nobis, Domine,*
in these words :—

Praised be God, and not our strength for it !
                    King Henry V. Act iv. Sc. 7.

---

* i. e. God being our guide. · The phrase is used again by the
king in the same play, Act i. Sc. 2.

And soon after, when the English herald came and delivered more fully the particulars of the victory, more fully rose also from the royal lips the ascription of praise and thanksgiving .—

> O! God ; Thy arm was here,
> And *not to us, but to Thy arm alone*
> Ascribe we all. When, without stratagem,
> But in plain shock and even play of battle,
> Was ever known so great and little loss
> On one part and on the other ? Take it, God,
> For *it is only Thine.*
>
> *Exeter.*   'Tis wonderful !
> Come, go we in procession to the village :
> And be it death proclaimed through our Host,
> To boast of this, or *take that praise from God*
> *Which is His only.*   *Ibid.* Sc. 8.

And how he himself behaved in strict accordance with his own command, is reported by the chorus at the opening of the next and concluding Act ; the description refers to his return and entry into London :—

> Where that his lords desire him to have borne
> His bruised helmet, and his bended sword,
> Before him through the city, he forbids it,
> Being free from vainness, and self-glorious pride,
> Giving full trophy, signal, and ostent,
> *Quite from himself to God.*

In like manner, his son and successor, out of *the fulness of the thankful heart* for which he had prayed, thus signifies the acknowledgments which he desires to make upon hearing of the suppression of the insurrection headed by Jack Cade :—

Then, Heàven, set ope thy everlasting gates,
To entertain my vows of thanks and praise !
King Henry VI. 2nd Pt. Act iv. Sc. 9.

The same pious and grateful character is ascribed, more than once, in the *First Part* of the same play, to the gallant Lord Talbot. See Act iii. Sc. 2 and Sc. 4.

The occasion of ordinary occurrence to which I referred as one upon which our poet appears to have felt, in an especial manner, that thankfulness was due, is the receiving of our ' daily bread.' Although, as Cicero has said—I forget of whom—' non tàm hominis fuit ista virtus quàm temporum,' so the praise of this is due, not more to our poet himself, than to the age in which he lived. It is indeed greatly to the credit of our forefathers that they recognised the duty of saying grace at meals, certainly not less, and performed it, I imagine, far more efficiently than we in this generation are wont to do. This is evident partly from the forms which were in use for such occasions, and which have come down to us in the Primers and other Devotional Manuals of the reigns of Edward VI. and Elizabeth, and partly from such as are still retained, mostly in Latin, in some of our college halls at the English universities and public schools. Still Shakspeare must also have the credit of giving to this duty its due prominence, and of indicating, as we shall presently see, again and again, the sense which he

doubtless entertained of its propriety and importance.   A century later it would seem that a change
had come over the manners of our countrymen—if
we may trust the testimony of Pope, speaking, too,
of poets—for the worse:—

> Then cheerful healths,   .   .   .
> And, *what's more rare,* a poet shall say grace.

And again, in another poem :—

> Sons, sires, and grandsons, all will wear the bays,
> Our wives read Milton, and our daughters plays ;
> To theatres and to rehearsals throng,
> And *all our grace at table is a song.*

At the same time I must not omit to add that
we have the authority of Dr. Warton,* in an observation upon the former of these passages, for the
statement, that if saying grace was 'rare' with Pope,
it was not so with Dean Swift.   He 'always did it,'
says the doctor, and (which one is glad to hear of
anything that he did) 'with remarkable decency and
devotion.'

But to return to Shakspeare.   Our two first illustrations are derived from the ancient days of
Greece and Rome—from *Timon of Athens,* and
from *Coriolanus* ; and in these instances it may be
thought that our poet has again been guilty of an
impropriety—similar to   that   which   we   before
noticed †—in attributing to men and women among
the heathen, 'sentiments and practices' which are

---

* *Essay on Pope,* vol. ii. p. 306.   † See above, p. 98.

to be found only among Christians. But if so, this much at least may be said in his defence. If there be one redeeming feature in the spirit of the old Classical mythology, it is the disposition which it tended to form, of habitual thankfulness * to a Superior Being. That it went so far as to teach men to *say grace at meals*, I am not prepared to maintain; but that it taught what was in effect the same— *not to taste the cup till a libation had been poured to Jove*, and *not to put the sickle to the corn till sacred songs had been sung to Ceres*—this, Homer, Il. vii. 480, and Virgil, Georg. i. 350, without going further, may suffice to prove.

One grace in *Timon of Athens* is a long one. Timon himself offers it, upon occasion of giving an entertainment in his own house. He introduces it thus, speaking to the guests. ' The gods require our thanks ; ' and it begins in these words :

You great benefactors! sprinkle our society with thankfulness.
Act iii. Sc. 6.

This of course is in prose ; but on a previous occasion, in the same play, another grace occurs, said by Apemantus, the 'churlish philosopher,' which is in verse, much after the style of some of the metrical graces in the old primers; and the manner in which it is introduced, apparently as a *Benedictio post cibum*, or at least after the entertain-

---

* See the beautiful passage in the fourth book of the *Excursion* to this effect.

ment has commenced, may possibly be intended to reflect upon the omission of grace-saying at public banquets, or at the tables of the rich—a suspicion which the words, spoken by Apemantus immediately before, would seem to confirm :—

Feasts are too proud to give thanks to the gods.

Act i. Sc. 2.

However this may be, and however we may question the propriety of putting such a sentiment as I am about to quote from *Coriolanus*, into the mouth of a Volscian soldier, there can be no doubt that the sentiment itself implies great familiarity on the part of our poet with the practice of saying grace both before and after meals. The scene is *a camp, at a small distance from Rome. Enter Aufidius,* General of the Volscians, *and his Lieutenant.*

Aufid. Do they still fly to the Roman?*
Lieut. I do not know what witchcraft's in him ; but
Your soldiers use him as *the grace 'fore meat,*
Their talk at table, and *their thanks at end* ;
And you are darkened in this action, sir,
Even by your own. Act iv. Sc. 7.

But to come to Christian times. I think we shall not be far wrong in supposing that our poet designed to satirize the Puritanism which had begun to prevail in his own day, when he put the following lines into the mouth of Gratiano, in the *Merchant of Venice.* Bassanio, whom he had proposed to accompany to Belmont, the house of Portia, con-

---

* i. e. to Coriolanus.

sented, but at the same time required of him 'to allay his skipping spirit with some cold drops of modesty :'—

> *Grat.*   Signior Bassanio, hear me :
> If I do not put on a sober habit,
> Talk with respect . . . . .
> Wear prayer-books in my pocket, look demurely ;
> Nay more, *while grace is saying, hood mine eyes*
> *Thus with my hat, and sigh and say, Amen ;*
> Use all the observance of civility,
> Like one well-studied in a sad ostent,
> To please his grandam—never trust me more.
>   Act ii. Sc. 2.

It is somewhat remarkable that no one of Shakspeare's commentators, so far as I have seen, has a word to say in illustration of the dialogue, which I am about to quote, between Lucio and the two Gentlemen, in the second scene of *Measure for Measure* :—

> *1st Gent.* There's not a soldier of us all that, in *the thanksgiving before meat,* doth relish the petition well that *prays for peace.*
> *2nd Gent.* I never heard any soldier dislike it.
> *Lucio.* I believe thee ; for I think thou never wast where grace was said.
> *2nd Gent.* No? A dozen times at least.
> *1st Gent.* What? in metre?
> *Lucio.* In any proportion, or in any language.

'*Proportion,*' Warburton says, here signifies *measure* ; but I rather think it means *prose or verse,* *chant* or *hymn,** as 'in any language' means especially,

---

* Mr. Bowdler omits the two last speeches, and much more that follows—partly with and partly without sufficient reason.

I imagine, *Latin* or *English*. However, it is of more interest to point out that the petition,

Give peace in our time, O Lord!

taken from the Versicles in the Prayer Book, before the Collect for the day, is still used, as it appears from the above passage to have been in Shakspeare's time, as part of the grace (probably from the connexion between *Peace* and *Plenty*) in some of our college halls; e. g. at Winchester, at election time, the concluding portion of the grace, *Post cibum,* which is *chanted,* runs thus, being formed out of three of the said Versicles.

Fac Reginam salvam, Domine ; *Da pacem in diebus nostris* ; et exaudi nos in die quocunque invocamus te. Amen.

Lucio had meant to insinuate that the 2*nd Gentleman* was a *graceless* fellow. The same jest passes somewhat more broadly, as might be expected, between Falstaff and Prince Hal :—

Fals. I pray thee, sweet wag, when thou art king—as, God save thy grace—majesty, I should say ; for grace thou wilt have none—

P. Hen. What, none?

Fals. No, by my troth ; not so much as will serve to be *prologue to an egg and butter* :—

King Hen. IV. 1st Part, Act i. Sc. 2.

where the speaker, with logic more characteristic than reverent, would imply that a short grace may suffice for a scanty meal.

There remains one more passage to be produced

under this head ; and it is one from which we might perhaps infer that in the time of Shakspeare the master of the house sometimes devolved the duty of saying grace upon his wife. In *Taming of the Shrew,* Petruchio says to Katharina, when the supper is brought in :—

> Come, Kate, sit down; I know you have a stomach.
> *Will you give thanks, sweet Kate,* or else shall I ?
> Act iv. Sc. 1.

SECT. 7. *Of the Duty and Efficacy of Prayer.*

There are few subjects of literary contemplation more interesting or more profitable than to observe the hold which a great practical subject like that of Prayer had upon a mind like that of Shakspeare. We know that some of our distinguished poets have unhappily allowed themselves, at one time or other, if not throughout their career, to imagine difficulties in the way of the performance of this duty; but we have no evidence in any of Shakspeare's plays, from first to last, that he ever entertained any but the truest and most just conceptions of it. First, in *Hamlet,* we learn the twofold force of Prayer, as obtaining either grace to prevent us from sinning, or pardon when we have sinned :—

> What's in Prayer, but this two-fold force,—
> To be forestalled, ere we come to fall,
> Or pardoned, being down ?   Act iii. Sc. 3.

Next, in the epilogue to the *Tempest*, this latter efficacy is represented as an antidote to despair :—

> My ending is despair,
> Unless I be relieved by Prayer;
> Which pierces so, that it assaults
> Mercy itself, and *frees all faults.*

It was probably not without some reference, in his own mind, to the practice of Daniel, vi. 10, and to the ancient *hours* of the church, that our poet puts into the mouth of Imogen, one of his sweetest and most attractive characters, those touching lines in which she represents herself as offering up prayers, ' three times a day,' for her lover,* and as having intended to enjoin the same practice upon him, in her behalf, before they parted, had not her father interposed to prevent the interview. Otherwise she would—

> Have charged him
> At the *sixth hour of morn,* at *noon,* at *midnight,*
> To encounter me with orisons, for then
> *I am in heaven for him.*   *Cymbeline,* Act i. Sc. 4.

And the same devotional character is kept up, when, after she had become, in disguise, the page of Belarius, now supposed to be slain, she attaches herself to Lucius, the Roman general, in the same capacity :—

> But first, an't please the gods,
> I'll hide my master from the flies, as deep
> As these poor pickaxes † can dig : and when

---

* See also *Tempest,* Act iii. Sc. 1.   † i. e. her fingers.

With wild wood-leaves and weeds I have strew'd his grave,
And on it said *a century of prayers,*
Such as I can, *twice o'er,* I'll weep, and sigh;
And, leaving ,so his service, follow you :
So please you entertain me.   Act iv. Sc. 2.

Nor is there any reason to suppose that our poet designed to exhibit examples of the practice of this duty only, or specially, in the weaker sex. On the contrary, it is kings and nobles whom he has chosen most of all to represent as men of prayer. This we expect in King Henry VI :—

Famed (as he was) for mildness, peace and prayer.
                     King Henry VI. 3rd Part, Act ii. Sc. 1.

And so, when Gloster stabs him in the Tower, the last words he is made to utter are these, in which he prays at once for himself and for his murderer :—

O God ! forgive my sins, and pardon thee.
                     Ibid. Act v. Sc. 6.

But the cruel and licentious Edward, who sup-planted and succeeded him—even *he* is introduced with words of prayer upon his lips, though words which breathe little (and this so far is meet) of the fervour and simplicity in devotion of a true servant of God :—

O! Warwick, I do bend my knee with thine ;
And ere my knee rise from the earth's cold face,
I throw my hands, mine eyes, my heart to THEE,
Thou setter up and plucker down of kings !
Beseeching Thee—if with Thy will it stands,

That to my foes this body must be prey—
Yet that Thy brazen gates of heaven may ope,
And give sweet passage to my sinful soul !
                                        Ibid. Act ii. Sc. 3.

It will be seen, however, that the occasion—it
was the morning of the battle of Towton, near
Ferrybridge, decisive in its issue against the oppo-
nents of Edward—was one in regard to which our
poet rarely fails to impress the duty of supplication
to the throne of grace. It is proper and incum-
bent upon us to have recourse to prayer before we
undertake any important business ; and more especially before we engage in war. This, I doubt not,
Shakspeare knew and felt ; and like a true Christian
patriot, he desired that others should know and feel
it. There is ample evidence to this effect, for example, in *King Henry V.* The good king, before he
sets out upon his expedition, is made to say :—

We have now no thought in us but France,
Save those to God, that *run before our business.*
                                        Act i. Sc. 2.

His prayer to the ' God of Battles,' before the
battle of Agincourt, has been already* quoted ; and
to that may be added here, that, while the Earl of
Salisbury previously exclaims, as the English forces
march into the field—

God's arm strike with us !   Act iv. Sc. 3.

---

* See above, p. 142.

the king himself thus humbly resigns himself to
the disposal of the Most High :—

> Now, soldiers, march away ;
> And how Thou pleasest, GOD, dispose the day !

A similar character is given, in *King Richard III.*
to the Earl of Richmond, afterwards King Henry
VII.   Before the battle of Bosworth field, in which
the wicked usurper was overthrown, not only does
Richmond exhort his followers to ' march in God's
name,' Act v. Sc. 2, and bids them—

> Remember this,—
> God, and our good cause, fight upon our side ;
> The prayers of holy saints and wronged souls,
> Like high-rear'd bulwarks stand before our faces ;—
>
> *Ibid.* Sc. 3.

but he himself makes a set prayer to the same
effect, when he retires to rest upon the night before
the battle :—

> O THOU ! whose captain I account myself,
> Look on my forces with a gracious eye ;
> Put in their hands Thy bruising irons of wrath,
> That they may crush down with a heavy fall
> The usurping helmets of our adversaries !
> Make us Thy ministers of chastisement,
> *That we may praise Thee in Thy victory !*
> To Thee I do commend my watchful soul,
> Ere I let fall the windows of mine eyes ;
> Sleeping, and waking, O ! defend me still !

And when God had given him the victory, and
the Lord Stanley came in, bearing the crown which

he had taken from the head of Richard, now dead, and presented it to Richmond, his first exclamation is—

> Great God of Heaven, say *Amen* to all;

and he concludes his last speech, with which the play ends, in prayer for lasting peace, summed up with a repetition of the same sentiment ;—

> O! now, let Richmond and Elizabeth,
> The true succeeders of each * royal house,
> By heaven's fair ordinance conjoin together!
> And let their heirs, GOD, if Thy will be so,
> Enrich the time to come with smooth-fac'd peace,
> With smiling plenty, and fair prosperous days!
> Abate the edge of traitors, gracious Lord,
> That would reduce these bloody days again,
> And make poor England weep in streams of blood!
> Let them not live to taste this land's increase,
> That would with treason wound this fair land's peace !
> Now civil wounds are stopped, peace lives again ;
> That she may long live here, God say—AMEN.

But besides the obligation of offering up prayer for divine aid on all important occasions, our poet had a no less clear conception of the duty and value of intercession in behalf of those who need and desire our prayers. This appears, for instance, in the picture which he draws of the end of the Duke of Buckingham, in *King Henry VIII*. The duke, having been found guilty of high treason, when led forth to execution, thus entreats the few that loved him :—

---

* i. e. of the houses of Lancaster and York.

Go with me, like good angels, to my end;
And as the long divorce * of steel falls on me,
Make of *your prayers one sweet sacrifice,*
And lift my soul to heaven.   Act ii. Sc. 1.

It is pleasant to think (and it goes some way to prove that Shakspeare was brought up in an atmosphere of religious sentiment at least), that in the very first scene of what was, if not the first, certainly one of his first written plays—the *Two Gentlemen of Verona*—he introduces the notion of friends praying for each other, in the case of the two young men, Proteus and Valentine, the latter of whom was on the point of setting out upon his travels :—

> *Proteus.*   In thy danger,
> If ever danger do environ thee,
> Commend thy grievance to my holy prayers,
> For I will be *thy beadsman*, Valentine.

Johnson interprets *Beadsman*, 'a man employed in praying, generally *in praying for another.*'

Moreover, among the various occasions for the exercise of the duty of intercessory prayer, Shakspeare had learnt, and desired to teach, that it is most especially—   ,

> A virtuous and *Christian-like* conclusion,
> To *pray for them that have done scath†* to *us.*
>   *King Richard III.* Act i. Sc. 3.

i. e. 'for them which despitefully use us.' Matt. v. 44.

---

* The axe that was to divorce the soul from the body.
† Injury.

M

And, as though he would teach this duty most effectually, he allots to Macbeth the odious task of attempting to decry it, and that in colloquy with one whom he designed to employ for the murdering of Banquo :—

> Do you find
> Your patience so predominant in your nature,
> That you can let this go ?   Are you *so gospelled*
> *To pray for this good man*, and for his issue,
> Whose heavy hand hath bowed you to the grave,
> And beggared yours for ever? *Macbeth*, Act iii. Sc. 1.

On the other hand, it is assigned as a fitting office for one of the most charming and most perfect* of our poet's characters, to exemplify this difficult duty in the most trying of all circumstances. When it is suggested to Desdemona, in order to account for Othello's vile and cruel language towards her, that some one must have slandered her to him, she meekly replies—

> If there be any such, *Heaven pardon him !*
> *Othello*, Act iv. Sc. 2.

There are two other points in regard to the duty of Prayer, which we should expect that Shakspeare would not overlook. One is, that our prayers should be *real*; not lip-service merely ; and must proceed from a heart sincerely desirous to please

---

* In our admiration for Desdemona, however, we must not forget that her tragical end represents the unhappy issue of a marriage entered into by a daughter without her father's consent, and in deceitful opposition to his authority.

God. The other is, that, if we do not receive the things for which we pray, we ought not therefore to conclude that we have been unheard ; for it often happens that the denial of our requests may prove a greater benefit to us than the granting of them would have been. Accordingly, the former of these points is brought before us in *Hamlet,* where the wicked king, after kneeling and attempting to pray, rises with the confession :—

> My words fly up, my thoughts remain below ;
> *Words without thoughts never to Heaven go.*
> Act iii. Sc. 3.

And again, in *Measure for Measure,* the duplicity is exposed of professing to offer up prayer while the heart is bent upon yielding to temptation, in the person of the licentious Deputy :—

> When I would pray, and think, I think and pray
> To several subjects : Heaven hath *my empty words* ;
> Whilst my intention,* hearing not my tongue,
> Anchors on Isabel. Act ii. Sc. 4.

He had before said, in the consciousness of suffer-ing himself to be overcome—

> I am that way going to temptation,
> Where *prayers cross* ;— *Ibid.* Sc. 2.

words which, doubtless, contain a reference to the petition in the Lord's Prayer against temptation, as Mr. Henley has observed ; but of which it is not

---

* Substituted by Warburton for *invention.*

easy to give altogether a satisfactory interpretation, if we must be content to take them as they stand.

The latter point, which I just now mentioned, is one with which scholars will be familiar, as forming the subject of that most remarkable production of heathen antiquity—the 10th Satire of Juvenal—so vigorously imitated by Johnson; and, therefore, there is at least no impropriety in putting it, as Shakspeare has done, into a dialogue, in *Antony and Cleopatra*, between Sextus Pompeius and his friend Menecrates :—

> *Pomp.* If the great gods be just, they shall assist
> The deeds of justest men.
> *Mene.* Know, worthy Pompey,
> That *what they do delay, they not deny.*
> *Pomp.* While we are suitors to their throne, decays
> The thing we sue for.
> *Mene.* We, ignorant of ourselves,
> *Beg often our own harms, which the wise powers*
> *Deny us for our good;* so find we profit
> By losing of our prayers. Act ii. Sc. 1.

Sect. 8. *Of the Domestic Relations.*

We should be glad to be able to feel assured that the marriage of our poet, though formed at such an early age (before he was 19), and in one respect disproportionate (his wife being eight years older than himself), did not prove an unhappy one. Doubtless it assisted to give him, when he was still young, his deep insight into female character; and the draught of his female personages, ón the whole, would rather lead us to suppose, that as he had been prepossessed in favour of the sex, so the experience which he afterwards enjoyed tended to confirm, rather than to remove, the good impression. The views which he has expressed of the conjugal union are such as do him honour ; and it is only fair, therefore, to conclude, that though he married early, he did not do so * unadvisedly, or without a due regard to the sacredness of the tie, which it is certain he had learnt in his maturer years to regard in its proper light. Thus, in *King Henry V.*, Isabel, Queen of France, is made to say, at the marriage of the king with her daughter Katharine :—

> God, *the best maker of all marriages,*
> Combine your hearts in one.   Act v. Sc. 2.

And the words that follow are not less worthy of the

---

* It must, however, be confessed, that in one of his last-written plays, *Twelfth Night*, he has left us a warning against the step which he himself had taken—yet a warning put in such a way that, with true delicacy of feeling, it reflects upon himself more than upon the lady who had been the object of his choice :—

> *Duke.*   *Let still the woman take*
> *An elder than herself*; so wears she to him,
> So sways she level in her husband's heart.
> For, boy, however we do praise ourselves,
> Our fancies are more giddy and unfirm,
> More longing, wavering, sooner lost and worn,
> Than women's are.
> Then *let thy love be younger than thyself,*
> *Or thy affection cannot hold the bent.*   Act iv. Sc. 4.

On Shakspeare in his own domestic relations, see Wise's *Shakspere and his Birthplace*, p. 72, *sq.*

subject and the occasion, though she who uttered
them proved untrue :—

> *I have forgot my Father ;*
> I know no touch of consanguinity,
> No kin, no love, no blood, no soul so near me
> As the sweet Troilus.
>
> *Troilus and Cressida,* Act iv. Sc. 2.

In this last quotation the first half line will remind us of a passage in the Psalms, xlv. 10 ; and
what I am next to quote would, probably, never
have been written if a passage of S. Paul, Eph. v.
23, had not been running in our poet's mind. I
allude to the dialogue between the Provost and
Clown, in *Measure for Measure* :—

> *Prov.* Come hither, sirrah, can you cut off a man's head ?
> *Clown.* If the man be a bachelor, sir, I can ; but if he be a
> married man, *he is his wife's head,* and I can never cut off a
> woman's head. Act iv. Sc. 2.

But there is a speech in which, besides repeating
this apostolic sentiment, it would seem that our poet
set himself to draw out at length all that the Scripture
teaches of the duty of wives towards their husbands,
with such additional touches to the picture as his
own imagination—or the contrast (let us hope)
afforded by his wife's good qualities—would readily
suggest. Katharina, having ceased to be *a shrew,*
under the discipline of Petruchio, gives the following good advice to one who was married, but had
not yet learned to be obedient to her husband :—

Fye, fye ! unknit that threat'ning unkind brow,
And dart not scornful glances from those eyes,
To wound thy lord, thy king, thy governor :
It blots thy beauty, as frosts bite the meads ;
Confounds thy fame, as whirlwinds shake fair buds ;
And in no sense is meet or amiable.
A woman moved is like a fountain troubled,
Muddy, ill-seeming, thick, bereft of beauty ;
And, while it is so, none so dry or thirsty
Will deign to sip, or touch one drop of it.
Thy husband is thy lord, thy life, thy keeper,
Thy head, thy sovereign ; one that cares for thee;
And for thy maintenance, commits his body
To painful labour, both by sea and land ;
To watch the night in storms, the day in cold,
While thou liest warm at home, secure and safe ;
And craves no other tribute at thy hands,
But love, fair looks, and true obedience,—
Too little payment for so great a debt.
Such duty as the subject owes the prince,
Even such a woman oweth to her husband ;
And when she's peevish, froward, sullen, sour,
And not obedient to his honest will,
What is she but a foul contending rebel,
And graceless traitor to her loving lord ?
I am asham'd, that women are so simple
To offer war, where they should kneel for peace ;
Or seek for rule, supremacy, and sway,
Where they are bound to serve, love, and obey.
Why are our bodies soft, and weak, and smooth,
Unapt to toil and trouble in the world,
But that our soft * conditions, and our hearts,
Should well agree with our external parts ?
          Taming of the Shrew, Act v. Sc. 2.

Some of my fair readers will think, perhaps, that

---

* The gentle qualities of our minds.—MALONE.

this lady's tongue has run on much too fast, and
much too far—not unintentionally, I dare say, on
the poet's part, in order to show how the characteristic weapon of the sex may be turned against
themselves. It will be well, therefore, to pass on
to a scene in which another Katharine will show, in
much fewer words, and as exemplified in her own
person, what is the perfect character of a good wife,
and that too, while her ' loving lord ' must, unhappily, be pronounced ' the graceless traitor:'—

> Have I lived thus long—a wife, a true one,
> A woman (I dare say, without vain-glory)
> Never yet branded with suspicion?
> Have I with all my full affections,
> Still met the king? loved him next Heaven? obeyed him?
> Been, out of fondness, superstitious to him?
> Almost forgot my prayers to content him?
> And am I thus rewarded? 'tis not well, lords.
> Bring me a constant woman to her husband,
> One that ne'er dreamed a joy beyond his pleasure;
> And to that woman, when she has done most,
> Yet will I add an honour—a great patience.
>
> *King Henry VIII.* Act iii. Sc. 1.

It is a curious instance of our author's tact that
he employs women to teach wives their conjugal
duty. We have seen this already in the *Taming of
the Shrew*; and there is another example in the
Comedy of Errors (if that play be Shakspeare's), where
Luciana takes to task her married sister Adriana,
for want of obedience and submission to her husband.
See Act ii. Sc. 1.

From the consideration of the duties which arise out of the marriage tie, we naturally proceed to the relationship of parents and children ; and there again our poet may speak to us from his own experience, in both relations. He was himself the eldest of eight children—four of either sex—but three of the sisters died in infancy ; and his own family consisted of two daughters and a son, the son* and the younger of the daughters being twins. These bare facts furnish nearly all the materials which we now possess, or can hope to obtain, of our poet's family history. It will be interesting to supply the deficiency, in however slight a degree, so far as we may be able, from his works. In these, accordingly, we may discover the tenderness of a parent's heart ; where the clown, in *All's well that ends well,* quotes the proverb, 'Bairns are blessings,'† Act i. Sc. 3 ; and, again, where Lady Constance, in *King John,* says to Cardinal Pandulph, Act iii. Sc. 4 :—

> *He* talks to me *that* never had a son.

In these, too, we seem to read that our author had learnt, and practised, and desired in his own turn to teach, the duty of children towards their parents. How pathetically, for instance, is this lesson read to Coriolanus by his mother Volumnia :—

> Say my request's unjust,
> And spurn me back ; but if it be not so,

---

* He died when only twelve years old.
† See Psalm cxxvii. 6, cxxviii. 5, *sq.*

> Thou art not honest; and the gods will plague thee,
> That thou restrainst from me the duty, which
> To a mother's part belongs. *Coriolanus*, Act v. Sc. 3.

And how forcibly is Goneril admonished by the Duke of Albany, that no good can be expected either *from* or *by* an undutiful child :—

> O Goneril!
> You are not worth the dust which the rude wind
> Blows in your face. I fear your disposition:
> *That nature, which contemns its origin*
> *Cannot be bordered certain in itself:*

i. e. cannot be restrained within any certain bounds, and will eventually shrink from no excess of sin.

> She that herself will sliver * or disbranch
> From her material sap, *perforce must wither,*
> *And come to deadly use.*

In these last words Warburton suggests that there is a reference to the use that witches and enchanters are said to make of withered branches in their charms. On the other hand, no less forcibly and pathetically does our poet teach us, we may suppose from his own feelings, the affection which parents cherish, or ought to cherish, towards their offspring, in the rebuke which Clifford administers to King Henry VI. :—

> My gracious liege, this too much lenity
> And harmful pity must be laid aside.
> Whose hand is that the forest bear does lick?
> Not his that spoils her young before her face.

---

* Tear off.

The smallest worm will turn, being trodden on,
And doves will peck in safeguard of their brood.
Unreasonable creatures feed their young,
And tho' man's face be fearful to their eyes,
Yet, in protection of their tender ones,
Who hath not seen them (even with those wings
Which sometimes they have used with fearful flight),
Make war with him that climbed unto their nest,
Offering their own lives in their young's defence?
For shame, my liege, make them your precedent!

K. Henry VI. 3rd Part, Act ii. Sc. 2.

A rebuke which, whether just or no, elicited from the king in reply, the noble sentiment about which there can be no question—that the good deeds of parents are the best inheritance which they can bequeath to their children :—

I'll leave my son my virtuous deeds behind.

What man had ever more reason than the son of Shakspeare to rejoice over the heirloom which his father left him? And besides the heritage of his name, and of his works, that father, I doubt not, bequeathed to his children—if nothing else—yet at least the effectual *blessing* of a good Christian. This I say, because I doubt not also that the pious practice of children receiving benedictions from their parents—a practice common in our poet's time —was observed in his own family. That such must have been the case we may not unreasonably infer from his frequent mention of it, and from the easy natural manner in which it is introduced. We find it in the *Two Gentlemen of Verona,* in *Coriolanus,* in

Cymbeline, in *Titus Andronicus*, in *King Lear*, in *Hamlet*, in *King Richard III*. But before we turn to the passages, let me produce a few examples in illustration of the custom from other sources.

In the Life of Sir Thomas More, published in the late Dr. Wordsworth's *Ecclesiastical Biography*, read:—

> Towards his father he gave many proofs of his natural affection and lowly mind. Whensoever he passed through Westminster to his place in the Chancery, by the Court of King's Bench, if his father, who sat there as judge, had been set down ere he came, he would go to him, and reverently kneeling down in sight of all, ask him blessing. *This virtuous custom he always solemnly observed*; tho' then men after their marriages thought themselves not bound to these duties of younger folks.

Such was the humility and filial reverence of the then Lord High Chancellor of England! Stapleton, in his *Tres Thomæ*, bears witness to the same fact, and in recording it speaks of the practice as *peculiar to the English people*. His words are worth quoting at the present day :—

> Solent apud nos liberi *quotidie, mane ac vesperi*, benedictionem flexo poplite *ab utroque parente* petere. Qui mos si apud alias quasdam gentes obtineret, haberent *Parentes* filios magis morigeros, haberet *Respublica* subditos magis obsequentes, haberet *Ecclesia* fideles magis obedientes.*

Nicholas Ferrar was born when Shakspeare began to write, viz. in 1592; and we are told of

---

* *Eccl. Biog.* ii. 73. Compare the testimony of Meric Casaubon, quoted in *Christian Institutes*, iv. 565.

him, when he was 27 years old, and his mother
came to visit him at Little Gidding, that 'though
he was of that age, and had been engaged in many
public concerns of great importance, had been a
distinguished member of Parliament, and had con-
ducted with effect the prosecution of the Prime
Minister of the day, at first approaching his mother,
he knelt upon the ground to ask and receive her
blessing ;' and he kept up the same practice in his
own family; as did also, we read,* Mr. Philip
Henry, who died in 1696 : so that we have evidence
of the existence of the custom during two centuries.
Bishop Sanderson, in 1657, mentions it as one of
the observances which, in that disordered and dis-
tempered time, were cried down as 'rags of Popery. '† And there can be no doubt that during
the Cromwellian usurpation our old English
manners suffered not a little, and 'many practices
which were themselves part and instruments of piety,
were exploded and lost by being branded under that
odious name.' ‡

But to return to Shakspeare. There could not
be a more striking illustration of the custom of
which I have been speaking, than that Caius Mar-
cius, on his return from the capture of Corioli, and
victory over the Volscians, should be made, as he
is, to kneel and beg his mother's blessing :—

---

* See *Ibid.* iv. 173, 181.   † Works, vol. ii. p. 35.
‡ *Eccl. Biog.* iv. 180. *Christian Institutes*, iv. 561.

All. Welcome to Rome, renowned Coriolanus!
Cor. No more of this, it does offend my heart :
Pray now, no more.
    *Com.**   Look, sir, your mother!
    Cor.   O !
You have I know petitioned all the gods
For my prosperity.   [*Kneels.*
    Vol.†   Nay, my good soldier, up!
                           Act ii. Sc. 1.

In *Cymbeline*, we naturally expect the same from
a son like Guiderius, see Act iv. Sc. 4 ; and from a
daughter like Imogen, see Act v. Sc. 5. It is a
daughter, too, who in *Titus Andronicus* says to her
father, upon his return to Rome, after conquering
the Goths :—

O bless me here with thy victorious hand.   Act i. Sc. 2.

On the other hand, remembering the treatment
which King Lear had received from his two unnatural daughters, Goneril and Regan, we are not
surprised that the Fool should say to him, while
they are out together in the pitiless storm upon the
heath :—

Good nuncle, in, and *ask thy daughter's*‡ *blessing* ; here's a night
pities neither wise men nor fools.   Act iii. Sc. 2.

While remembering also how he himself had acted
towards his good daughter, Cordelia, we are not dis-

---

* Cominius, general in command with Coriolanus, against the
Volscians.
  † Volumnia, mother to Coriolanus.
  ‡ So Mr. Malone prints it ; but surely it should be ' daughters.'
Lear goes on to speak of ' two pernicious daughters.'

pleased that he should say to her, at the last, when moved to repentance :—

> When *thou dost ask me blessing,* I'll kneel down,
> And ask of thee forgiveness ;—   Act v. Sc. 3.

nor that she, on her part, should beseech and protest :—

> O ! look upon me, sir,
> And *hold your hands in benediction o'er me.*
> No, sir, *you* must not kneel.   Act iv. Sc. 7.

In the *Two Gentlemen of Verona,* when Launce, the servant of Proteus, is to leave Rome in attendance upon his master, he ludicrously describes all the particulars of the mournful scene, and among the rest:—

> Now come I to my father ; *Father, your blessing.*
>   Act ii. Sc. 3.

In like manner, we have already seen,* in *Hamlet,* Polonius laying his hand upon his son Laertes' head, and blessing him before he set out upon his travels; and in the same play, Hamlet says to the unhappy queen his mother, whom he had urged to repentance and reformation :—

> .   Once more, Good night !
> And when you are desirous to be blessed,
> *I'll blessing beg of you* :—   Act iii. Sc. 4.

that is, I'll beg your blessing, when you yourself are desirous to amend, and so shall be in a condition to receive blessing from God.

Once more, in *King Richard III.,* the wicked

---

* Above, p. 116.

Gloster, as he then was, has the hypocrisy to go through the same pious form towards his mother :—

> *Glos.* Madam, my mother, I do cry you mercy !
> I did not see your grace—*Humbly on my knee*
> *I crave your blessing.*
>   *Duch.* God bless thee! and put meekness in thy breast,
> Love, charity, obedience, and true duty !
>   *Glos.* Amen!   And make me die a good old man.
> *That is the butt-end of a mother's blessing,*   [*Aside.*
> *I marvel that her grace did leave it out.*   Act ii. Sc. 2.

It would be interesting to descend to the relations which exist in a family between the master and mistress and their domestics; and to endeavour to trace the notions which our poet entertained of the reciprocal duties that flow from that relationship. But I must be content to observe that he has drawn no purer or better character than that of old Adam, the servant, in *As you like it* ; and that in *Cymbeline* he takes occasion, in a speech of Posthumus to his servant Pisanio, to lay down the just and important principle, that no servant is bound to please his master by doing what is wrong :—

> Every good servant does not all commands:
> *No bond, but to do just ones.*   Act v. Sc. 1.

SECT. 9.   *Of Charity and Mercifulness.*

If we are to lay a solid foundation of moral duty, we must first learn to entertain a just abhorrence of its opposite. 'O ye that *love* the Lord, see that ye

hate the thing that is evil.' Ps. xcvii. 10. Thus
of the Ten Commandments, not only the three first,
but the five last also, are all couched in the negative
form, as though the prohibition of vice was designed to form the foundation of virtue. And thus,
too, we learn, even from a heathen poet—

> *Virtus est vitium fugere,* et sapientia *prima*
> Stultitiâ caruisse.

*The beginning of Virtue is to flee Vice, and the be-
ginning of Wisdom to have escaped from Folly.*
  In this and the four next sections I propose to
test the teaching of Shakspeare by this rule ; and,
following the order of the second table of the moral
law, to show how, after the model of Scripture, he
would teach us : (1) from the prohibition of murder to build up the grace of charity; (2) from the
prohibition of adultery to build up the grace of
chastity and sobriety ; (3) from the prohibition of
stealing to build up the grace of honesty ; (4) from
the prohibition of false witness to build up the grace
of truth ; and (5) from the prohibition of covetousness to build up the grace of contentment.
  The subject then of this section corresponds
with the scope of the *sixth* Commandment, as deve-
loped by our Lord in the sermon on the mount.
  In *K. Richard III.* Clarence thus speaks to one of
the men who were sent by Gloster to murder him
in the Tower :—

N

Erroneous vassal! The great KING OF KINGS
Hath in the *Table of His law* commanded
That *thou shalt do no murder*; wilt thou then
Spurn at His edict, and fulfill a man's?
Take heed; for He holds vengeance in His hand,
To hurl upon their heads that break His law.

Act i. Sc. 4.

There is, however, a well-known passage in *Hamlet*, in which our poet would seem not only to justify the taking of blood for blood by private assassination, but to go much further, by teaching to postpone such an act, out of 'a refinement of revenge,' with the view of securing, at the same time, as far as possible, the everlasting perdition of the murderer. And Johnson, accordingly, has condemned the speech—more especially coming, as it does, from 'a virtuous character'—as one 'too horrible to be read or to be uttered.' This is a grave charge to bring against our author; and though the commentators in general appear to have acquiesced in it as just, I would venture to offer a few remarks in arrest of so severe a judgment. For this purpose it will be necessary to produce at least a portion of the speech alluded to. When the wicked king, in attempting to repent,* retires and kneels, Hamlet entering unobserved, says to himself—with reference to the act of murder which he was contemplating—

Now might I do it, pat, now he is praying;
And now I'll do't :—and so he goes to heaven :—

---

* See above, pp. 140, 163.

And so am I revenged? That would* be scanned :
A villain kills my father : and, for that,
I, his sole son, do this same villain send
To heaven.
Why this is hire and salary, not revenge.
He took my father grossly, *full of bread,*
With all his crimes broad blown.

I may observe, by the way, that the expression
‘ full of bread’ affords a remarkable instance of
Shakspeare’s intimate acquaintance with Holy Scripture. I had noticed the parallel to Ezekiel, xvi.
49, and ‘I find that Mr. Malone has done the
same.

And am I then revenged
To take him in the purging of his soul,
When he is fit and season’d for his passage ?
No.
Up, sword; and know thou a more horrid hent.†—

And he concludes by saying *aside* to the king—

This physic but prolongs thy sickly days.

Now, first, I would borrow the observation of Mr.
M. Mason, that though ‘ this speech of Hamlet’s,
as Johnson observes, is horrible indeed, yet some
moral may be extracted from it, as all his subsequent calamities were owing to this savage refinement of revenge.’ But further ; it has been pointed
out, with great truth, that in times of less civiliza-
tion revenge was regarded as a sacred duty. *The*

---

* That *should* be, *requires to be* well considered.
† Hold, seizure.

more fell and terrible the retributive act the more meritorious it seems to have been held. The king himself, in a subsequent scene (Act iv. Sc. 7), when stimulating Laertes to kill Hamlet, says: ' Revenge should have no bounds.' These remarks are confirmed by many unhappy incidents in our Scotch history. The following is told by Sir Walter Scott, in his Review* of the Culloden Papers :—

> So deep was this thirst of vengeance impressed on the minds of the Highlanders, that when a clergyman informed a dying chief of the unlawfulness of the sentiment, urged the necessity of his forgiving an inveterate enemy, and quoted the Scriptural expression, ' Vengeance is mine, saith the Lord,' the acquiescing penitent said, with a deep sigh—' To be sure it is too sweet a morsel for a mortal.' Then added, ' Well, I forgive him, but the *deil take you*, Donald (turning to his son), if *you* forgive him!

Other stories are told by Sir Walter to the same effect in the same place, and 'we could add an hundred,' he writes, ' of that insatiable thirst for revenge which attended *northern* feuds.' Under ' northern,' we may well include ' Danish ; ' especially when we consider the close affinity that existed between this country and Denmark in early times. In like manner, Mr. P. F. Tytler, in his *History of Scotland*,† tells us of the ' sacred *duty* of feudal vengeance ; ' and again, of the ' deep *principle* of feudal vengeance which demanded blood for blood ; ' a principle which he describes, in another

---

* See *Quarterly Review*, vol. xiv. p. 288.
† See vol. ix. pp. 15, 65, 309.

place, as ' so universally felt that it may be regarded
almost as the *pulse* of feudal life.' That our poet
had fully realized the existence and the energetic
character of this principle may be inferred from
scenes and sentiments which he has introduced elsewhere; as in *Romeo and Juliet*, where Tybalt, as a
Capulet, says of a Montague—

> Now by the stock and *honor of my kin*,
> *To strike him dead, I hold it not a sin.* Act i. Sc. 5.

But there, too, the entire plot and catastrophe of
the play turns upon the fatal results which may be
expected to overtake those who act upon such a
sentiment; while its corrective is early (Act iii. Sc. 1)
administered by the prince himself in those weighty
words :—

> Mercy but murders, pardoning those who kill—

which faithfully embody the teaching of Scripture,
as we find it in Genesis ix. 5, 6 ; Numbers xxxv. 16,
31. And in *Hamlet*, even the wicked king is made
to substantiate the same truth :—

> No place indeed should murder sanctuarize;
> Act iv. Sc. 7.

i. e. should afford sanctuary to a murderer.

But to return to the speech of Hamlet. In addition to what has been already said, we are to
remember that Hamlet was a man of *unsettled
mind*, and that what had unsettled him was the duty
of *dealing in some way* with the murderer of his

father and the usurper of his throne. I do not deny, what Dr. Johnson asserts, and would, of course, maintain as essential for the support of his unfriendly criticism, viz. that Hamlet's madness was 'feigned;' but it was not, in my opinion, so feigned as to have *no foundation* in actual derangement; and what more proper or more natural than that the cause which gave occasion for his derangement should lead him to harbour an idea so monstrous, and to express himself in terms so shocking, as to be defensible only upon that ground? I agree with Goethe and others who conceive that Shakspeare meant, in the case of Hamlet, to represent the effects of a great action laid upon one who was inadequate to the performance of it. And part of this inadequacy, I imagine, is made to lie in his looking for the redress which he had to seek only in personal revenge of the meanest kind—secret assassination; while, in justice to the really good and amiable features of his character, a veil is in some sort thrown over this *meanness* by accompanying it with sentiments which would indeed be 'too horrible' for any man, much more a man of 'virtuous character,' *not disordered in his mind,* to entertain or express.

At the same time it is to be noted that Shakspeare had prepared us from the first not to expect in Hamlet, however virtuous on the whole, *the perfection of Christian principle* in bearing up against the grievous wrongs done to both his parents, and through them to himself. In the second scene of the play, speaking to his friend Horatio, of his mother's marriage with the murderer of his father—before the ghost had assured him of the fact and circumstances of the murder—he has recourse to a sentiment which contains the germ of all that shocks us most in the speech so gravely censured by Dr. Johnson, and gives the first indication of *excited* feeling, in the direction not of discontent merely, but of maliciousness, of revenge:—

> Would I had met *my dearest* foe in heaven,*
> Or ever † I had seen that day, Horatio! Act i. Sc. 2.

How different the language put by our poet into the mouth of Wolsey, as a Christian bishop, now penitent and at the close of life:—

> *Cherish* those hearts that hate thee!
> *K. Henry VIII.* Act iii. Sc. 2.

And again this truly Christian character is given to the first reformed Anglican archbishop, Cranmer, in the same play, the king himself bearing witness of him in these words:—

> The common voice, I see, is verified
> Of thee, which says thus: *Do my Lord of Canterbury*
> *A shrewd turn, and he is your friend for ever.*
> Act v. Sc. 2.

The precept to *love our enemies* aims at a height to which the most perfect teaching of morality among

---

* i. e. greatest, worst.   † See above, p. 36.

the heathen made no pretension.* But the doctrine
of forgiveness was not altogether unknown to them,
as we may gather from Cicero :—

> Sunt quædam officia etiam adversus eos servanda a quibus in-
> juriam acceperis. Est enim ulciscendi et puniendi modus.
> Atque haud scio an satis sit *eum qui lacessierit, injuriæ suæ*
> *pœnitere.*   *De Officiis,* lib. 1, cap. xi.

Our poet therefore was at liberty to put such words
as these into the mouth of Volumnia, the mother
of Coriolanus :—

> Why dost not speak ?
> Think'st thou it *honorable for a noble man*
> *Still to remember wrongs ?*   *Coriol.* Act v. Sc. 3.

Compare Prospero in the *Tempest,* Act v. Sc. 1.

On a par with *Revenge* for the *evil* we have received is *Ingratitude* for the *good.* 'Religion groans
at' both ; though it is with reference to the latter
that our poet has used this expressive figure, in
Timon of Athens :—

> 1*st Stranger.* O ! see the monstrousness of man,
> When he looks out in an ungrateful † shape.
> 2*nd Stranger.* RELIGION GROANS AT IT.   Act iii. Sc. 2.

On the other hand, Religion SMILES at every attempt to overcome or to remove not only the more

---

* On Shakspeare's own practice in this respect, see Mr. Wise, p. 145.

† Compare the strong condemnation of Ingratitude in *Twelfth
Night* :—

> I hate ingratitude more in a man
> Than lying, vainness, babbling, drunkenness,
> Or any taint of vice, whose strong corruption
> Inhabits our frail blood.   Act iii. Sc. 4.

grievous instances of uncharitableness such as those, but whatever is at variance with brotherly kindness and good will. She has taught our poet to write :—

> Blessed are the peacemakers on earth.
> > *K. Henry VI. 2nd Part,* Act ii. Sc. 1.

And, further, she has taught him, as we saw above in Section 7, that one great instrument of making peace, is to *pray for those who despitefully use us.* Moreover, she has taught him that the foundation of love or charity to others is the sense of our own liability to want; and the true motive for exercising charity the remembrance that we ourselves do constantly need effectual relief and loving comfort, and *do constantly receive them* from God :—

> Thou shalt not oppress a stranger, *for ye know the heart of a stranger,* seeing ye were strangers in the land of Egypt.
> > Exodus xxiii. 9.
> The Lord your God loveth the stranger in giving him food and raiment. Love ye *therefore* the stranger : *for ye were strangers in the land of Egypt,* from which the Lord delivered you.
> > Deut. x. 17–19.

King Lear confesses that in the day of prosperity he had given too little heed to these considerations :

> O! I have ta'en
> Too little care of this! Take physick, Pomp ;
> Expose thyself to feel what wretches * feel ;
> That thou may'st shake the superflux to them,
> And show the Heavens more just. Act iii. Sc. 4.

---

* The general duty of sympathy is expressed in the very words of Scripture, Rom. xii. 15, 'to weep with them that weep,' in *Titus Andronicus,* Act iii. Sc. 1.

But Shakspeare makes use of Gloster, in the same play, to teach this same lesson still more effectually. Turned out of doors, with his eyes put out, he meets on the heath, without knowing him, his son Edgar, as Mad Tom. Learning from the old man who led him that Mad Tom was a beggar, he says to him:—

> Here, take this purse, thou whom the heaven's plagues
> Have humbled to all strokes: that I am wretched,
> Makes thee the happier—

i. e. because my wretchedness now teaches me to compassionate those who are in distress :—

> Heavens, deal so still!
> Let the superfluous and lust-dieted man
> That slaves * your ordinance, that will not see
> *Because he doth not feel,* feel your power quickly :
> So distribution should undo excess,
> And each man have enough.   Act iv. Sc. 1.

These last words may remind us of S. Paul's argument in favour of alms-giving, ' that there may be an equality ' between rich and poor, in 2 Cor. viii. 13–15.

Once more, in the same play, Edgar, who had been made to drink deeply of the ' physic ' of adversity, tells the happy effect which it had produced upon him. When asked, ' Now, good sir, what are you ?' he answers:—

---

* Makes a slave of, instead of obeying, the divine ordinance of charity to the poor.

> A most poor man, made tame by fortune's blows :
> Who, *by the art of known and feeling* sorrows,*
> *Am pregnant to good pity.* Give me your hand,
> I'll lead you to some biding.† Act iv. Sc. 6.

I have already‡ had occasion to quote the well-known speech of Portia, in the *Merchant of Venice,* which bears upon this point :—

> We do pray for mercy :
> And that same prayer doth teach us all to render
> The deeds of mercy. . Act iv. Sc. 1.

And if we fail to do so, Portia again, in the same scene, warns us what we may expect :—

> As thou urgest justice, be assured
> Thou shalt have justice, *more than thou desir'st.*

We know that, according to the teaching of Scripture, charity or love is the sum of all virtue. There is something singularly striking in the way in which our poet carries on the idea, and makes *kindness* the sum not only of all virtue, but of all beauty :—

> In nature there's *no blemish,* but the mind;
> None can be called *deformed,* but the *unkind* :
> VIRTUE IS BEAUTY. *Twelfth Night,* Act iii. Sc. 4.

Shakspeare was doubtless no stoic ; but by some means or other he has contrived to appropriate and improve upon the best ideas of the stoical phi-losophy.

---

* Either 'feeling' is used for 'felt,' as Malone is inclined to think, or 'known and feeling' is to be understood of 'past and *present* sorrows,' as Warburton interprets.
† Place to abide in. ‡ See p. 96.

Flowing from a kindly and considerate disposition, the duty of hospitality is one which the
Bible, we know, frequently enjoins and commends.
See 1 Peter iv. 9; Hebrews xiii. 2; Romans xii.
13. But there is a passage more solemn and more
impressive than any of these, spoken by our Lord
Himself with reference to the great day of account.
'I was a stranger, and ye took me in;' and 'I
was a stranger, and ye took me *not* in,' Matt. xxv.
35, 43; which I cannot help thinking was present
to our poet's mind when he made Corin say, in
As you like it :—

> My master is of churlish disposition,
> And little reeks *to find the way to heaven,*
> By doing deeds of hospitality.   Act ii. Sc. 4.

Copious, however, and emphatic as the Bible is
in giving us lessons upon all the parts and exercises
of duty which relate to charity and brotherly love,
it does not omit to give us, at the same time, all
needful caution in regard to the mistakes that may
be made and the danger incurred by the indulgence
of kind feelings, or a social disposition, without dis-
cretion and respect of persons. We are to be
careful in the choice of those with whom we associate; careful in making and trusting friends; careful,
above all, not to 'walk in the counsel of the ungodly, nor stand in the way of sinners, nor sit in the
seat of the scornful.' I feel that it is carrying out
the subject of this section somewhat beyond its

proper limit to extend it to points such as these;
I shall not therefore attempt to illustrate them in
detail; only, as a warning upon the choice of friends,
I venture to quote the dying speech of the Duke of
Buckingham, in *King Henry VIII.* :—

> You that hear me,
> This from a dying man receive as certain :
> Where you are *liberal* of your loves and counsels,
> Be sure you be not *loose*, for those you make friends,
> And give your hearts to, when they once perceive
> The least rub in your fortunes, *fall away*
> *Like water* * from ye, never found again,
> But where they mean to sink ye.   Act ii. Sc. 1.

Falstaff gives us another and still weightier reason
for the same precept :—

> It is certain that either wise bearing or ignorant carriage is
> caught, as men take diseases, one of another: therefore let men
> take heed of their company.

Compare with this sentiment the verse of Menander
quoted by S. Paul in 1 Cor. iii. 18.

And that *a multitude is not to be followed in doing
evil,* where could we find a more just, though
laughable illustration, than in the words of Fluellen
in the English camp before the battle of Agincourt ?—

> If the enemy is an ass and a fool and a prating coxcomb, is it
> meet, think you, that *we should also, look you, be an ass and a fool
> and a prating coxcomb* :—in your own conscience now?
>   *K. Henry V.* Act iv. Sc. 1.

---

* See Psalm lviii. 6, Prayer-Book version.

Sect. 10. *Of Diligence, Sobriety, and Chastity.*

I have already been led to speak, in the eighth section of this chapter, on the close connection and sacredness of the Conjugal Relationship. It is a relationship whereby the wife becomes, in the highest and noblest sense, the property of the husband, and the husband the property of the wife. A British Churchman may be allowed to please himself in fancying Shakspeare as an occasional hearer of Bp. Andrewes *—the greatest poet listening to the greatest preacher of the age—and had he been present when that admirable divine delivered his ' Exposition of the Seventh Commandment,' he could not have laid down its first principles more accurately than he has done in *Troilus and Cressida*, where Hector thus speaks respecting the duty of restoring Helen to her husband Menelaus :—

> Nature craves
> All dues be rendered to their owners ; now,
> *What nearer debt* † *in all humanity*
> *Than wife is to the husband?* If this law
> Of nature be corrupted thro' affection,.
>
> . . . .
>
> There is a law in each well-order'd nation,
> To curb those raging appetites that are

---

* Born in 1555 ; one of the translators of the Bible, 1611.

† Mr. Malone interprets the word ' propriety' as used by Olivia in *Twelfth Night*, Act v. Sc. 2, in this sense, viz. to mean the right of *property* which a married couple have in each other, and which Milton speaks of as the ' sole *propriety* in Paradise ; ' but I rather think it means in that place, ' proper state.'

Most disobedient and refractory.
If Helen then be wife to Sparta's king—
As it is known she is—these *moral laws*
Of nature and of nations speak aloud
To have her back returned :—Thus to persist
In doing wrong, extenuates not wrong,
But makes it much more heavy.　　　Act ii. Sc. 2.

And in *Measure for Measure* our poet follows the severity of the Mosaic Law, that those who commit the sins more immediately forbidden by this commandment are worthy of death,* no less than they who commit murder :—

It were as good
To pardon him, that hath from nature stolen
A man already made, as to remit †
Their saucy ‡ sweetness, that do coin Heaven's image
In stamps that are forbid ;—　　　Act ii. Sc. 4.

an aphorism not the less profound because enunciated by a hypocrite, of which the author gives us intimation, with admirable skill, by the phrase chosen to describe the sin which is at once palliated and proscribed. In like manner, no exception can be taken against the truth of what follows—in regard either to the imprudence of hasty marriage or the criminality of divorce—however we may abhor the speaker, the wicked Gloster :—

Hasty marriage seldom proveth well.
Yet God forbid that I should wish them severed,
Whom God hath joined together.
　　　　　K. Henry VI. 3rd Part, Act iv. Sc. 1.

---

* See also *King Lear*, Act iv. Sc. 6.　But comp. S. John viii. 11.
† Pardon.　　　　‡ Inordinate indulgence of sensual appetite.

There is a sentiment, too often realised in the experience of inordinate affection and unhallowed intercourse between the sexes, which our poet might have adopted from the miserable history of Amnon and Tamar, recorded in 2 Samuel xiii. 2–15 :—

> Sweet love, I see, changing his property,
> Turns to the sourest and most deadly hate.
>
> *K. Richard II.* Act iii. Sc. 2.

And where shall we find the unhappy passion which sometimes seizes upon true and pure affection, and which Shakspeare has delineated with over-whelming power in *Othello,** and again in *Winter's Tale* and *Comedy of Errors,* more justly character-ised, though in so few words, than in the Song of Solomon ?—

> Jealousy is cruel as the grave ; the coals thereof are coals of fire, which hath a most vehement flame. viii. 6.

That the plays of Shakspeare are not free from passages which may minister food to an impure imagination,† cannot be denied ; but that their

---

* In mitigation of the horror which the conduct of Othello inspires, it would be well if it could be proved that he was not a Christian. Schlegel regards him so, and points this out as an instance in which Shakspeare has improved upon the novel, the Moor of which he says ' is a baptised Saracen.' But to say nothing of the language which Othello himself uses in Act ii. Sc. 3, quoted in the next page ; or of the reference which Iago (who surely must be considered of the same religion as his general) makes to ' proofs of Holy Writ ' in Act iii. Sc. 3 ; it is plain that Schlegel must have overlooked the passage in Iago's soliloquy (Act ii. Sc. 3) where he speaks of Othello as ready even ' to renounce *his baptism* ' for the love of Desdemona.

† He writes as if penitently conscious of this in his *Sonnets* cx. and cxi. But compare my remarks below in the *Conclusion.*

general tendency is of an opposite and wholly virtuous character, is no less certain. Nor has he
omitted, on fit occasions, to give us the best of
lessons for the control of passion,* and the avoiding
of excess : as, for instance, in *Measure for Measure*,
the severe rebuke which the Duke, disguised as a
friar, administers to the Clown upon his profligate
course of life, Act iii. Sc. 2; and in *Othello*, where
Cassio, after he had been betrayed into intoxication,
delivers the following lecture against intempe-
rance :—

> Oh! that men should put an enemy to their mouths to steal
> away their brains! that we should with joy, revel, pleasure and
> applause, transform ourselves into beasts!
> *Iago.* Why, but you are now well enough. How came you
> thus recovered ?
> *Cassio.* It hath pleased the devil Drunkenness to *give place to
> the devil*† wrath : one imperfectness shows me another, to make
> me frankly despise myself. . . . To be now a sensible man,
> by and by a fool, and presently ‡ a beast! O strange! *Every
> inordinate cup is unblessed*, and the ingredient is a devil.
>
> Act ii. Sc. 3.

The drinking bout had ended in a quarrel, and
in the midst of the disturbance, Othello, coming in,
exclaims :—

---

* See the earnest caution to lovers before marriage in *Tempest*,
Act iv. Sc. 1, and the Song of the Fairies in *Merry Wives of Windsor*,
Act v. Sc. 5.

† See Ephes. iv. 27.

‡ Compare what the clown, in *Twelfth Night*, says of a drunken
man : that he is 'like a drowned man, a fool, and a madman.'
Act i. Sc. 5.

> Why, how now, ho! from whence ariseth this?
> Are we turned Turks, and to ourselves do that
> Which Heaven hath forbid the Ottomites ?*
> For Christian shame, *put by this barbarous brawl.*

The last line is one of those which make it difficult
to believe that Shakspeare had altogether forgotten
his schoolboy † classics.   Surely when he wrote it
he was thinking of Horace :—

> Natis in usum lætitiæ scyphis
> Pugnare Thracum est ; *tollite barbarum*
> *Morem,* verecundumque Bacchum
> *Sanguineis* prohibite *rixis.*

In like manner we are warned against idleness,
as the certain mother of all evil, and especially of
such sins as are pointed at under this head, in
Antony and Cleopatra, where Antony resolves :—

> I must from this enchanting queen break off :
> Ten thousand harms, more than the ills I know,
> *My idleness* doth hatch.   Act i. Sc. 2.

Where again it is not impossible that Shakspeare
had in mind another Roman poet of high authority
in such matters :—

---

* Mahometans.

† The subject here hinted at is a tempting one even after Dr.
Farmer's essay. Let me be allowed to give only one instance in
addition to those produced above, and elsewhere in the text of these
pages. In *K. Henry VIII.,* Griffith says to Q. Katharine, with reference to Wolsey, ' Men's evil manners live *in brass* ; their virtues
we *write in water.*'

Mr. Reed has a long note in illustration of this latter figurative
expression, but neither he nor any of the critics has quoted a parallel
to it nearly so close, as is afforded by the following from Catullus :—

> ' Dicit ; sed mulier cupido quod dicit amanti,
>   In vento, et *rapida scribere oportet aquâ.*'

See, however, *Supplementary Note* at end of this volume.

Quæritur Ægisthus quare sit factus *Adulter* ?
    In promptu causa est ;—*desidiosus erat.*

But the most impressive lesson of all in this respect
is the picture which our poet draws of the deathbed
of one whom he has made the type of a merry, but
sensual and ungodly life ; and being put into the
mouth of a worthless woman (for it could scarcely
have been represented otherwise) the description of
the scene is made more touching, more melancholy.
I allude to Act ii. Sc. 3 in *King Henry V.* The
reader of Burnet, of Evelyn's Memoirs, and of the
Life of Bp. Ken will be at no loss to compare a
parallel scene of real life, only exhibited on the most
elevated stage and in the highest rank, the death-
bed scene of the 'Merry Monarch,' King Charles II.
' Truly the end of that mirth is heaviness.' Prov:.
xiv. 13.

I will only add here that as idleness is the root
of vice, so diligence and the desire of self-improve-
ment is, with the guidance of Divine grace, the best
road to virtue. And this too our poet would teach
us, if I do not misinterpret him, in these comprehensive and emphatic words :—

> Ignorance is the curse of God,
> *Knowledge the wing wherewith we fly to heaven.*
> *K. Henry VI.* 2nd *Part,* Act iv. Sc. 7.

Or to take only the lower and merely practical view
which a heathen could exhibit :—

                              Ni
    Posces ante diem librum cum lumine, si non

Intendes animum *studiis* et *rebus honestis,*
Invidiâ vel *Amore* vigil torquebere :—

in other words, with *such things* as, he leaves us to
conclude, are *not* 'honest,' *not* 'virtuous,' *not* 'of good
report.' By 'invidia' we may understand all those
evil affections which belong to the *irascible,* as by
' amor ' those which belong to the *concupiscible* part
of our nature.

Sect. 11.   *Of Justice and Honesty.*

We are told in *Measure for Measure* of a certain
'sanctimonious pirate that went to sea with the *Ten
Commandments,* but scraped one—the *eighth*—out of
the Table,' Act i. Sc. 2. *Thou shalt not steal* ' was a
commandment to command the captain and all the
rest from their functions.' I am afraid that conduct
similar in effect to this pirate's is still only too common—among landsmen; as we may conclude it was
in Shakspeare's day. ' To be honest, as this world
goes,' says Hamlet* to Polonius, ' is to be one man
picked out of ten thousand,' Act ii. Sc. 2. And in
Timon of Athens, it is the remark of one of the three
strangers that 'Policy sits above conscience,' Act iii.
Sc. 2. And yet how often have we been taught, in
regard not only to dishonest and unjust but to harsh
and ungenerous treatment of others, that ' with
what measure ye mete, it shall be measured to you
again !' Matt. vii. 2.

---

* See above, p. 119.

Measure for measure must be answered.
Henry VI. Act ii. Sc. 6.
Like doth quit like, and measure still for measure.
Measure for Measure, Act v. Sc. 1.

We know that even heathen moralists, such as
Cicero, regarded illiberality as a species of injustice;
and though we have a proverb which bids us to be
just before we are generous, yet we also know that, as
Christians, we can never be said to be *truly* just,
until we are also really bountiful. It is the twofold
stigma of prodigality that it has a direct tendency,
by disabling us from giving, to make us unjust both
toward God and towards man. Hence it is that
while the duty of a charitable temper and disposition
belongs rather to the sixth Commandment, the
practical exhibition of that duty in regard to alms-
giving may be said to fall more properly under the
eighth. In the parable of *the rich man and Lazarus*
we see the *measure* which will hereafter be *measured
again* to those who *mete* as Dives did to the poor.
How often our poet has alluded to that parable I
shall have occasion to mention in a later section.*
The parable of *the prodigal son* has another, and
more blessed lesson to teach, besides the evils and
injustice of prodigality—a lesson fitted for the pulpit rather than for the stage ; but the stage may
seize at least upon that portion of the story which
represents how ' the drunkard and the glutton shall

---

* See below, Sect. 16.

come to poverty,' Prov. xxiii. 21, and how 'want
shall come as an armed man' upon the sluggard
and the dissolute, Prov. vi. 11.

> All things that are,
> Are with more spirit chased than enjoy'd.
> How like a younker, or *a prodigal,*
> The scarfed bark puts from her native bay,
> Hugg'd and embraced by the strumpet wind !
> How *like the prodigal doth she return* ;
> With over-weather'd ribs, and ragged sails,
> Lean, rent, and *beggar'd* by the strumpet wind !
>
> *Merchant of Venice,* Act ii. Sc. 6.

Mr. Bowdler has not spared this beautiful passage,
but he has allowed what follows to stand without
curtailment.   Oliver is speaking, in *As you like it,*
to his unkind and unnatural brother, Orlando :—

> Shall I keep your *hogs,* and *eat husks* with them ?   What
> *prodigal portion have I spent, that I should come to such penury ?*
>
> Act i. Sc. 1.

There is another reference to the same parable,
which again Mr. Bowdler has omitted, in the *First
Part of King Henry IV.* Act iv. Sc. 2.

On the other hand, the poor widow who, in
putting her two mites into the treasury, gave ' all
her living,' Mark xii. 44, was evidently in our
poet's thoughts, when he wrote :—

> *Fool.* How now, nuncle ? Would I had two coxcombs,* and
> two daughters !
> *Lear.* Why, my boy ?
> *Fool.* If I *gave them all my living,* I'd keep my coxcombs my-
> self.

---

* Fool's caps.

With regard to the administration of justice, I have noted only the following passages as coming within the scope of my design. We read in the *Acts* how that

King Agrippa and Bernice came unto Cesarea to salute Festus. And when they had been there many days, Festus declared Paul's cause unto the king, saying, ' There is a certain man left in bonds by Felix, about whom, when I was at Jerusalem, the chief priests and the elders of the Jews informed me, desiring to have judgment against him. To whom I answered, it is not the manner of the Romans to deliver any man to die, before that *he which is accused have the accusers face to face,* and have licence to answer for himself concerning the crime laid against him.' xxv. 13–16.

Well therefore does Archbishop Cranmer urge, in *King Henry VIII.,* before the Lords of Council who were assembled to condemn him unheard :—

> I do beseech your lordships,
> That in this case of justice, my *accusers,*
> Be what they will, may stand forth *face to face,*
> And freely urge against me. Act v. Sc. 2.

And well too does the Bishop of Carlisle, in *King Richard II.,* urge the same in behalf of his sovereign against those who had conspired to dethrone him :—

> Thieves are not judged, but *they are by to hear,*
> Altho' apparent guilt be seen in them :
> And shall the figure of God's majesty,
> His captain, steward, deputy elect,
> Anointed, crowned, planted many years,
> Be judged by subject and inferior breath,
> And *he himself not present ?* Act iv. Sc. 1.

SECT. 12. *Of the use and abuse of the Tongue.*

'I will speak daggers,' says Hamlet, Act iii. Sc. 2, using a metaphor which the Bible has made familiar to us. 'Swords are in their lips,' says the Psalmist, lix. 7. And again, 'Who whet their tongue like a sword, and bend their bows to shoot their arrows— even bitter words,' lx. 3. And no doubt there are many cases in which this is found by experience to be too true. For instance :—

> 'Tis *slander* ;
> Whose *edge is sharper than the sword*; whose tongue
> Out-venoms all the worms of Nile ; whose breath
> Rides on the posting winds, and doth belie
> All corners of the world : kings, queens, and states,
> Maids, matrons, nay, the secrets of the grave
> This viperous slander enters. *Cymbeline*, Act iii. Sc. 4.

And the heinousness of slander lies in this, that nothing is more precious to a man than his good name. There is an admirable sermon of Bishop Sanderson* upon the text, 'A good name is better than precious ointment,' Eccles. vii. 1 ; in which he observes—the more precious a good name is, the more grievous is their sin who seek to rob others of it. 'Neither thieves nor murderers are more cruel and injurious than slanderers, backbiters, and false accusers are.'† This is vigorously put by that great divine, but not so effectively as our poet has

---

* Born 1587, died 1662.   † *Works*, vol. i. p. 21.

expressed the same ; and he has added the original idea, that though so much is lost by him against whom the sin is committed, nothing is gained by him who commits it :—

> Good name in man or woman, dear my lord,
> Is the immediate jewel of their souls :
> Who steals my purse, steals trash ; . . .
> But he that filches from me my good name,
> Robs me of that which not enriches him,
> And makes me poor indeed.   *Othello,* Act iii. Sc. 3.

Where Mr. Malone quotes Proverbs xxii. 1, ' A good name is rather to be chosen than great riches.'

S. Paul has taught us, that in judging others the consequence is we condemn ourselves, Rom. ii. 1 ; an idea which our poet has caught and admirably intensified, when he makes Timon ask—

> Wilt thou whip thine own faults in other men ?
> *Timon of Athens,* Act v. Sc. 1.

At the same time he does not deny that censure and reproof, even of the greatest severity, may be sometimes necessary, and that charity itself may require us to administer them :—

> I must be cruel, only to be kind.
> *Hamlet,* Act iii. Sc. 4.

But with regard to censures in general there is no reflection more just or more profound than that the judgment we form and the estimate we express of the conduct of others depends upon our own moral state ; and how happily has our poet embodied this truth !—

> Wisdom and goodness to the vile seem vile.
>
> *King Lear,* Act iv. Sc. 2.

It follows, as a consequence from this remark, that praise is often a doubtful benefit, and we know that in warning us against it, our Lord himself has gone so far as to say—

> Woe unto you when all men shall speak well of you !
>
> Luke vi. 26.

And how ingeniously again has this sentiment been adopted and assigned to the character to whom, of all others, it is most appropriate !—

> *Timon.* If I hope well, I'll never see thee more.
> *Alcibiades.* I never did thee harm.
> *Timon.* Yea, *thou spok'st well of me.*
> *Alcibiades.*   Call'st thou that harm ?
> *Timon.* Men daily find it such.*
>
> *Timon of Athens,* Act iv. Sc. 3.

See also the dialogue between the Duke and the Clown, in *Twelfth Night* :—

> *Duke.* How dost thou, my good fellow ?
> *Clown.* Truly, sir, the better for my foes, and the worse for my friends.
> *Duke.* Just the contrary ; the better for thy friends.
> *Clown.* No, sir, the worse.
> *Duke.* How can that be ?
> *Clown.* Marry, sir, they praise me and make an ass of me; now my foes tell me plainly I am an ass ; so that by my foes, sir, I profit in the knowledge of myself; and by my friends I am *abused.*†   Act v. Sc. 1.

---

* See S. Chrys. *on Acts,* Hom. lii.   † i.e. deceived, imposed upon.

And if the praise of others is harmful, still less
will our own praise of ourselves do us good :

Let another man praise thee ; and not thine own mouth.
Prov. xxvii. 2.

It is not good to eat much honey ; so for men to search their
own glory is not glory. xxv. 27.

The worthiness of praise disdains his worth,
If that the praised himself bring the praise forth.
Troilus and Cressida, Act i. Sc. 3.

Pride is his own glass, his own trumpet, his own chronicle ;
and whatever praises itself but in the deed, devours the deed in
the praise. *Ibid.* Act. ii. Sc. 3.

We have had occasion, in former sections, to
speak of the efficacy of prayer and intercession,
and also of the practice of *Parental Benediction*,
which our pious forefathers doubtless regarded as
not altogether unavailing. That they should have
attributed some effect to *malediction* likewise, when
solemnly pronounced in a righteous cause, is not to
be wondered at ; and for my own part I feel at
least no sympathy with the scrup.es which induced
Mr. Bowdler to omit the last line of the passage I
am about to quote :—

Q. Mar. O! princely Buckingham, I kiss thy hand ;—
Thy garments are not spotted with our blood,
Nor thou within the compass of my curse.
Buck. Nor no one here ; for curses never pass
The lips of those that breathe them in the air.
Q. Mar. I'll not believe but they ascend the sky,
And there awake God's gentle sleeping peace.
King Richard III. Act i. Sc. 3.

Instead of omitting these last words, it would

have been a wiser course to have drawn attention to the enormity of the crimes, some committed already, and others remaining to be committed by Richard—and the solemn appeal to God's all-seeing eye, in a *public* cause, which especially concerned His own majesty, as King of Kings. If malediction could ever be justifiable, it was justifiable—I had almost said it was charitable—in the case and under the circumstances in which Shakspeare has introduced it; and put it into the mouth of a woman— that woman a mother, and that mother once a queen.

The connection between speaking truth and integrity of action, and on the other hand, between falsehood and unrighteousness, is strongly marked in Holy Scripture, and it has not escaped the notice of Shakspeare.* In the 3rd chapter of S. John's Gospel our Lord first uses the expression, ' every one that doeth evil,' and then, as the reverse of it, ' he that *doeth truth.*' In like manner the same Apostle writes, in his first Epistle, ' If we say that we have fellowship with Him, and walk in darkness, we lie, and *do not the truth,*' i. 8, where the falsehood of speech and the falsehood of action, i. e. unrighteousness, are both combined. And so again, in his second Epistle, he speaks of ' walking *in truth,*' v. 4, i. e. in righteousness and holiness of life. Once more. S. Paul puts the question in the mouth of a disputer of this world :—

---

* Nor of Lord Bacon. See his 6th Essay.

If the truth of God hath more abounded through *my lie* (i. e. my sinfulness) unto His glory, why yet am I also judged as *a sinner?*
                                                        Rom iii. 7.

It is the same principle which led our poet to use the word ' untruth ' for *disloyalty*, i. e. *sin against a king*, in the following passage of *King Richard II.*, where the Duke of York exclaims—

> God for His mercy! what a tide of woes
> Comes rushing on this woeful land at once!
> I know not what to do : I would to God,
> (So *my untruth* had not provoked him to it)
> The king had cut off my head with my brother's.
>   Act ii. Sc. 2.

SECT. 13. *Of Humility, Contentment, and Resignation.*

We may well believe that Shakspeare's own experience of life, even in his early days, had sufficiently confirmed the truth, which he might have learnt from Scripture, that happiness, if it is to be expected at all in this world, is not to be looked for merely in external circumstances :—

Take heed (said our Lord) and beware of covetousness ; for a man's life consisteth not in the abundance of the things which he possesseth.   Luke xii. 15.

The scene in the *Third Part of King Henry VI.*, which is laid in a chase in the north of England, and in which the dethroned monarch enters disguised, with a Prayer Book in his hand, and is accosted by the two keepers who were on the look-out to apprehend him, affords our poet an excellent opportunity for introducing sentiments such as we are now to speak of :—

> *2nd Keep.* Say, what art thou, that talk'st of kings and queens?
> *K. Hen.* More than I seem, and less than I was born to :
> A man at least, for less I should not be ;
> And men may talk of kings, and why not I ?
> *2nd Keep.* Ay, but thou talk'st as if thou wert a king.
> *K. Hen.* Why, so I am *in mind*, and that's enough.
> *2nd Keep* But if thou be a king, where is thy crown ?
> *K. Hen.* My crown is *in my heart*, not on my head ;
> Not deck'd with diamonds and Indian stones,
> Nor to be seen ; my crown is called CONTENT ;
> A crown it is that seldom kings enjoy.   Act iii. Sc. 1.

In illustration of this, Mr. Steevens quotes that excellent old song in Percy's *Reliques of Antient English Poetry*, i. 213, beginning with :—

> My minde to me a kingdome is.

But here again I cannot help suspecting that our poet's school-learning was running in his head, and reminded him of some one of those numerous passages * which represent the stoical notion that the *wise man* is the truly *royal* personage—' King of kings, and inferior only to Jove himself.' See Horace 1 *Epist.* i. 106, *sq.*; or what comes nearer

---

* The most remarkable perhaps is that in the *Thyestes* of Seneca : the chorus beginning
         'Tandem Regia nobilis,' v. 336 ;
which might have been known, if not to Shakspeare, to the author of the song in Bp. Percy's collection.

to the circumstances before us, the well-known
stanzas in the *2nd Book of Odes* :—

> Redditum Cyri solio Phraaten
> Dissidens plebi numero beatorum
> Eximit Virtus, populumque falsis
> Dedocet uti
> Vocibus ; *regnum et diadema tutum*
> Deferens uni propriamque laurum,
> Quisquis ingentes oculo irretorto
> Spectat acervos.

Nor does it seem unreasonable to conjecture,
considering the superabundant evidence before us of
Shakspeare's familiarity with the ideas of Scripture,
that the text—' Behold, the *kingdom* of God is
within you,' Luke xvii. 21, and others of a similar
character, may have contributed to the sentiment
which he has put into King Henry's mouth.   It is
in the same vein, though carried somewhat further,
that the ' honest chronicler,' Griffith, speaks of Cardinal Wolsey, after his decease :—

> His overthrow heaped happiness upon him,—
> For then, and not till then, he felt himself,
> And found the *blessedness of being little.*
>   *K. Henry VIII.* Act iv. Sc. 2.

And the churlish Apemantus, in *Timon of Athens*,
philosophizes for once to some purpose when he
says:—

> *Best* state, *contentless,*
> Hath a distracted and most wretched being,
> Worse than *the worst, content.*   Act iv. Sc. 3.

In other words, as the old lady in attendance upon
Anne Bullen testifies, in *King Henry VIII.,*

> Our content
> Is our *best having* :   Act ii. Sc. 3.

i. e. our best possession.   But to return to *King
Henry VI.*   In an earlier part of the play before
quoted, and on the very day of the battle of Towton,
which established his antagonist Edward on the
throne, and while the fight was raging in the distance, we have that pious but feeble-minded prince
thus moralizing :—

> Here on this molehill will I sit me down.
> To whom God will, there be the victory.
>
> .   .   .   .
>
> Would I were dead ! if God's good will were so ;
> For what is in this world, but grief and woe ?
> O God ! methinks it were a happy life,
> To be no better than a homely swain :
> To sit upon a hill, as I do now,
> To carve out dials quaintly point by point.
>
> .   .   .   .   .   .
>
> So minutes, hours, days, weeks, months and years,
> Pass'd over to the end they were created,
> Would bring white hairs unto a quiet grave.
> Ah ! what a life were this ! how sweet ! how lovely !
> Gives not the hawthorn bush a sweeter shade
> To shepherds, looking on their silly sheep
> Than doth a rich embroider'd canopy
> To kings that fear their subjects' treachery ?
> O ! yes it doth ; a thousand times it doth.
> And to conclude—the shepherd's homely curds,
> His cold thin drink out of a leather bottle,
> His wonted sleep* under a fresh tree's shade,

---

* See Eccles. v. 12, and compare *K. Henry V.* Act iv. Sc. 1.

All which secure and sweetly he enjoys,
Is far beyond a prince's delicates ;
His viands sparkling in a golden cup,
His body couched in a curious bed,
Where care, mistrust, and treason wait on him.   Act ii. Sc. 5.

The argument here adduced in favour of a humble station of life is its comparative freedom from anxiety and alarm. And such an argument, just because it is superficial rather than substantial, comes with propriety enough from a weak though amiable character like that of King Henry VI. But our poet was well aware that deeper, and I may add, more Scriptural motives were to be assigned for the choice which such a character would make out of mere pusillanimity. The greater exposure to temptation, already alluded to in the case of Wolsey, and to which all are liable in proportion to the elevation and grandeur they attain, affords a ground for contentment in moderate, and even in lowly circumstances, which minds, not the weakest, but the strongest and best, will be most ready to appreciate. The Danish courtiers Rosencrantz and Guildenstern gave a wise return to Hamlet's salutation—' My excellent good friends—how do ye both ? '—when they replied, or rather, the latter said, speaking for them both :—

Happy, in that we are not *over happy*.
Hamlet, Act ii. Sc. 2.

So too, Nerissa, in the *Merchant of Venice*, remarks, ' It is no mean happiness to be seated *in the*

P

mean.' Act i. Sc. 2. The blinded Gloster, in *King Lear,* when the old man leading him observes,

> Alack, sir, you cannot see your way;

makes answer, as a conscience-stricken penitent ;—

> I have no way, and therefore want no eyes;
> I *stumbled when* * I *saw.* Full oft 'tis seen,
> *Our means*† *secure us*; and *our mere defects*
> *Prove our commodities.* Act iv. Sc. 1.

It is in a calmer, but not less truthful spirit of Christian Philosophy that King Henry V., on the night before the battle of Agincourt, teaches us how ' our defects,' i. e. *our wants,* our deficiencies in the comforts and conveniences of life, may ' prove our commodities,' and so suggests an additional motive, not merely for contentment in a humble, but for resignation in an adverse lot, when he argues :—

> There is some soul of goodness in things evil,
> Would men observingly distil it out;

---

* See John ix. 39—41 ; Matt. xiii. 13.

† I retain the reading of the original editions, both quarto and folio. Mr. Malone does so likewise, but he understands 'means' (plural) in the same sense as those do who have adopted Pope's emendation ' our mean secures us,' i. e. *our middle state,* as Warburton interprets. It does not seem to have occurred to any of the critics that the verb ' secure ' may here not improbably signify *make careless,* and then ' means ' will be opposed to ' defects,' and signify *the things we have,* ' our commodities,' and in Gloster's case, *his sight.* Compare the use of ' gentle ' as a verb, in *King Henry V.* Act. iv. Sc. 3—

'This day *shall gentle* his condition '—

i. e. make him a gentleman. I am surprised that Bp. Hurd, in his note (highly commended by Mr. Hallam) upon Horace's 'callida junctura' of words, though he instances Shakspeare's art in converting *substantives* into *verbs,* says nothing of the same conversion in regard to ' adjectives.'—See Hurd's Works, vol. i. p. 78.

> For our bad neighbour makes us early stirrers,
> Which is both healthful and good husbandry :
> Besides, they are our *outward consciences,*
> And preachers to us all ; admonishing
> That we should dress us fairly for our end.
> Thus may we gather *honey* from the *weed,*
> And make a moral of the devil himself.
>
> *K. Henry V.* Act iv. Sc. r.

On a former occasion the same king had taught us :—

> In peace there's nothing so becomes a man
> As modest *stillness* and *humility.*   Act iii. Sc. 1.

According to the Apostolic precept that we should ' study to be *quiet,*' 1 Thess. iv. 11. In like manner, the advice of the ' good Duke Humphrey' of Gloster to his Duchess, under the disgrace and punishment which she had brought upon herself—

> Thy *greatest help is quiet,* gentle Nell ;
> I pray thee, sort thy heart to patience—
>
> *K. Henry VI. 2nd Part,* Act ii. Sc. 4.

may be compared with the admonition of the Evangelical Prophet :—

> Their strength is to sit still. In quietness and in confidence shall be your strength.   Isaiah xxx. 7, 15.

Nor can we reasonably doubt that when our poet wrote in *King Richard II.,*—

> Pride must have a fall,   Act v. Sc. 5.

he had in his mind that saying in the Book of Proverbs :—

> Pride goeth before destruction, and an haughty spirit before a fall. xvi. 18.

Meanwhile, amid all his commendations of a low estate, our poet was fully sensible of the contemptuous and unworthy treatment which poverty too often meets with at the hands of a vain and mammon-serving world. He knew the testimony of Solomon :—

> The poor is hated even of his own neighbour. Prov. xiv. 20. All the brethren of the poor do hate him : how much more do his friends go far from him ? He pursueth them with words, yet they are wanting to him. xix. 7.

This is a sad picture, and it is made more melancholy by the addition of ingratitude when a rich and bountiful man, having fallen into poverty, meets with no better return from those whom he has benefited—the case of *Timon of Athens* :—

> *2nd Serv.*   As we do turn our backs
> From our companion thrown into his grave;
> So his familiars *to* * his buried fortunes
> Slink all away; leave their false vows with him,
> Like empty purses pick'd, and his poor self,
> A dedicated beggar to the air,
> With his disease of *all-shunn'd poverty*,
> Walks, like contempt, alone. ·   Act iv. Sc. 2.

And for one who had not the lessons and consolations of revealed religion to fall back upon, such a trial is not improperly represented as too great. But it is not so with the Christian hero, like S. Paul, who ' has learnt, in whatsoever state he is, therewith to be content ; ' nay, who ' in every thing

---

* Sir T. Hanmer's reading, ' from,' seems preferable.

gives thanks.' And Hamlet describes his friend
Horatio as approaching, at least, to that high
standard :—

> Thou hast been
> As one, in suffering all, who suffers nothing ;
> A man that fortune's buffets and rewards
> Has ta'en *with equal thanks.* Act iii. Sc. 2.

And, looked at from this point of view, we may
accept the sentiment of Hamlet, which otherwise
would savour of an infidel philosophy:—

> There is nothing either good or bad but thinking makes it so.
> Act ii. Sc. 2.

He is not speaking of *moral* good and evil. He
had before said ' Denmark's a prison ;' to which
Rosencrantz demurred—' We think not so, my
lord.' Hamlet replies, ' Why then 'tis none to you:
for there is nothing,' &c., &c. So that the passage
becomes parallel to Horace's :—

> Quod petis, hic est ;
> Est Ulubris, *animus* si te non deficit *æquus.*

And to Milton's :—

> The *mind* is its own place ; and in itself
> Can make a heaven of hell, a hell of heaven.

That our poet is entitled to the full benefit of
this interpretation—unless we will suppose that he
designed, in this single instance * to give a sceptical

---

* Warburton has given a semi-infidel interpretation to another
saying of Hamlet, in Act v. Sc. 2 : ' Since no man, of aught he
leaves, knows,' &c., but without sufficient reason. The reading is

turn to Hamlet's philosophical character—we may
reasonably conclude from (among other proofs) a
sentiment which he assigns to Troilus, and which
sufficiently indicates belief in the essential and ob-
jective character of moral truth :—

> We may not think the justness of each act
> Such and no other than event doth form it.
> *Troilus and Cressida*, Act ii. Sc. 2.

Nor was this beyond what was to be expected
from a heathen. Shakspeare might have remembered the Ovidian distich :—

> Careat successibus, opto,
> Quisquis ab eventu facta probanda putet.

The proverb that *Sorrows never come single* is one
which I am tempted to recur* to in passing, on account of the felicitous and at the same time varied
forms in which our author has expressed it. Thus,
in *Hamlet* :—

> When sorrows come, they come not single spies,
> But in battalions. Act iv. Sc. 5.

And again, in the same play :—

> One woe doth tread upon another's heel,
> So fast they follow. *Ibid.* Sc. 7.

---

doubtful. Johnson's interpretation is much more satisfactory ; but
I am inclined to think that Hamlet, in his morbid state of mind,
means to say, that since we can attain to no true knowledge in this
life—since no man *really knows* about anything which goes on in
this world—secretly alluding to the plausible, but most wicked,
character and doings of his uncle—'to leave (it) betimes' can be no
great loss. In short we neither *know* what *is* here, nor, as he has
remarked elsewhere, what *is to be* hereafter. See his famous soliloquy
in Act iii. Sc. 1, alluded to below, p. 224.

* See above, p. 132.

Again in *Pericles, Prince of Tyre* :—

> One sorrow never comes, but brings an heir
> That may succeed, as his inheritor.   Act i. Sc. 4.

But however thick misfortunes may come upon us, the same author who thus leads us to expect them, has not failed to prescribe, no less plainly and frequently, the remedy which a Christian knows it is his duty to apply, when occasion requires, in his own case. When news is brought to King Henry VI. that he is utterly bereft of all that the English crown had possessed in France, his reply is :—

> Cold news, Lord Somerset; but *God's will be done!*
> *King Henry VI. 2nd Part,* Act iii. Sc. 1.

When Brandon announces to the Duke of Buckingham that he is arrested for high treason, and must go as a prisoner to the Tower, his reply is :—

> *The will of Heaven*
> *Be done in this, and all things!* I obey.
> *King Henry VIII.* Act i. Sc. 1.

To his mother, the Duchess of York, in her affliction for the death of her sons (King Edward IV. and the Duke of Clarence), the Marquess of Dorset thus administers consolation, founded upon the well-known passage in the Book of Job, i. 21.

> Comfort, dear mother; God is much displeased
> That you take with unthankfulness his doing;
> In common worldly things 'tis called—ungrateful,
> With dull unwillingness to repay a debt,
> Which with a bounteous hand was kindly lent;

> Much more to be thus opposite with Heaven,
> For * it requires the royal debt it lent you.
> > *King Richard III.* Act ii. Sc. 2.

Finally, it is left to a heathen to teach the elementary lesson† that no distresses or afflictions, however many or great, should be allowed to provoke us into destruction of the life, of which, as no one (except by just authority) can lawfully deprive us, so neither can we lawfully deprive ourselves:—

> *Gloster.* You ever gentle gods, take my breath from me;
> Let not my worser ‡ spirit tempt me again
> To die before you please.　　*King Lear,* Act iv. Sc. 6.

Even in the mouth of Brutus (who is eventually represented as putting an end to his own life,§ much as King Saul had done, and as Antony afterwards did), our poet has ventured to place substantially the same sentiment:—

> *Cassius.* If we do lose this battle, then is this
> The very last time we shall be together;
> What are you then determined to do?
> *Brutus.* Even by the rule of that philosophy
> By which I did blame Cato for the death
> Which he did give himself:—I know not how,
> But I do find it *cowardly and vile,*
> For fear of what might fall, *so* to prevent ‖
> ·The time of life :—*arming myself with patience,*
> To stay ¶ the providence of some high powers,
> That govern us below.　　*Julius Cæsar,* Act v. Sc. 1.

---

* i. e. Because.　　† See above, p. 129.
‡ See above, p. 20.　　§ See above, p. 129.
‖ i.e. to anticipate the full, appointed time. See above, Pt. I. ch. ii.
p. 10.　　¶ i. e. stay for, wait upon.

SECT. 14. *Of Holy Scripture, the Christian Ministry, and Church Membership.*

For Shakspeare's own estimation of Holy Scripture, we have no occasion to look beyond the evidence contained in every page of the present volume. To him, I doubt not, it was—what it is to every faithful reader—' the Word of God unto Salvation.' His habitual regard for its authority may be traced in language such as that which he has put into the mouth of Iago :—

> Trifles light as air
> Are to the jealous confirmations strong
> As *proofs of Holy Writ.*   *Othello,* Act iii. Sc. 3.

At the same time, the age in which he lived would not suffer him to be ignorant how liable men are, from various causes, to pervert God's Word, and give to it a meaning which it was never meant to convey.

> In religion,
> What damned error, but some sober brow
> Will bless it, and *approve* * *it with a text*
> Hiding the grossness with fair ornament ?
>   *Merchant of Venice,* Act iii. Sc. 2.

And again, his own study of the Bible had discovered to him how much judgment and caution are required in reconciling and adjusting texts which, though susceptible of perfect harmony, to a hasty

---

* Justify it.

and superficial reader may appear discordant, or even contradictory. When King Richard II. is confined in the dungeon of Pomfret Castle, he amuses himself by comparing his prison to the world, and he imagines his own thoughts to form the population, which is necessary to give verisimilitude to the comparison :—

> And these same thoughts [are, he says,]
> In humours like the people of this world,
> For no thought is contented. The better sort—
> As thoughts of things divine—are intermixed
> With scruples, and do set the THE WORD itself
> Against THE WORD.—
> As thus—*Come, little ones;** and then again—
> *It is as hard to come, as for a camel*
> *To thread the postern of a needle's eye.*†
>
> > K. *Richard II.* Act iv. Sc. 5.

The three last lines are omitted by Mr. Bowdler. Surely they savour of no irreverence; and, when taken with the context, they point not unprofitably to difficulties and dangers which every reader of the Scriptures must expect to encounter, and which every well-disposed and well-instructed reader will be enabled to overcome.

And as no intentional irreverence towards Holy Scripture, often as he quotes or refers to it, is to be found in our poet's works, so neither does he ever allow himself to speak of the ministers of religion, as other play-writers have done, with disrespect,

---

* See Matt. xi. 28. † See Matt. xix. 24.

still less with derision. That he entertained indeed a just sense of the dignity and responsibility of their sacred office, and of the mischiefs that must ensue whenever it is disgraced by insufficiency, or perverted by unfaithfulness ; that he regarded them as ambassadors for Christ, and as intercessors, through Him, in behalf of man, we need no further proof than the speech of Prince John of Lancaster, in the *Second Part of King Henry IV.* He is addressing Scroop, Archbishop of York, who had joined the Earl of Northumberland's party against King Henry, the Prince's father, in the Forest of Gualtree :—

> My Lord of York, it better showed with you,
> When * that your flock, assembled by the bell,
> Encircled you to hear with reverence
> Your exposition on the holy text,
> Than now to see you here an iron man,†
> Cheering a rout of rebels with your drum,
> Turning the word to sword, and life to death.
> That man that sits within a monarch's heart,
> And ripens in the sunshine of his favour,
> Would he abuse the countenance of the king,
> Alack, what mischiefs might he set abroach,
> In shadow of such greatness ! With you, lord bishop,
> It is even so.   Who hath not heard it spoken,
> How deep you were within the BOOKS OF GOD ?
> To us, the speaker in HIS parliament ;
> To us, the imagined voice of GOD HIMSELF ;
> The very opener and intelligencer
> Between the grace, the sanctities of Heaven,

---

* See above, Pt. I. ch. i. p. 22.   † i.e. clad in armour.

And our dull workings.* O! who shall believe,
But you misuse the reverence of your place;
Employ the countenance and grace of Heaven,
As a false favourite doth his prince's name,
In deeds dishonourable? You have taken up,†
Under the counterfeited zeal of God,
The subjects of His substitute, my father;
And both against the peace of Heaven and him,
Have here upswarmed them.   Act iv. Sc. 2.

After reading this speech, it is sad to think that the same Prince John, in the next scene, would seem to father upon God his own treachery towards the rebels, when he says :—

Heaven, and not we, hath safely fought to-day.

So prone are we all to make religion the cloak, or even the minister of sin !

But our poet, however well disposed towards the clergy, does not fail to preach out of his own *pulpit,* that if they would retain the respect to which they are entitled by their office, they must themselves give good heed to the instruction which they deliver to others. Thus, King Henry VI. rebukes his great-uncle, Cardinal Beaufort, Bishop of Winchester :—

Fye, uncle Beaufort! I have heard you preach,
That malice was a great and grievous sin :
And will not you maintain the thing you teach,
But prove a chief offender in the same ?
                    K. Henry VI. 1*st Part,* Act iii. Sc. 1.

Or, as S. Paul expresses it, 'Thou which teachest

---

* i. e. ' Labours of thought.'—Steevens.   † Levied.

another, teachest thou not thyself?' Rom. ii. 21.
Thus too the amiable Ophelia, when she had
listened to the good advice of her brother Laertes,
assures him :—

> I shall the effect of this good lesson * keep,
> As watchman to my heart. But, good my brother,
> Do not, as some ungracious pastors do,
> Show me the steep and thorny way to heaven,
> Whilst, like a puffed and reckless libertine,
> Himself the primrose path of dalliance treads,
> And *recks not his own read.*† *Hamlet*, Act i. Sc. 3.

At the same time, our poet is not unreasonable.
He knew that the duty of the clergy requires them
to *teach*, and that charitable allowance is to be made
for them, if, not in wilfulness or in hypocrisy, but
from the imperfection incident to our common
nature, they fall short, in practice, of their own
lessons :—

> If to do were as easy as to know what to do, chapels had been
> churches, and poor men's cottages princes' palaces. *It is a good
> divine that follows his own instructions.* I can easier teach twenty
> what were good to be done than be one of the twenty to follow
> mine own teaching. *Merchant of Venice*, Act i. Sc. 2.

An observation which must find an echo in every
clergyman's breast.

---

* It was a saying of the pious Bp. Wilson, that the only true
proof of a good sermon is *its making people better.* Shakspeare has
anticipated the remark, in substance, when he writes, in the *Merchant
of Venice* :—

> ' *Portia.* Good sentences, and well pronounced!
> *Nerissa.* They would be better, *if well followed.*'
> Act i. Sc. 2.

† ' Heeds not his own lessons.'—Pope. Read=counsel.

There can be no reasonable doubt that Shakspeare was a member of the Reformed Church of England ; in other words, that he was a true Catholic Christian ; and as such, a Protestant against the errors and corruptions of the Church of Rome. Yet, strange to say, the attempt has been made to represent him as a Romanist ! So at least it would seem from the ' Copy of Shakspeare's Will ' which used to be exhibited not many years ago—and perhaps* still is—in the room at Stratford-upon-Avon, where the so-called ' Shakspeare's relics ' are preserved and shown to visitors. That this ' copy ' is a forgery has been proved by comparing it with the real will, which is deposited in Doctors' Commons, from which the document commonly prefixed to editions of our poet's works, and truly called ' Shakspeare's Will,' is taken. The supposititious document has a preamble much longer than the genuine one ; from which also it differs widely both in tone and expression — the differences being mostly such as to leave no doubt that the forger's design was to claim our poet for the Romish Church !† That such a claim is utterly groundless might be proved abundantly from the internal evidence of his works. Not to lay stress upon the expression ' Popish tricks‡ and ceremonies ' in *Titus*

---

* But see *Supplementary Note* at end of the volume.

† See Preface to *Religious and Moral Sentences from Shakspeare*, by a member of the Shakspeare Society, 1843.

‡ Mr. Bowdler has altered this into ' *idle* tricks.'

Andronicus, Act v. Sc. 1 (because that play, as I have said before, is most probably not Shakspeare's), it is sufficient to refer to the character of Cardinal Beaufort in the *First Part of King Henry VI.,* and to the manner in which the pretended supremacy of the Pope is not only repudiated in *King John,* but, moreover, is shown, in *King Henry VIII.,* to be destructive of the just authority of the episcopate. I allude to the passage in which the Earl of Surrey begins his charge against Wolsey :—

> First, that, without the king's assent or knowledge,
> You wrought to be a legate, by which power
> You maimed the jurisdiction of all bishops.
>
> Act iii. Sc. 2.

It is remarked by A. W. Schlegel, in his admirable *Lectures on Dramatic Literature,* that Shakspeare, amidst the rancour of religious parties, takes a delight in painting the condition of a monk, and always represents his influence as beneficial.* With regard to the monk in *Romeo and Juliet,* I quite agree that ' the discourse of the pious old man is full of deep meaning.'† But what are we to think of the duke disguised as a monk, in *Measure for Measure,* and who, according to Schlegel, carries out the disguise so perfectly, that, ' contrary to the well-known proverb, the cowl (in his case) seems really to make a monk ? ' Ministering to Claudio in prison, and encouraging him against the fear of death, he is made to say :—

---

* Vol. ii. p. 169.   † *Ibid.* p. 188.   See above, p. 108.

> Thy best of rest is sleep,
> And that thou oft provok'st, yet grossly fear'st
> Thy death,* *which is no more*— Act iii. Sc. 1.

A sentiment which calls forth the 'indignation' of Johnson, and which our poet's most indulgent critics have been somewhat puzzled to account for. But what if he intended to represent the monk as in reality an unbeliever? There can be no doubt that Popery, from the excess and exorbitancy of its demands upon the faith of its adherents, has a tendency to produce reaction which has often led to open, and still more to secret infidelity,† especially in the monastic orders,‡ and in the priesthood. The same sentiment occurs to Hamlet in his famous soliloquy :—

> To die—to sleep—
> *No more,*—

But then he presently corrects the thought :—

> To die—to sleep—
> To sleep! perchance to dream ; ay, there's the rub ;
> For in that sleep of death what dreams may come,
> When we have shuffled off this mortal coil,§
> Must give us pause.‖ Act iii. Sc. 1.

Returning to the Church-membership of our poet, if we are persuaded he was not a Romanist, we are

---

* Compare Lucretius, lib. iii. 1058, *sq.* and 990.

† See *Supplementary Note* at end of the volume.

‡ The Jesuits are nowhere mentioned by name in Shakspeare ; but there is a passage in *Macbeth*, Act ii. Sc. 2, in which Warburton supposes them to be meant, and in which (if so) they are satirised as ' the inventors of the execrable doctrine of equivocation.'

§ Turmoil, bustle.

‖ Make us hesitate, and think of what may come after death.

equally certain he was no Puritan. 'Young Char-
bon *the Puritan*, and old Poysam *the Papist*,' are
named together in a passage of *All's well that
ends well*, Act i. Sc. 3, not illnaturedly, but as if
the writer had no more sympathy with the one
than with the other. Probably, if the truth were
known, of the two he had less liking for the new-
fangled species of religionism which had sprung up
within his own time. We must not lay any great
stress upon what passes in conversation between two
such worthies as Sir Andrew Ague-Cheek and Sir
Toby Belch; yet the following dialogue indicates,
no doubt, a certain amount of popular feeling ; and
I think we may gather from it that our poet desired
to side with those who could feel respect for piety
and earnestness *in any shape*, rather than with the
ignorant multitude who, without knowing why,
would be prepared to persecute * it :—

Sir Toby. Possess † us, possess us ; tell us something of him.
Maria. Marry, sir, sometimes he is a kind of Puritan.
Sir Andr. O, if I thought that, I'd beat him like a dog.
Sir Toby. What, for being a Puritan ? thy exquisite reason, dear
knight.
Sir Andr. I have no exquisite reason for't, but I have reason
good enough. *Twelfth Night*, Act ii. Sc. 3.

At the same time he does not attempt to withhold
from view, what he must have discovered from his
own experience, that religious zeal, such as was

---

* Our poet's just dislike of *all* religious persecution may be inferred from *Winter's Tale*, Act. ii. Sc. 3, ' It is an heretic,' &c.
† Inform us.

Q

manifested by the Puritans, is often hollow, and often both mistaken in its principles and mischievous in its results. We may not be able to determine the precise drift, or even the true reading —for Tyrwhitt and Malone concur in questioning the present text—of a speech of the Clown in *All's well that ends well*; but we cannot doubt, I think, that it implies distrust, to some extent at least, of the Puritanical character :—

> Though honesty be no Puritan, yet it will do no hurt; it will wear the *surplice of humility* over the *black gown of a big heart.*
> Act i. Sc. 3.

That is, as I suppose, an honest man will not be troubled with unnecessary scruples, especially in a case where his obedience is required to a lawful command, however the command may be distasteful to himself. He will put on the surplice—to which the Puritans objected. But still when he has done so, though so far not a Puritan, this is no security that he may not be all the while, ' intus et in cute,' as bad as if he were—having as proud a heart as if he wore a black gown. Shakspeare generally uses the word ' big,' where moral qualities are concerned, in a bad sense. This is in character with the petulance of the Clown ; but here again I could suspect that our poet wished to intimate that though he had no liking for the Puritans, yet he would not suffer others who might be as bad or worse to run them down. In this, as in other countless instances,

he shows himself the *thorough Englishman*; who,
though he has his likes and dislikes, and will not
conceal them, yet, above them all, *loves to see fair
play*. We have another Clown in *Winter's Tale*,.
who cannot quite let the Puritans alone, and yet
alludes to them in a good-humoured way. Mr.
Bowdler, however, in *his* love of fair play, having
altered ' Popish tricks,' thought it necessary to *omit*
the words to which I allude. They occur in Act iv.
Sc. 2, where the Clown,. son of the old shepherd,.
reputed father of Perdita, gives account of the
preparations made by his supposed sister for the:
sheep-shearing feast :—

> She hath made * me four-and-twenty nosegays for the shearers :.
> three-man † song-men all, and very good ones . . . but one
> Puritan amongst them, and he *sings psalms to hornpipes*.
> Act iv. Sc. 2.

The utmost offence which appears to be com--
mitted in these words is, that the Clown playfully·
satirizes the objectional practice which the Puritans·
introduced, which is still, unhappily, kept up in
some places, of singing sacred songs to *jiggish·
tunes*.‡ There are other passages of a more serious·
caste in which Shakspeare, without mentioning the·
Puritans, may be thought to have them in his view.
Such is the case,. for instance, as Warburton has

---

* See above, Pt. I. Ch. i. p.15.

† i. e. Singers of catches in three parts.

‡ Compare *Merry Wives of Windsor*, Act ii. Sc. 1. There is
also a reference to the Puritans in *Pericles, Prince of Tyre*, Act iv.
Sc. 6.

Q 2

remarked, in *Timon of Athens*, where Timon's servant, speaking of Sempronius, one of his master's
false friends, observes :—

How fairly this lord strives to appear foul ! takes virtuous copies
to be wicked : *like those that under hot ardent zeal would set
whole realms on fire !*   Act iii. Sc. 3.

A remarkable prediction of what actually came to
pass less than thirty years after our poet's death !
And it is not improbable that they are alluded to
in what follows from the mouth of Polonius :—

> We are oft to blame in this,—
> *'Tis too much proved*, that with devotion's visage
> And pious action, we do sugar o'er
> The devil himself.   *Hamlet*, Act iii. Sc. 1.

We may now inquire what positive evidence is
to be produced respecting Shakspeare's conformity
as a member of the Church of England. The
familiar use of the response *Amen* (the τὸ 'Αμὴν of
S. Paul, Cor. xiv. 16), which occurs in our author's
plays *more than sixty times*, may alone be regarded
as a sufficient indication to that effect. There is
something singularly solemn and impressive in
his employment of it towards the close of *King
Henry V.* :—

> That English may as French, French Englishmen,
> Receive* each other—GOD speak to this AMEN.

And again, at the end of *King Richard III.* :—

> That peace may long live here—GOD say AMEN.

---

* See Rom. xv. 7.

From our poet's allusion to the observance of Sunday not much is to be inferred—except that it would seem, in his time, to have been the most usual day for the celebration of marriages. In *Taming of the Shrew*, Petruchio, in answer to Baptista's question *how he had sped* with his daughter Katharina, replies :—

> We have 'greed so well together,
> That upon *Sunday* is the wedding day.   Act ii. Sc. 1.

Whether this remark may help to throw any light upon a passage in *Much ado about nothing*, over the meaning of which critics have disagreed, I will not undertake to say ; but it may be worth considering.   Benedict says to Claudio :—

> Shall I never see a bachelor of threescore again ?   Go to, i'
> faith : an thou wilt needs thrust thy neck into a yoke, wear the
> print of it, and *sigh away Sundays*.   Act i. Sc. 1.

i. e. sigh away the days which, if married on Sunday, will serve to remind you most of all of the mistake you made.   Neither Warburton's explanation that even Sundays, the days formerly (he says) of most ease and diversion, will be passed uncomfortably ; nor Steevens', that there is probably an allusion to the strict manner in which the Sabbath was observed by the Puritans, appears satisfactory.   It would be simpler to suggest that Sunday is the day of the week which is generally spent *most domestically*.   It is hardly to be supposed, that at the court of Cleopatra the difference was understood between Sundays

and working days, unless it could be supposed
that the notion had come down by tradition from
the captivity of the Israelites in Egypt ; and then
it would go far to settle an important question in
theology !—but our poet has not scrupled to speak,
in *Antony and Cleopatra*, of ' a worky-day fortune ;'
meaning a fortune not rich and splendid, but ordinary and common place, see Act i. Sc. 2 ; just as,
with a propriety which admits of no question, he
makes Marcellus to ask Horatio, in *Hamlet* :—

> Why such impress of shipwrights, whose *sore task*
> *Does not divide the Sunday from the week ?*
>> Act i. Sc. 1.

In the same play we have a reference to the
season of Christmas, and to the traditions, that at
that season, the cock—

> The bird of dawning singeth all night long :
> And then, they say, no spirit dares stir abroad ;
> The nights are wholesome ; then no planets strike, .
> No fairy * takes, nor witch hath power to charm :
> So hallowed and so gracious is the time !

This passage, so beautiful in its simplicity, could
only have been written by one who had the sense
and feeling of a true Christian and loyal member
of the Church in regard to the nativity of our
Blessed Lord. Of the two other great festivals I
am not aware that our poet makes mention, except
to let us know, in *Romeo and Juliet*, Act iii. Sc. 5,

---

* i. e. Strikes with lameness or diseases.

that 'new doublets' were worn at Easter; and, in
King Henry V. Act ii. Sc. 4, that Whitsuntide—
called, in *Two Gentlemen of Verona*, Act iv. Sc. 4,
Pentecost—was the season for 'morris dances,' and
'pageants of delight.'

It remains to notice here, that Shakspeare appears
to have received and held, without misgiving, the
doctrine of Baptismal Grace, which he would have
been taught as an orthodox member of the Anglican
Church. 'We will believe,' says King Henry V.
to the Archbishop of Canterbury and Bishop of
Ely—

> That what you speak is in your conscience washed
> *As pure as sin with baptism.*
> > *K. Henry V.* Act i. Sc. 2..

And, in *Othello*, the villainous Iago is made to
represent Desdemona's influence to be such, that it
would be easy for her, if she wished—

> To win the Moor—wer't to renounce *his baptism*—
> *All seals and symbols of redeemed sin.* Act ii. Sc. 3.

The judicious reader will be surprised—and not,
I think, well pleased—to learn that Mr. Bowdler,
in his 'Family Shakspeare,' has seen reason to omit
the latter of these two lines.

And passing from the first scene of the Christian
life to the last, from baptism to burial, we find, in
Cymbeline, the *rationale* of interment with the head
towards the east alluded to, and also the beautiful
custom of strewing the grave with flowers, described

in language no less beautiful.   The two brothers, Guiderius and Arviragus (Cadwal) are engaged in burying Fidele :—

> *Guid.* Nay, Cadwal, we must lay his head to the east:
> My father hath a reason for't.   Act iv. Sc. 2.

The 'reason' could not properly have been, in the mouth of a Pagan—the Christian one—and therefore no further explanation is given :—

> *Arvig.*   With fairest flowers,
> Whilst summer lasts, and I live here, Fidele,
> I'll sweeten thy sad grave.   Thou shalt not lack
> The flower that's like thy face, pale primrose; nor
> The azured hare-bell, like thy veins; no, nor
> The leaf of eglantine, *whom* * not to slander,
> Out-sweeten'd not thy breath : the ruddock † would,
> With charitable bill, bring thee all this;
> Yea, and furr'd moss besides, when flowers are none,
> To winter-ground thy corse.   .   .   .
>   [*Re-enter Belarius.*
> *Bel.* Here's a few flowers; but about midnight, more :
> The herbs that have on them cold dew o' the night
> Are strewings fitt'st for graves.

SECT. 15.   *Of Politics—Peace and War.*

We cannot conceive of Shakspeare otherwise than as a Conservative and a Royalist—if the anachronism involved in the use of both names may be pardoned.   We may safely attribute to him a deep reverence for antiquity ; and we need not doubt

---

* See above, p. 19.   † Redbreast.

that the precept of Solomon, 'My son, fear thou the Lord and the King, and meddle not with them that are given to change,' Prov. xxiv. 21, approved itself thoroughly to his large heart and marvellous understanding. How just is the sentiment which ascribes to 'reverence' (or due regard for subordination) *the power that keeps peace and order in the world*, to borrow the gloss of Johnson upon the words that follow :—

> Tho' mean and mighty, rotting
> Together, have one dust ; yet reverence
> (That ANGEL of the world) doth make distinction
> Of place 'tween high and low.
>
> *Cymbeline*, Act iv. Sc. 2.

And where shall we find a more effective protest against the spirit of innovation and continual change, or the value of antiquity and custom more truly estimated and described, than in what follows; where a rash political movement is objected to—

> As tho' the world were now but to begin,
> *Antiquity* forgot, *custom* not known,
> *The ratifiers and props of every word.*

The critics have been somewhat puzzled by 'word,' as here used, and have proposed to alter it ; Warburton suggesting 'ward,' Johnson 'weal,' and Tyrwhitt 'work.' Had any one of them read the Bible as attentively, and known it as well as Shakspeare did, I imagine he would have recognized the expression as borrowed, probably, from Scripture, where 'word' occurs not unfrequently as put for 'thing.' The Greek ῥῆμα, properly *word*, and so translated in Matt. xviii. 16—'that in the mouth of two or three witnesses *every word* may be *established*'—is translated 'thing' in Luke i. 37, 'With God *nothing* shall be impossible;' in the Prayer Book, *Office for Visitation of the Sick*, however, the old and more exact translation is retained, 'We know, O Lord, that there is *no word* impossible with Thee.' The truth is, that *word* and *work*, or *deed*, though very different, as we know, in the case of man, are *synonymous with regard to God*, and therefore synonymously used in the Book of God.

Our poet's moral estimate of a mere worldly politician, without faith in God, as the governor of the world, may be gathered from an observation of Hamlet, in the grave-digger's scene, where, when one of the clowns had thrown up a skull, he says—

This might be the pate of a politician, which this ass now over-reaches, one that *would circumvent God*, might it not?

Act v. Sc. 1.

Surely not too bold a supposition, when we consider how statesmen have been known to act in defiance of God's laws.

I have already had occasion, much oftener than I could have wished, to invite my reader's attention to the manner in which omissions and even alterations of our poet's words have been made, in 'The Family Shakspeare.' But what will be thought of the strange obtuseness (for I can call it nothing

less) which has changed the name of ‘ God ’ into
the word ‘ anybody ’ in the foregoing quotation—
a change by which the *ne plus ultra* of bathos is
fathered upon Shakspeare, and the grand meaning
of the speaker that, however man may scheme and
plot for the government of states, God Himself is
the only true politician in the universe, is entirely
lost !

No one who has not been present at a coronation, or who has not read *the authorised Coronation
Service*, can have a just idea of the punctilious
accuracy with which Shakspeare has described what
took place at the crowning of Queen Anne Bullen,
and was repeated, only with such additions as would
be proper for a queen-regnant, on the crowning of
our present most gracious sovereign Queen Victoria. I have before me a printed copy of *the
Form and Order of the Service performed, and Ceremonies observed* on this latter occasion ; and when I
have presented to the reader Shakspeare’s description, as we find it in *King Henry VIII.*, I will make
some extracts from the said formulary, which may
serve to illustrate what our poet has written ; none
of his critics, so far as I am aware, having said a
word upon the matter, which is surely a most interesting one to every British subject. The place
is Westminster Abbey :—

> At length her Grace rose, and with modest paces
> Came to the altar : where she kneel’d, and saint-like,

Cast her fair eyes to heaven, and prayed devoutly.
Then rose again, and bowed her to the people;
When by the Archbishop of Canterbury
She had *all the royal makings of a queen,*
As *holy oil, Edward Confessor's crown,*
The rod, and bird of peace, and *all such emblems,*
Laid nobly on her : which performed, the choir,
With all the choicest music of the kingdom,
Together sung *Te Deum.*   Act iv. Sc. 1.

The authorised *Coronation Service* is divided into nineteen sections. A Rubric in the first section will partly explain the first three lines of the fore-going description:—

The queen . . . having passed by her throne, makes her humble adoration, and then kneeling at the faldstool set for her before her chair, uses some short private prayers.

The eighth section is entitled 'THE ANOINTING,' which follows immediately after the Queen has kissed 'the Holy Gospel in the great Bible,' and signed the Coronation 'Oath.' It is commenced with the hymn *Veni Creator.* Then follows a prayer by the Archbishop for the consecration of the oil, and for the blessing and sanctification of her who is to be anointed therewith. The unction is performed on *the crown of the head,* and on *the palms of both the hands.* It was made also *on the breast,* previously to the two last female corona-tions of Queen Adelaide and Queen Victoria. The putting on of 'Edward Confessor's CROWN' does not come till the twelfth section, and meanwhile— besides 'THE ROD' (not to be confounded with the sceptre) 'and BIRD OF PEACE,' i. e. the Dove, which is delivered into the Queen's left hand, with these words, by the Archbishop :—

Receive the rod of equity and mercy ; and God, from whom all holy desires, all good counsels, and all just works do proceed, direct and assist you in the administration and exercise of all those powers which He hath given you :—

besides these — the other 'emblems laid nobly on her' are 'THE SPURS AND SWORD,' in Sect. ix. ; 'THE ROYAL ROBE, AND ORB' with the cross above it, to signify 'that the whole *world* is *subject* to the power and empire of Christ our Redeemer,' in Sect. x. ; 'THE RING, the ensign of kingly dignity, and of defence of the Catholic Faith;' and 'THE ROYAL SCEPTRE, the ensign of kingly power and justice,' in Sect. xi. After the crowning, comes first 'THE PRESENTING* OF THE HOLY BIBLE,' in Sect. xiii. ; and then the 'TE DEUM,' in Sect. xiv; followed by 'THE INTHRONIZATION.' It is scarcely necessary to add that the service is concluded with the celebration of the Holy Eucharist, for which the Queen 'offers' the bread and wine.

It will have been noticed in the preceding extracts that the Coronation 'Ring' is described as 'the ensign of kingly dignity, &c. ;' and before I pass on to other matters I am tempted to observe,

* This was omitted at the coronation of James II.! See Macaulay's *History*, vol. ii. p. 49.

in reference to that description, that the Rubric requires the Ring to be one 'in which a *table-jewel* is enchased,' meaning, I suppose, a flat jewel capable of serving as a seal.* In that same play of *King Henry VIII.* we have the King's ring given to Cranmer, Act v. Sc. 1, and presented by him, Sc. 2, as a security against the machinations of Gardiner and others of the Council who were plotting to destroy him. It was anciently the custom, as Mr. Reed remarks, for every monarch to have a ring, the temporary possession of which invested the holder with the same authority as the owner himself could exercise; and not for every monarch only. In *King Richard II.*, the Duke of York gives this order to his servant :—

> Sirrah, get thee to Plashy, to my sister Gloster ;—
> Bid her send me presently a thousand pound :
> Hold, *take my ring*. Act ii. Sc. 2.

There is a curious relic of the same custom still kept up in the ancient College of William of Wykeham at Winchester. When the captain of the school petitions the head master for a holiday— and obtains it—he receives from him a ring, in token of the indulgence granted, which he wears during the holiday, and returns to the head master when it is over. The inscription upon the ring

---

* Such rings, I imagine, were always signet rings; and the wearing of them is a custom of great antiquity. Compare Gen. xxxviii. 18 ; Jerem. xxii. 24 ; Daniel vi. 17 ; Hagg. ii. 23.

was formerly 'Potentiam fero, geroque.' It is now 'Commendat rarior* usus.'

Imbued as the mind of our poet was with Scriptural principles, we shall not be surprised to find that he places upon the very highest ground both the prerogative and the responsibility of kings and governors. If, on the one hand, he would warn us that—

> Divinity doth hedge a king;   *Hamlet,* Act iv. Sc. 5.

that

> Kings are earth's gods ;   *Pericles,* Act i. Sc. 1.

and 'deputies,' though 'unworthy,' of God himself, *King Henry VI.* Act. iii. Sc. 2 ; that 'The King's name is a tower of strength,' *King Richard III.* Act. v. Sc. 3, even as 'the name of the Lord is a strong tower,' Prov. xviii. 10 :—On the other hand, he does not fail to teach that—

> He who the sword of Heaven will bear,
> Should be as holy as severe ;
> *Measure for Measure,* Act iii. Sc. 2.

where we are reminded of S. Paul, Rom. xiii. 4.

---

* From Juvenal, Sat. xi. 208.
> 'Voluptates commendat rarior usus :'
which our poet thus renders, very appropriately—
> ' If *all the year were playing holidays,*
> To sport would be as tedious as to work ;
> But *when they seldom come, they wished for come.*'
> *K. Henry IV.* 1st Part, Act i. Sc. 2.
See also the quotation from his 52nd sonnet above, Pt. I. ch. i. p. 22, ' the fine point of *seldom pleasure.*'

In like manner, if on the one hand he teaches that there can be no security for usurped and illegitimate authority :—

> For though usurpers sway the rule awhile,
> Yet Heavens are just, and time suppresseth wrongs :—
> *King Henry VI. 3rd Part*, Act iii. Sc. 3.

on the other hand, he warns us that the loyalty and obedience which are due to lawful governors must be duly paid; for

> Every subject's duty is the King's.
> *King Henry V.* Act vi. Sc. 1.

That it is an unhappy thing for a country when its king is under age is a thought which might occur to many minds ; but that the thought should be expressed in words so precisely parallel as those which I am about to quote could not have happened without actual contact of the mind of the one writer with the mind of the other :—

> Woe to thee, O land, when thy king is a child.
> Ecclesiastes, x. 16.

> Woe to that land that's governed by a child.
> *K. Richard III.* Act. ii. Sc. 3.

Among the countless marvels of Shakspeare's mind, it is not the least remarkable that he appears equally at home in regard to matters that must have been alien from his own experience and to those that came within it. For instance, whether he has to speak of the circumstances of peace or war, his sentiments and descriptions are equally just

and valuable; although of the latter he could
have known nothing from personal observation.
It would be beyond my purpose to enter into this
subject; and I shall content myself by à general
reference to *King Henry V.* and *King Richard III.*
But there are two points connected with it which
belong fairly to the design I have had in view, and
upon which, therefore, I shall venture to add a few
words. One is, that *war is a punishment sent by
God.* So the Bible teaches, see Ezek. v. and xiv.
21. And so Shakspeare teaches, see *King Henry V.*
Act iv. Sc. 1.

> War is His (God's) beadle; * war is His vengeance.

And again, see *King Henry VI. 2nd Part,* Act v.
Sc. 2 :—

> O! war, thou son of hell,
> Whom *angry Heavens do make their minister,*
> Throw in the frozen bosom of our part
> *Hot coals* of vengeance!

where Mr. Steevens has remarked that the last
phrase is scriptural, and he quotes Psalm cxl. 10
in the Prayer Book version :—

> Let hot burning coals fall upon them !

The other point is *the lawfulness of war.* This,
too, the Bible teaches ; see Eccles. iii. 8, Luke iii.
14, Acts x. And so Shakspeare teaches—with the
just and necessary provision—' if the cause be
good.' See *King Henry V.* Act. iv. Sc. 1. In

---

* This clause is omitted by Mr. Bowdler.

R

further proof of this point, the reader may consult a sermon* preached by Bishop Andrewes before Queen Elizabeth, at Richmond, in 1609, ' at what time the Earl of Essex was going forth upon the expedition for Ireland,' to quell the insurrection excited by the Earl of Tyrone—a sermon, therefore, which our poet might have heard; although, as I have said, we have no reason to suppose that he took part in that or any other warlike expedition.

SECT. 16.   *Of Death, the Intermediate State, and Day of Judgment.*

In the famous soliloquy of Hamlet, ' To be, or not to be,' when he comes to speak of

> The undiscovered country *from whose bourn*
> *No traveller returns,*   Act iii. Sc. 1.

Mr. Douce suspects, not without reason, that Job x. 21, was present to our poet's mind :—

> I go *whence I shall not return,* even to the land of darkness and the shadow of death.

And here let me introduce an observation which has occurred, I doubt not, to the minds of many of my readers in the course of this and the preceding chapter.

There can be little doubt that our forefathers, in

---

* Bp. Andrewes' Works, vol. i. pp. 321–337.

and before Shakspeare's time, and even Shakspeare himself, derived, not altogether unprofitably, some portion of their knowledge of Holy Scripture from the exhibitions of religious plays, called miracles, or mysteries; and consequently that much which would strike us now-a-days as irreverent, or at best of questionable propriety, when spoken upon the stage, did not appear to them in the same light. I imagine that when Justice Shallow observed to Silence, his brother justice,

> Death, *as the Psalmist saith*, is certain to all; all shall die ;—
> *King Henry IV. 2nd Part,* Act iii. Sc. 2.

neither the author nor the actor would be conscious of any irreverence in thus introducing the Psalmist's name; but times are changed, and Mr. Bowdler, by omitting the clause printed in italics, gives us to understand that now it ' cannot with propriety be read' even ' in a family ! '

Together with the certainty of death, the Psalmist also teaches us that the rich man ' shall carry nothing away with him when he dieth, neither shall his pomp follow him ; ' xlix. 17. And the apostle, that ' As we brought nothing into this world, so it is certain we can carry nothing out ; ' 1 Tim. vi. 7. Their words require no confirmation ; and yet the great Earl of Warwick is well chosen to speak as follows when he comes to die :—

> Lo, now my glory smeared in dust and blood !
> My parks, my walks, my manors that I had,

> Even now forsake me, and of all my lands
> Is nothing left me * but my body's length!
> Why what is *pomp*, rule, reign, but earth and dust?
> And live we how we can, yet *die we must.*
> > *K. Henry VI. 3rd Part,* Act v. Sc. 2.

The Lord Talbot, speaking of the death of ' the noble Duke of Bedford,' tells us the same truism, with the addition of a melancholy sentiment, to which most of us, sooner or later, will be inclined to respond :—

> Kings and mightiest potentates must die,
> For that's the end of human misery.

We find both the truism and sentiment (which our poet is fond of introducing where he has occasion to mention death) repeated at greater length in the Dirge over Fidele, sung by Guiderius and Arviragus :—

> *Gui.* Fear no more the heat † o' the sun,
> > Nor the furious winter's rages ;
> Thou thy worldly task hast done,
> > *Home art gone,* and ta'en thy wages :
> Golden lads and girls all must,
> As chimney-sweepers, come to dust.
> *Arv.* Fear no more the frown o' the great,
> > Thou art past the tyrant's stroke ;
> Care no more to clothe, and eat ;
> > To thee the reed is as the oak :
> The sceptre, learning, physic, must
> All follow this, and come to dust.
> > *Cymbeline,* Act iv. Sc. 2.

But these were heathens. In the case of Chris-

---

* A frequent sentiment in the Greek tragedians.
† See Revel. vii. 16.

tians, our poet fails not to introduce a touch of holier consolation :—

> *Ch. Just.* How doth the king?
> *War. Exceeding well*; his cares are now all ended.
> *Ch. Just.* I hope not dead?
> *War.*   He's walk'd the way of nature;
> And, *to our purposes*, he lives no more.
> *King Henry IV. 2nd Part*, Act v. Sc. 2.

As much as to say, *not* however to *his own purposes*, now that his true and immortal life has begun. So, too, in *Winter's Tale*, Dion says, with reference to the supposed death of Hermione, wife of King Leontes :—

> What were more holy
> Than to rejoice, the former queen *is well*?   Act v. Sc. 1.

This happy notion and expression of our poet that it is ' well'—' exceeding well'—with the departed, was perhaps * derived from the reply which the good Shunamite gave to the Prophet Elisha, when he asked her,—

> Is it well with the child? And she answered, *it is well*—
> 2 Kings, iv. 26.

though the child was dead.

But, in order that it may be really ' well ' with us when we come to die, Shakspeare will also tell us—no man better—what is the one thing needful. And with what a lightning flash of condensed thought and language does he teach the lesson !—

---

* Since the above was written, I find that Mr. Henley has made the same conjecture. The phrase in question, as applicable to the dead, occurs also in *Antony and Cleopatra*, ii. 5; and twice in *Romeo and Juliet*, iv. 4, and v. 1.

> Men must endure
> Their going hence, even as their coming hither : .
> *Ripeness is all* : come on.   *King Lear*, Act v. Sc. 2.

'Ripeness,' i. e. to be prepared to die, at the appointed time. As Hamlet expresses the same idea:—

> If it (death) be not now, yet it will come : *the readiness is all.*
> Act v. Sc. 2.

And what minister of the gospel ever discoursed
more justly of the value of such preparation than
does, in Shakspeare's words, King Henry V., when,
passing through the camp in disguise, before the
battle of Agincourt, he holds discourse with Wil-
liams, one of the common soldiers of his army ?—

> Every soldier in the wars should do as every sick man in his
> bed—*wash every mote out of his conscience* ; and dying so, death
> is to him * advantage : or not dying, the time was blessedly lost
> wherein such preparation was gained.   And in him that escapes,
> it were not sin to think, that making God so free an offer, He
> let him outlive that day to see His greatness, and *to teach others
> how* they should prepare.   Act iv. Sc. 1.

And now—if we wish to see the end of worldly
ambition in a death-bed scene, what sermon is to
be compared to the representation which our poet
gives of the death of Cardinal Beaufort, in the *Second
Part of King Henry VI.* ; its effect being heightened
by the charity of the king in declining to judge,
and in proposing to turn it to the edification of the
survivors !   I give the scene entire—for, as with
the Scripture itself (if the comparison may be made

---

* To die is gain.—Phil. i. 2.

without irreverence), it would be wrong to take anything from it, or to add anything to it. Johnson has truly observed, the beauties of it are such that the superficial reader cannot miss them, and the profound can imagine nothing beyond them.

SCENE.—*Cardinal Beaufort's bedchamber.*
Enter K. HENRY, SALISBURY, WARWICK, &c. *The Cardinal in bed.*

K. Hen. How fares my lord? speak, Beaufort, to thy sovereign.
Car. If thou be'st Death, I'll give thee England's treasure,
Enough to purchase such another island,
So thou wilt let me live, and feel no pain.
K. Hen. Ah, what a sign it is of evil life,
Where death's approach is seen so terrible!
War. Beaufort, it is thy sovereign speaks to thee.
Car. Bring me unto my trial when you will.
Died he * not in his bed? where should he die?
Can I make men live, whe'r they will or no?—
O! torture me no more, I will confess.—
Alive again? then show me where he is;
I'll give a thousand pound to look upon him.—
He hath no eyes, the dust hath blinded them.—
Comb down his hair; look! look! it stands upright,
Like lime-twigs set to catch my winged soul!
Give me some drink; and bid the apothecary
Bring the strong poison that I bought of him.
K. Hen. O thou eternal Mover of the heavens,
Look with a gentle eye upon this wretch!
O, beat away the busy meddling fiend,
That lays strong siege unto this wretch's soul,
And from his bosom purge this black despair!
War. See, how the pangs of death do make him grin.
Sal. Disturb him not, let him pass peaceably.

---

* Humphrey, Duke of Gloster, murdered by Beaufort's order.

K. Hen. Peace to his soul, if God's good pleasure be!
Lord cardinal, if thou think'st on heaven's bliss,
Hold up thy hand, make signal of thy hope.
He dies, and makes no sign ; O God, forgive him !
War. So bad a death argues a monstrous life.
K. Hen. Forbear to judge, for we are sinners all.
Close up his eyes, and draw the curtain close ;
And let us all to meditation.

K. Henry VI. 2nd Part, Act iii. Sc. 3.

With this harrowing picture it will be some relief
to compare the death-bed of another Cardinal, also
the victim of inordinate ambition,* but partly, too,
of the fickleness of royal favour—I mean Cardinal
Wolsey :—

Kath. Pr'ythee, good Griffith, tell me how he died :
If well, he stepp'd before me, happily,
For my example.
Grif.　　　　　Well, the voice goes, madam :
For after the stout earl Northumberland
Arrested him at York, and brought him forward
(As a man sorely tainted) to his answer,
He fell sick suddenly, and grew so ill,
He could not sit his mule.
Kath.　　　　　Alas! poor man!
Grif. At last, with easy † roads, he came to Leicester,
Lodg'd in the abbey ; where the reverend abbot,
With all his convent, honourably receiv'd him ;
To whom he gave these words,—*O, father abbot,*
An old man, broken with the storms of state,
Is come to lay his weary bones among ye ;
Give him a little earth for charity !
So went to bed : where eagerly his sickness
Pursued him still ; and, three nights after this,

---

* The death-bed scene of a sensualist, as exhibited in the case of
Falstaff, has been alluded to above.　See p. 195.　† i. e. stages.

About the hour of eight (which he himself
Foretold should be his last), full of repentance,
Continual meditations, tears, and sorrows,
He gave his honours to the world again,
His blessed part to heaven, and slept in peace.
    Kath. So may he rest; his faults lie gently on him !

Griffith afterwards adds :—

His overthrow heap'd happiness upon him ;
For then, and not till then, he felt himself,
And found the blessedness of being little :
And, to add greater honours to his age
Than man could give him, *he died fearing God.*
               King Henry VIII. Act iv. Sc. 2.

The place to which the spirits of good men are
admitted immediately upon their dissolution is twice
mentioned by our poet under the figure* by which
we find it represented in the New Testament ; see
Luke xvi. 23.

Boling. Why, bishop, is Norfolk dead?
Carlisle. As sure as I live, my lord.
Boling. Sweet peace conduct his sweet soul *to the bosom
Of good old Abraham* !   *K. Richard II.* Act iv. Sc. 1.

K. Rich. The sons of Edward sleep in *Abraham's bosom.*
               K. Richard III. Act iv. Sc. 4.

On the other hand, the torment of bad men after
death, as represented in the case of the rich man in
the same parable, is twice alluded to in *King Henry
IV.* (viz. 1*st Part,* Act iii. Sc. 3 ; 2*nd Part,* Act i.
Sc. 2), and on both occasions the allusion is put
into the mouth of Falstaff, who handles it, as might

---

* There is also a reference to our Lord's promise to the penitent
thief (Luke xxiii. 43), in *K. Henry VI.* 2*nd Part,* Act v. Sc. 1.

be expected, with such characteristic levity, that in these instances I cannot complain of Mr. Bowdler for omitting it, as he has done. There is also from the mouth of Falstaff a reference to Lazarus (*1st Part*, Act iv. Sc. 2), which is *partly* dealt with by Mr. Bowdler in the same way. This also may be justified. But there are two other passages of a similar character, and bearing upon the same point, not to be found in 'the Family Shakspeare,' the omission of which is, I think, to be regretted. One is the speech of the Clown in *All's well*, &c., Act iv. Sc. 5 :—

I am for the house *with the narrow gate*, which I take to be too little for pomp to enter ; some that humble themselves may ; but *the many* will be too chill and tender ; and they'll be for the flowery way, that *leads to the broad gate*, and the *great fire*.

The other is spoken by the porter at Macbeth's castle :—

I had thought to have let in some of all professions that go *the primrose way to the everlasting bonfire*.

Macbeth, Act ii. Sc. 3.

Mr. Steevens, in his note upon the former passage, condemns this 'as impious stuff.' For my own part, as I do not doubt it was written with earnestness, and with a wonderful knowledge of human nature— the latter passage, especially, as put into the mouth of a drunken man—so I believe it may be read with edification.

With regard to the condition and circumstances of the departed in the intermediate state, we have no Scriptural authority for *concluding* that they are *not* conscious of what is passing here. Our poet therefore has not exceeded the bounds which the Anglican Church allows to the *pious opinions* of her members, when, at the conclusion of *King Henry VIII.*, he makes the King to say, on the occasion of the christening of his infant daughter—afterwards Queen Elizabeth:—

> When I am in heaven, I shall desire
> To see what this child does, and praise my Maker.
>
> Act v. Sc. 4.

Still less can we object to that which is put into the mouth of the Lady Constance, in *King John*, to the effect that the recognition of those whom we have known and loved in this world will be among the causes of our happiness in the world to come. Addressing Pandulph, the Pope's legate, she says:—

> Father cardinal, I have heard you say
> That we shall see and know our friends in heaven :
> If that be true, I shall see my boy again.   Act iii. Sc. 4.

Strange, indeed, would it be, if we Christians might not entertain the hope which was the earnest expectation, the comfort, and the joy of the great and good among the heathen ! ' Equidem,' says Cato to Scipio and Lælius, in the *De Senectute* of Cicero, ' Equidem efferor studio patres vestros, quos colui et dilexi, videndi,' i. e. after death. And he proceeds in this noble strain : ' O ! præclarum diem, quum ad illum divinum animorum concilium cœtumque proficiscar, quumque ex hac turbâ et colluvione discedam ! ' And then, like Constance, he thinks of seeing again the son whom he had lost. ' Proficiscar enim non ad eos solum viros, de quibus ante dixi, verum etiam *ad Catonem meum* ; ' whom he goes on to praise, as she has praised Arthur. So much is there of the same truth and nature where great minds, no matter how different their respective circumstances, are led to speak upon the same subjects !

But we pass on to still more solemn truths, fully certified to the Christian only, through the Revelation he has received. *We* know that after the intermediate state, and before the final and complete reward of God's true servants, will come the Judgment ; and we also know that that judgment will differ from the trials which take place in this world, in two respects ; 1st. It will be incorruptibly and infallibly just, and 2nd. The accused will be made to give evidence against themselves :—

> In the corrupted currents of this world,
> Offence's gilded hand may shove by justice ;
> But 'tis not so above.
> There is no shuffling : there the action lies
> In *his* * true nature ; and *we ourselves compelled*,
> *Even to the teeth and forehead of our faults,*
> *To give in evidence.*   *Hamlet*, Act iii. Sc. 3.

It is very remarkable that Shakspeare should have seized upon this latter point. He is supported in the view he takes by Bishop Pearson,† than

---

* See above, p. 17.   † Born, 1612 ; died, 1686.

whom the Anglican Church has no higher authority upon theological questions. That learned divine, expounding the seventh article of the Creed, thus writes, in an argument upon conscience :—

It followeth that this conscience is not so much a judge as *a witness,** bound over to give testimony, for or against us, at some judgment after this life to pass upon us.

And he refers to S. Paul, Rom. ii. 14-16.

It was to be expected that the circumstances of the judgment day, as they are revealed to us in Scripture, would make a deep and lasting impression upon a mind like Shakspeare's. Accordingly, when he desires to give more than ordinary effect to deep passion, to indignation and abhorrence at crime committed, or to affliction and distress at calamity incurred, he has recourse to images which are associated with the final doom—the sounding of the last trump, the discomfiture of creation, the dissolution of the heavens and the earth. Thus, first, in the concluding scene of *King Lear*, where the fact that the personages of the play are all Pagans, would not allow of more than a general and indistinct allusion to ' the promised end,' we read as follows :—

> *Enter* Lear, *with* Cordelia *dead in his arms.*
>
> *Lear.* Howl, howl, howl, howl ! O, you are men of stones :
> Had I your tongues and eyes, I'd use them so

---

* Juvenal, though a heathen, expresses the same truth, and so confirms S. Paul, where he says that wicked men—

' Nocte, dieque suum gestare in pectore *testem.*'— Sat. xiii. 198.

That heaven's vault should crack.

*   *   *   *   *   *

Kent.   Is this the promis'd end?
Edgar. Or image of that horror?   Act v. Sc. 3.

See Matt. xxiv. 6, ' The end is not yet; ' and
1 Pet. iv. 7., ' The end of all things is at hand.'

There is the same kind of indistinct reference to
the gospel record of our Lord's combined prophecy
of the destruction of Jerusalem, and of the end of
the world, in a speech of Gloster's, towards the beginning of the same play :—

> These late eclipses in the sun and moon portend no good to
> us : . . . *love cools,* friendship falls off, *brothers divide* : in cities,
> mutinies ; in countries, discord ; in palaces, treason ; and *the bond
> cracked between father and son.* This villain of mine comes
> under the *prediction* ; there's *son against father* : the king falls
> from bias of nature ; there's *father against child.* Act i. Sc. 2.

In answer to the objection that such references
are out of place in the mouth of Pagans, it is to be
remembered that the heathen had their Sibylline
verses and prophetical books, and that both Lucan
and Ovid foretell of prodigies, and of the conflag-
ration of the world at the last day.

In *Macbeth* we advance a step farther towards a
fuller exhibition of the same comparison, when
Macduff enters, and discovers the dead bodies of
King Duncan and his attendants, all murdered :—

> *Macduff.* O horror! horror! horror!
> Tongue, nor heart, cannot conceive, nor name thee!

*   *   *   *   *   *

.   .   .   .   .   . Murder! and treason!
Banquo, and Donalbain! Malcolm! awake!
Shake off this drowsy sleep, death's counterfeit,
And look on death itself! Up, up, and see
The great doom's image!——Malcolm! Banquo!
As *from your graves rise up,* and *walk like sprites,*
To countenance this horror!

> *Enter* LADY MACBETH.

Lady M. What's the business,
That such a hideous *trumpet* calls to parley
The sleepers of the house? Act ii. Sc. 3.

Again the same image is invoked to give expression to other but no less violent and absorbing
emotions, in *Romeo and Juliet* :—

Juliet. Is Romeo slaughtered, and is Tybalt dead;
My dear-loved cousin, and my dearer lord?
Then *dreadful trumpet, sound the general doom!*

Act iii. Sc. 2.

When the young Lord Clifford, in the *Second
Part of King Henry VI.*, sees, after the battle of St.
Albans, the hopes of his party blasted, and his
father killed, he exclaims :—

O! let the vile world end!
And the *premised* * *flames of the last day
Knit earth and heaven together!*
Now let the *general trumpet blow his blast,*
Particularities and petty sounds
To cease! † Act v. Sc. 2.

The incestuous marriage of the queen, in *Hamlet*,
with the murderer of her husband and his own
brother, might well seem to call forth from the

---

* i. e. Sent before their time.   † To stop.

young prince the utmost abhorrence which words
can express :—

> Heaven's face doth glow :
> Yea, this solidity and compound mass
> With tristful visage, as * *against the doom,*
> Is thought-sick at the act.   *Hamlet,* Act iii. Sc. 4.

I see nothing in this last passage to justify the
doubts and objections which Warburton and other
critics have raised.   I imagine that *the glowing of
Heaven's face* is to be understood to imply *shame*
at the Queen's act.   Mr. Malone timidly asks—
' Had not our poet S. Luke's description of the
last day in his thoughts ? '   No doubt, he had ; but
why not also the parallel descriptions of S. Matthew and S. Mark ?   Yes, and still more, of
S. Peter, 2 Ep. iii. 7–11 ; and S. John, Rev.
xx. 11.   The truth is, I fear, that whatever else
our poet's critics have been strong in, they have,
for the most part, not† been strong in knowledge
of the Scriptures ; and that the book which they
should have looked to first and most for help in
the illustration of his works, is the book which has
been generally looked to last and least.

That the passage of S. Peter just referred to
had attracted his attention is evident from a speech
of Prospero in the *Tempest* :—

---

* See above, p. 23.

† I speak of the critics in the Variorum edition.   Among these
Mr. Henley is, I think, the only one who deserves to be exempted
from the above censure.

Our revels now are endcd : these our actors,
As I foretold you, were all spirits, and
Are melted into air, into thin air :
And, like the baseless fabric of this vision,
The cloud-capp'd towers, the gorgeous palaces,
The solemn temples, *the great globe itself,*
Yea, *all which it inherit, shall dissolve,*
And, like this insubstantial pageant faded,
Leave not a rack* behind.   Act iv. Sc. 1.

Compare also Isaiah li. 6, ' The heavens shall vanish away like smoke,' &c.

And now the curtain of our great teacher drops, as it ought, before the happiness of Heaven. We know, though imperfectly, what we now are; we know not, even with the help of Revelation, what we shall be hereafter :—

Beloved, now are we the sons of God; and it doth not yet appear what we shall be.   1 John iii. 2.

Ophelia has caught this up in her touching way, where she says to the king, in *Hamlet* :—

Well, God 'ield † you! They say, the owl was a baker's daughter. Lord, we know what we are, but *know not what we may be.* God be at your table!   Act iv. Sc. 5.

We can have no doubt that the last of these expressions (which, by the bye, Mr. Bowdler has omitted) is to be understood as a deranged person's version of ' May you be at God's table,' according

---

* i. e. A vapour. But, notwithstanding the elaborate argument of Horne Tooke, I confess I should prefer to read *track,* supported as it is by the parallel in *Timon of Athens.*
† Yield, i. e. reward you.

S

to the Scriptural notion,* which represents the happiness of heaven under the figure of a feast, with God for our host. See Matt. viii. 11, Luke xii. 37. There can be no doubt, too, that the preceding clause in Ophelia's speech is taken from the latter clause of S. John's text. What if the eccentricity of thought, natural to mad people, should have converted—in the presence of the wicked king —the Christian's *sonship to God*, with which the apostle's text begins, into the owl's *daughtership to the baker*, which Ophelia first introduces? I am inclined to think this not impossible, more especially as the legend referred to is a Christian one, in which, according to Mr. Steevens, our Saviour being refused *bread* by the daughter of a baker (which again would suggest the notion of the *blessedness of him that shall eat bread in the kingdom of God*, Luke xiv. 15) is described as punishing her by turning her into an owl. Mr. Douce has given the story more at length, and represents it as still current among the common people in Gloucestershire.

But though ' it doth not yet appear what we shall be' in heaven, we know that comfort and happiness are to be looked for *there*, and *only there*. When the

---

* And classical also. Compare Virg. Ecl. iv. 62 :

'Cui non risere Parentes,
Nec *Deus hunc mensâ*, Dea nec dignata cubili est.'

See also Hor. iv. Od. viii. 29, and elsewhere.

Queen, in *King Richard II.*, says to the Duke of York,

> For Heaven's sake, speak comfortable words;

he replies in language which many passages of the Bible fully justify :—

> Should I do so, I should belie my thoughts;
> *Comfort's in heaven* : and we are on the earth,
> Where nothing *lives* but crosses, care, and grief.'
>
> Act ii. Sc. 2.

And yet we must not be impatient to quit this scene of trial, so long as our remaining here may tend in any way to promote God's glory, or to be serviceable to our fellow men. Shakspeare, from the mouth of Hamlet, will teach us this, after the measure of the wisdom and the love of this world; but we must go to the Bible, and sit at the feet of S. Paul, if we would learn it more perfectly.

The dying Prince of Denmark speaks to his friend Horatio :—

> If thou didst ever hold me in thy heart,
> Absent thee from felicity awhile,
> And in this harsh world draw thy breath in pain,
> To tell my story. Act v. Sc. 2.

The great apostle of the Gentiles, in bondage at Rome, writes to his Philippian converts :—

> I am in a strait betwixt two, having a desire to depart, and to be with Christ, which is far better : Nevertheless to abide in the flesh is more needful for you. Phil. i. 23, 24.

Meanwhile may our 'names be written *in the Book of Life*!' This expression, which is used frequently by S. John in the Revelation, and once by S. Paul, Phil. iv. 3, could only have occurred to one who had often in his hand the sacred volume, which is *to us in this world* ‘ the Book of Life.’ We find it in *King Richard II.*   The speaker is Mowbray, Duke of Norfolk :—

> No, Bolingbroke ; if ever I were traitor,
> My *name be blotted from the Book of Life,*
> And I from heaven banished, as from hence !
>
> Act i. Sc. 3.

CHAPTER III.

Of the Poetry of Shakspeare as derived from
the Bible.

 COME now, in the last place, to speak of passages in which Shakspeare has been indebted to Holy Writ, not only for poetical diction and sentiment, but for some of the most striking and sublime images which are to be found in his works.

1. We are familiar with that simple, but most affecting apostrophe with which the vision of Isaiah opens :—

Hear, O heavens, and give ear, O earth ; for the Lord hath spoken—I have nourished and brought up children, and they have rebelled against Me.   i. 2.

See also Deut. xxxii. 1, Jerem. ii. 12, vi. 19. All creation is summoned to listen to a tale of un-dutifulness, which was felt by the prophets to be without parallel. It was under the influence of a similar feeling that Hamlet exclaims upon his mother's hasty and incestuous marriage with his uncle, his father's murderer :—

Heaven and earth!
Must I remember? Why, she would hang on him,
As if increase of appetite had grown
By what it fed on : and yet within a month—
Let me not think on't.   Act i. Sc. 2.

And again the same feeling is aroused and vents itself in a similar exclamation, in the scene between Hamlet and his father's ghost :—

Ghost.   List, list, O list,
If thou didst ever thy dear father love.
Hamlet. O ! Heaven !
Ghost. Revenge his foul and most unnatural murder.
                                        Ibid. Sc. 5.

The exclamation is not idle or common-place, but sublime and full of intense passion.

2. It is a bolder flight of imagination which represents the elements and heavenly bodies taking part, as allies, in the conflict of human warfare. Thus, in that grandest of all lyrical compositions— the Song of Deborah and Barak, Judges v. 20 :—

They fought from heaven ; the stars in their courses fought against Sisera.

Compare Joshua x. 12-14.

The classical student will be reminded of a parallel and wonderfully magnificent passage in the poet Claudian, *De tert. Consul. Honor.* 93–98 :—

Te propter, gelidis Aquilo de monte procellis
Obruit adversas acies, revolutaque tela
Vertit in auctores, et turbine reppulit hastas.
O nimium dilecte Deo ! cui *militat æther,*
Et conjurati veniunt ad classica venti.

Claudian was a heathen; but he recognised what was believed to be the interposition of the Deity on behalf of the Emperor Theodosius against Eugenius, at the battle of Aquileia, fought on Sept. 6th, A.D. 394. See Augustin, *De Civit. Dei*, lib. v. cap. xxvi.; *Fleury's Church History*, book xix. c. xlix.

Let us now see the use which our poet has made of this sublime idea.

First, in *King Henry VI. 3rd Part*, it appears in its simplest and, so to speak, most elementary form, where Hastings says :—

'Tis better using France, than trusting France :
Let us be *backed with Heaven*, and *with the seas*,
Which God hath given for fence impregnable,
And *with their helps only defend ourselves* :
In them and in ourselves our safety lies :—

Act iv. Sc. 1.

a passage upon which Dr. Johnson truly remarks :

This has been the advice of every man who in any age understood and favoured the interest of England.

Next, in *King Richard II.*, we have a develop-ment of the idea, suggested probably by the destruction of the host of Sennacherib, recorded in 2 Kings xix. and Isaiah xxxvii. :—

K. Richard. And we are barren, and bereft of friends;
Yet know—my master, God omnipotent,
Is mustering in his clouds, on our behalf,
Armies of pestilence : and they shall strike
Your children yet unborn, and unbegot,
That lift your vassal hands against my head,
And threat the glory of my precious crown. Act iii. Sc. 3.

In like manner, the Lady Constance, in *King John*, on behalf of her son Arthur, with the fury of a Pythian prophetess enthroned upon her sacred tripod, cries out—

> *Arm, arm, you heavens,* against these perjur'd kings!
> A widow cries; be husband to me, heavens!
> Let not the hours of this ungodly day
> Wear out the day in peace.   Act iii. Sc. 1.

Once more, the aged King Lear, upon the sight of his unnatural daughter, Goneril, thus invokes the armed confederacy of heaven on his side against her :

> *K. Lear.*   .   Who comes here?—*O heavens,*
> If you do love old men, if your sweet sway
> Allow * obedience, if yourselves are old,
> Make it your cause; *send down and take my part.*
>   Act ii. Sc. 4.

See also 'I tax not you,' &c., in Act iii. Sc. 2.

3. To pass on from this mustering of elements of warfare to the incidents of war itself. In that most poetical of all the Books of Scripture, the Book of Job, the passage which describes the warhorse, ch. xxxix. 19–25, has ever been considered as one of the most sublime—superior even to the famous parallel of Virgil :—

> Tum, si qua sonum procul arma dedere,
> Stare loco nescit, micat auribus, et tremit artus,
> Collectumque premens volvit sub naribus ignem.
>   *Georg.* iii. 83–85.

The expression of the inspired writer which ap-

---

* See above, Pt. I. ch. ii. p. 29.

pears to have struck the fancy of our poet most is this :—

> He swalloweth the ground with fierceness and rage.

Thus in *King Henry IV. 2nd Part,* we read : —

> With that, he gave his able horse the head,
> And, bending forward, struck his armed heels
> Against the panting sides of his poor jade
> Up to the rowel-head ; and starting so,
> He seemed in running to *devour the way,*
> Staying no longer question.　　　　Act i. Sc. 1.

And afterwards, in *Hamlet,* we find the same image very appropriately introduced in the mouth of a Danish gentleman, to describe an occurrence to which the flat sea-board of that country would be liable, though not so frequently or so destructively perhaps as the coast of Holland :

> *Gent.* (To the king).　　Save yourself, my lord,
> The ocean, overpeering of his list,*
> *Eats not the flats* with more impetuous haste
> Than young Laertes, in a riotous haste,
> O'erbears your officers.　　　　Act iv. Sc. 5.

4. The transformation of weapons of war into implements of peace is a favourite image with the inspired prophets. Thus, Isaiah ii. 4, and Micah iv. 3 :

> They shall beat their swords into ploughshares, and their spears into pruning-hooks.

And the contrary transformation in the Prophet Joel, where, in a vein of irony, he challenges the heathens to make their utmost efforts in opposition to God's truth ; iii. 9, 10 : —

---

* i. e. bounds.

Proclaim ye this among the Gentiles : Prepare war ; wake up the mighty men : let all the men of war draw near ; let them come up—

Beat your ploughshares into swords, and your pruning-hooks into spears : let the weak say, I am strong.

A transformation which Virgil describes as actually taking place in the melancholy picture which he draws of the universal disorders caused throughout the world by the civil wars of Rome :—

> Tot bella per orbem ;
> Tam multæ scelerum facies : non ullus aratro
> Dignus honos ; squalent abductis arva colonis :
> Et curvæ rigidum falces conflantur in ensem.
>
> *Georg.* i. 505–508.

Our poet has given an original turn to the same idea, by applying it to women. I allude to the words of Philip Faulconbridge, in *King John*, where he represents the female part of the population as ready to rise, or rather as already risen, in the king's behalf :—

> Ladies, and pale-visaged maids,
> Like Amazons, come tripping after drums ;
> Their *thimbles into armed gauntlets change,*
> Their *neelds to lances,* and their gentle hearts
> To fierce and bloody inclination.   Act v. Sc. 2.

5. Another image of warfare which occurs more than once in the poetical portions of the Bible is that which describes the weapons of war, arrows and the sword, when used to execute God's vengeance, as ' drunk with blood.' See the Song of Moses, Deut. xxxii. 42, and the Lamentations of

Jeremiah xlvi. 10. Shakspeare has profited by this in the words which he puts into the mouth of the Earl of Warwick, when Richard Plantagenet had told him of his brother's death:—

Rich. Thy brother's blood the thirsty earth hath drunk.
Warw. Then let the earth *be drunken with our blood.*
K. Henry VI. 3rd Part, Act ii. Sc. 3.

The idea will be familiar to the reader of the Greek tragedians; who, possibly, may have derived it from the Mosaical account of the first murder, where the Lord is introduced as speaking to Cain:—

And now art thou cursed from the earth, which hath *opened her mouth* to receive thy brother's blood from thy hand.
Genesis iv. 2.*

6. From passages such as these it is a slight transition or advance in metaphor which ascribes feelings of sympathy to inanimate things, and especially when things animate have come short in that duty. We can all appreciate the strict human propriety, as well as the poetry of the language which our Lord made use of when the Pharisees appealed to Him to rebuke His Disciples for the acclamations which they raised upon his last entry into Jerusalem:—

He answered and said unto them, I tell you, if these should hold their peace, the stones would immediately cry out:—
Luke xix. 40.

Not without reference probably to the similar

---

* Comp. Revel. xvii. 6.

rebuke which the prophet Habakkuk announces
would be forthcoming against the covetousness of
the rich, who had exalted themselves and their
dwelling places, through covetousness, through
violence, and injustice :—

The stone shall cry out of the wall, and the beam out of the
timber shall answer it.   ii. 11.

This notion of the brute earth, with its products,
senseless and irrational, exhibiting, or, in the poet's
imagination, not unwilling to exhibit greater powers
of sympathy than are to be found among men, has
afforded matter for several of Shakspeare's most
effective passages. For example, when King Richard
II. returned from Ireland, to meet, and, if possible,
suppress the insurrection of Bolingbroke, afterwards
King Henry IV., he thus apostrophises the coast of
Wales, upon which he landed :—

I weep for joy,
To stand upon my kingdom once again.—
Dear earth, I do salute thee with mine hand,
Tho' rebels wound thee with their horses' hoofs :

.   .   .   .   .   .

Feed not thy sovereign's foe, my gentle earth,
Nor with thy sweets comfort his ravenous sense ;
But let thy spiders, that suck up thy venom,
And heavy gaited toads, lie in their way :

.   .   .   .   .   .

Yield stinging nettles to mine enemies :
And when they from thy bosom pluck a flower,
Guard it, I pray thee, with a lurking adder ;
Whose double tongue may with a mortal touch
Throw death upon thy sovereign's enemies.—

Mock not my senseless conjuration, lords ;
This earth shall have a feeling, and these stones
Prove armed soldiers, ere her native king
Shall falter under foul rebellion's arms.   Act iii. Sc. 2.

This is a noble passage. Ten years later, when our poet produced *Julius Cæsar*, he had recourse again to the same image, and gave effect to it in a strain which nothing can surpass. The reader will know that I am referring to the speech of Antony, spoken by permission of Brutus and the other conspirators, over the body which they had stabbed to death :—

Antony. I have neither wit,* nor words, nor worth,
Action, nor utterance, nor the power of speech,
To stir men's blood : I only speak right on ;
I tell you that which you yourselves do know :
Show you sweet Cæsar's wounds, poor, poor dumb mouths,
And bid them speak for me :   But were I Brutus,
And Brutus Antony, there were an Antony
Would ruffle up your spirits, and put a tongue
In every wound of Cæsar, that would move
The *stones of Rome to rise and mutiny.*   Act ii. Sc. 2.

7. As there are 'thoughts which lie too deep for tears,' so there have been stages of human existence in which even desire for sympathy has become extinct ; and nothing has seemed left to those whose hope was thus overclouded, but to wish that they had never been. This state of feeling, to which no faithful Christian should allow himself to be reduced, finds vent in expressions, the appalling sublimity of

---

* Malone reads ' writ,' which Johnson defends, not, I think, satisfactorily.

which has never been surpassed, in the 3rd chapter
of the Book of Job:—

> After this opened Job his mouth, and cursed his day.
>
> And Job spake and said :
>
> Let the day perish wherein I was born, and the night in which
> it was said, there is a man-child * conceived.
>
> Let that day be darkness ; let not God regard it from above,
> neither let the light shine upon it.
>
> Let darkness and the shadow of death stain it ; let a cloud
> dwell upon it ; let† the blackness of the day terrify it.
>
> As for that night, let darkness seize upon it, let it not be joined
> unto the days of the year, let it not come into the number of the
> months.
>
> Lo ! let that night be solitary, let no joyful voice come
> therein.
>
> Let the stars of the twilight thereof be dark ; let it look for
> light, but have none ; neither let it see the dawning of the day.

I think the readers of Shakspeare will agree with
me that there is no one of all his characters from
whom language of this kind would be more expected, or come with greater propriety, than from
the Lady Constance in *King John*.   And so we find
that he has put into her mouth a speech which I
cannot doubt was founded upon the poet's recollec-
tion of the foregoing passage of the Old Testament.
When King Philip had announced that the marriage
was agreed on between his son Lewis and the Lady
Blanch, whereby young Arthur, the son of Constance,
was to be excluded from succession to the English
throne—speaking of the contract as one that would

---

* See above, p. 36.   † But see margin.

ever reflect lustre upon the day then present, upon
which it had been made :—

> The yearly course, that brings this day about,
> Shall never see it but a holyday :—

Constance broke in upon him, thus :—

> A wicked day, and not a holyday !
> What hath this day deserved ? What hath it done,
> That it in golden letters should be set,
> Among the high tides,* in the kalendar ?
> Nay, rather, *turn this day out of the week,*
> This day of shame, oppression, perjury ;
> Or, if it must stand still, let wives with child
> Pray that their burdens may not fall this day.
>
> Act iii. Sc. 1.

And in *Hamlet*, written, according to Malone, in
the same year as *King John*, viz. 1596, we find the
sentiment of Job very nearly adopted, when he
says to Ophelia, speaking of himself :—

> I could accuse me of such things that *it were better†* *my mother
> had not borne me.* Act iii. Sc. 1.

To these passages may be added, from *Timon of
Athens*, the last words spoken by Timon, as he
goes out to put an end to his existence :—

> *Sun, hide thy beams !* Timon hath done his reign.
> Act v. Sc. 2.

8. The striking sublimity with which Paul, when
brought before Festus, replied to the Governor's
exclamation, ' that he was beside himself,' by the
simple denial, ' I am not mad, most noble Festus,'

---

* Times, seasons. † See Matt. xxvi. 24.

Acts xxvi. 25, was not likely to be lost upon our poet's imagination. In both the plays which I just now mentioned as contemporaneous, *Hamlet* and *King John*, it is copied with good effect. When the Queen accuses Hamlet, after the exit of the Ghost, which he had seen, of 'ecstacy,' he answers :—

> Ecstacy !
> My pulse as yours doth temperately keep time,
> And makes as healthful music : *It is not madness*
> *That I have uttered.*   Act iii. Sc. 4.

And in *King John*, when Pandulph says to Constance :—

> Lady, you utter madness, and not sorrow,

her reply is :—

> Thou art not holy to belie me so ;
> *I am not mad* : this hair I tear is mine ;
> My name is Constance ;   I was Geffrey's wife ;
> Young Arthur is my son, and he is lost—
> *I am not mad : I would to heaven I were !*
>   Act iii. Sc. 4.

9. The mention of S. Paul may remind us of another sublime passage in the writings of that Apostle, which appears to have been present to the mind of Shakspeare. I allude to the verse in the Epistle to the Galatians, i. 8 :—

> Though we, or an *angel from heaven*, preach any other gospel
> unto you than that ye have received, let him be accursed.

Compare with this what we read in *King John*, in that most affecting of all scenes, between Hubert and Arthur, when the young Prince says to him :—

> An * *if an angel should have come to me*
> *And told me,* Hubert should put out mine eyes,
> I would not have believed him. Act iv. Sc. 1.

Akin, in some degree, to the foregoing, are two remarkable passages in the *First Part of King Henry IV.* The former of these has perplexed the commentators more, I think, than it need have done, if they had considered the striking resemblance which it bears to a strain of bold and figurative language to be met with more than once in Holy Scripture. It is quite in keeping with the character of Hotspur to speak as follows :—

> By heaven, methinks, it were an easy leap
> To pluck bright honour from the pale-faced moon,
> Or dive into the bottom of the deep,
> And pluck up drowned honour by the locks;
> So he, that doth redeem her thence, might wear,
> Without corrival, all her dignities. Act i. Sc. 3.

We may be sure that Shakspeare had never seen the passage of Euripides which has been produced to justify and explain the so-called 'bombast' of these lines; and we may be no less certain that he *had seen and studied* those two grand chapters of Deuteronomy, and of the Epistle to the Romans, in which we read what I proceed to quote :—

For this commandment which I command thee this day, it is not hidden from thee, neither is it far off. It is not *in Heaven*;

---

* See above, p. 26.

T

that thou should'st say, who shall go up for us to heaven, and *bring it unto us*, that we may hear it, and do it? Neither is it *beyond the sea* that thou should'st say, who shall go over the sea for us, and *bring it unto us*, that we may hear it and do it? . But the word is very nigh unto thee, in thy mouth and in thy heart, that thou mayest do it.   Deut. xxx. 11–14.

The righteousness which is of faith speaketh on this wise : Say not in thine heart, who shall ascend into heaven? that is, *to bring Christ down from above*. Or, who shall descend into the deep? that is, *to bring up Christ again from the dead* : But what saith it? The word is nigh thee, even in thy mouth, and in thy heart ; that is, the word of faith, which we preach.

                                    Romans x. 6–8.

In the other passage of the same play, to which I last referred, we may also trace a similar use and adaptation of Scriptural ideas and modes of thought. In this instance, for a reason that will be obvious, let us take the Scripture first.

In Job xxi. 22, the solemn question is asked :—

Shall any teach God knowledge?

And in Isaiah xl. 13 :—

Who hath directed the Spirit of the Lord, or, being his counsellor, hath taught Him?

And in S. Paul, more than once, see Rom. xi. 34, 1 Cor. ii. 16 :—

Who hath known the mind of the Lord, or who hath been His counsellor?

When Owen Glendower desires to represent that he is something more than human :—

All the courses of my life do show
I am not in the roll of common men—

he endeavours to fortify the boast by making use
of the same image and attribute of Deity :—

> Where is he living . . .
> Which *calls me pupil*, or hath read to me ?
> And bring him out, that is but woman's son,
> Can trace me in the tedious ways of art,
> And hold me pace in deep experiments ?
>
> Act iii. Sc. 1.

10. Again : the sublime passages of the Old
Testament, in which the attributes of man, or of
angels, are assigned to Almighty God ;—as, for
instance, where He is said to ' ride upon the
heavens,' Deut. xxxiii. 26, Ps. lxviii. 4 ; or ' to
walk ' or ' fly upon the wings of the wind,' Ps.
civ. 3, xviii. 10 ; or that ' His hand is not
shortened,' Numb. xi. 23, Isai. l. 2, lix. 1 ;—might
expect to find their likenesses in Shakspeare, and
they do find them : yet so softened and disguised,,
that no comparison which might suggest thoughts.
of irreverence is provoked by the imitation.

It is Romeo who thus, from Capulet's garden,,
addresses Juliet at her window :—

> O ! speak again, bright angel, for thou art
> As glorious to this night, being o'er my head,
> As is a winged messenger of Heaven
> Unto the white upturned wondering eyes
> Of mortals, that fall back to gaze on him,
> When he *bestrides the lazy-pacing clouds,*
> And *sails upon the bosom of the air.*   Act ii. Sc. 2.

The shortening of the hand or arm is applied as a
metaphor to Danger, with great force and propriety,

T 2

in *Pericles, Prince of Tyre*, part of which, at least,
I take to have been written by Shakspeare when
a young man.

> Danger, which I feared, is at Antioch,
> Whose *arm seems far too short to hit me here.*
>
> Act i. Sc. 2.

Nor can I doubt that our poet had in his eye
that beautiful and most pathetic passage of the
prophet Isaiah, in which God's unfailing remembrance of his people is set forth, xlix. 15 ;—

> Can a woman forget her sucking child? . . . Yea, they
> may forget, yet will *I* not forget thee ;—

when he wrote, in *King Henry V.*, that well-
known speech of the king on the eve of the victory
at Agincourt :—

> This day is called the feast of Crispian!
> He that outlives this day, and comes safe home,
> Will stand a tip-toe when this day is named ;
>
> .   .   .   .   .   .   '
>
> .   .   .   .   .   .
>
> *Old men forget*, yea, *all shall be forgot*,
> *But he'll remember* with advantages
> What feats he did that day.   Act iv. Sc. 3.

I may observe that, in the received text of this
passage, the reading is '*yet* all shall be forgot;'
but with the parallel words of Isaiah before me,
I had no doubt that the true reading is 'yea' instead of 'yet:' and I have since discovered that
the same conjecture had occurred to Malone,
though he makes no mention of the confirmation

given to it by the turn of expression which the inspired prophet employs.

11. The reader who desires further illustrations
under this head is requested to compare the fine
description in *King Richard II.* of deeds of darkness shrinking and terrified at the return of day;—

> Then murders, treasons, and detested sins,
> The cloak of night being plucked from off their backs,
> Stand bare and naked, trembling at themselves;—
>
> Act iii. Sc. 2.

with the similar description in the Book of Job:—

> In the dark they dig thro' houses; . . they know not the
> light; for the morning is to them even as the shadow of death:
> if one know them they are in the terrors of the shadow of death.
>
> xxiv. 13–17.

And again, the grand passage in the *Third Part of
King Henry VI.*, where the Earl of Warwick com-
pares his own fall to that of the cedar,

> Whose arms gave shelter to the princely eagle,
> Under whose shade the ramping lion slept;
>
> Act v. Sc. 2.

was doubtless derived, as is pointed out in a note
of Steevens, from the prophet Ezekiel, who had
made a similar comparison between the fall of the
glory of Assyria and of a cedar in Lebanon:—

> All the fowls of heaven made their nests in his boughs, and
> under his branches did all the beasts of the field bring forth their
> young; under his shadow dwelt all great nations. xxxi. 6.

12. The following may be added as specimens

of less elaborate comparison, no less evidently drawn from the same sacred source.

In *Much ado about nothing*, Benedick says to Don Pedro, in answer to the latter's question :—

> Where's the count ?
> I found him here as melancholy as *a lodge in a warren.*
>
> Act ii. Sc. 1.

Where again the note of Steevens very properly refers us to the parallel in Isaiah :—

> The daughter of Zion is left as a cottage in a vineyard, as *a lodge in a garden of cucumbers*, as a besieged city ;—   i. 8.

a melancholy picture of loneliness and desolation.

In *Hamlet*, Polonius warns Ophelia not to trust too readily to the advances of the young prince, however accompanied with protestations of affection :—

> These blazes, daughter,
> Giving more light than heat, *extinct* in both,
> Even in their promise as it is a making,
> You must not take for *fire*.   Act i. Sc. 3.

And again, in the *First Part of King Henry IV.* the same image occurs to describe the companions of the sovereign whom Henry had supplanted :—

> The skipping king, he ambled up and down,
> With shallow jesters, and rash bavin wits,
> *Soon kindled and soon burnt.*   Act iii. Sc. 2.

' Bavin ' means *brushwood*.   In like manner David, in Psalm cxviii. 12, says of his enemies :—

> They are *extinct*, even as *the fire among the thorns*; for in the name of the Lord I will destroy them.

In *Othello*, the Moor speaks of Desdemona, we know how unjustly, as having been 'false *as water*,' Act v. Sc. 1. Was this simile derived from the character given by Jacob to his first-born son Reuben?

Unstable *as water*, thou shalt not excel. Gen. xlix. 4.

In *Timon of Athens*, the painter says to the poet, speaking of Timon :—

You shall see him *a palm* in Athens again, and *flourish* with the highest. Act v. Sc. 1.

The notion of ' flourishing like a palm tree ' is one with which we are familiar from Psalm xcii. 12.

13. In like manner the comparisons derived from animals, with which the Bible has familiarized us, are to be found no less in the pages of Shakspeare. For instance, in the last-named play, the description of the hostile approach of Alcibiades,

Who, *like a boar too savage, doth root up*
His country's peace ; Act v. Sc. 2.

is derived from the Psalmist's description of the enemies of Jerusalem represented as a vine :—

The wild boar out of the wood doth root it up ; and the wild beasts of the *field devour it.*
Ps. lxxx. 13, Prayer Book version.

So, too, 'the wolf in sheep's clothing,' of S. Matthew vii. 15, is reproduced in *Second Part of King Henry VI.*, Act iii. Sc. 1, where Queen Margaret enquires concerning Gloster :—

Is he *a lamb ?* his skin is surely lent him,
For he's inclined as are the ravenous *wolves.*

The 'dog returning to his vomit,' of S. Peter, 2 Ep. ii. 22, and of Proverbs xxvi. 11, is reproduced in *King Henry IV. 2nd Part*, Act i. Sc. 3 (where Mr. Bowdler, in omitting the allusion, has curtailed the passage in a manner singularly awkward and scarcely grammatical), and again (though still* not in Mr. Bowdler's edition) in *King Henry V.* Act iii. Sc. 7, where the text of S. Peter is given in French, almost exactly from the Genevan Bible of 1588 : a fact which renders one part, at least, of Dr. Farmer's conclusion in his celebrated essay very improbable, viz. that 'Shakspeare did not understand very common words in the *French* and *Latin* languages.' The 'deaf adder' has been already spoken of.† The cherished 'Serpent, that, at the last, biteth, and stingeth,' of Proverbs xxiii. 32, is reproduced in *King Henry VI. 2nd Part*, Act iii. Sc. 1 :—

> I fear me, you but warm the starved *snake*,
> Who, cherished in your breasts, will *sting your hearts.*

And as we are 'set to school to the ant' in Proverbs vi. 6, so are we also in *King Lear*, Act ii. Sc. 4.

14. Again, the metaphorical images of 'the tree known by its fruits;' of 'the axe laid to the root of the tree;' of causing our 'light to shine before

---

* This is mentioned not to complain of the omission in the present instance, but for the information of readers of that edition.

† See above, p. 48.

men,' in this naughty world; of 'the cheek to be given to the smiter;' and of 'the mote' in the mind's 'eye;'—each of them well known to us from the Bible—have been all pressed into service by our great poet: as may be seen by any one who will read *First Part King Henry IV.* Act ii. Sc. 4; *Third Part Henry VI.* Act ii. Sc. 2; *Merchant of Venice,* Act v. Sc. 1; *King Lear,* Act iv. Sc. 1; *Hamlet,* Act i. Sc. 1.

But the field of Scriptural metaphor is one over which we must track our poet still further. In the Bible, life is 'a pilgrimage,' Gen. xlvii. 9, and elsewhere; so it is in Shakspeare :—

> His time is spent, our *pilgrimage* must be.
> K. *Richard II.* Act ii. Sc. 1.

In the Bible, the human body is a 'temple,' John ii. 21, and elsewhere; so it is in Shakspeare :

> Nature, crescent, does not grow alone
> In thews and bulk, but, as *this temple* waxes,
> The inward service of the mind and soul
> Grows wide withal. *Hamlet,* Act i. Sc. 3.

In the Bible, that which infects and corrupts others is 'leaven,' 1 Cor. v. 6-8, and elsewhere; so it is in Shakspeare :—

> Thou, Posthumus,
> Wilt lay the *leaven* on all * proper men;
> Goodly and valiant shall be false and perjured
> From thy great fall;— *Cymbeline,* Act iii. Sc. 4.

---

* See above, p. 39. But here it seems to mean *handsome morally* and *inwardly*, like the Greek καλός.

i. e. shall not escape the imputation and character of being such. In the Bible, that which is appropriated and secured, is ' sealed,' Rom. xv. 28, and elsewhere; so it is in Shakspeare :—

> Since my dear soul was mistress of her choice,
> And could of men distinguish her election,
> She hath *sealed thee* for herself;   Act iii. Sc. 2.

says Hamlet to his friend Horatio, and, again, in the same play, the phrase which S. John uses, iii. 33, is adopted by our poet :—

> A combination and a form indeed,
> Where every god did seem to *set his seal,*
> *To give the world assurance* of a man;
> This was your husband.   Act iii. Sc. 4.

15. But further ; besides the broader and more important principles and sentiments treated of at large in the preceding chapter, we may notice here several minor instances in which Shakspeare has adapted the moral axioms of Scripture to his purposes as a dramatic poet. A remarkable example of this, and one which might be illustrated by a whole cento of Bible texts, as including references not only to Scriptural maxims, but to facts, is to be found in *All's well that ends well* :—

> He that of greatest works is finisher,
> *Oft does them by the weakest minister :*
> So holy writ in babes hath judgment shown,
> When judges have been babes : great floods have flown
> From simple sources; and great seas have dried,
> When miracles have by the greatest been denied.
> *Oft expectation fails, and most oft there*

Where most it promises ; and oft it hits
Where hope is coldest, and despair most sits.

Act ii. Sc. 1.

Here Mr. Malone has properly pointed out both the resemblance to the words of S. Paul, 'God hath chosen,' i. e. is wont to choose, 'the *weak things* of the world to confound the things which are mighty,' 1 Cor. i. 27 ; and the direct allusion to the words of our Lord :—

I thank Thee, O Father, because Thou hast hid these things from the wise and prudent, and hast revealed them unto babes.

Matt. xi. 25.

But in the latter case it would have been more apposite to have quoted Matt. xxi. 15, 16, containing the reference to Psalm viii. 2 ; because in that passage ' the judgment ' of the children in the temple, as contrasted with the unbelief of the chief priests and scribes, is actually ' shown.' Mr. Holt White suggests that the allusion is to Daniel's judging, when ' a young youth,' the two elders in the story of Susannah. I have remarked that Shakspeare had this story in view on another* occasion ; but I doubt whether he would have spoken of an apocryphal book as ' holy writ ; ' though some of the fathers, and our own Homilies (using the word ' Scripture ' in a laxer sense than prevailed in Shakspeare's time, or prevails now) did so speak. Returning to the speech of Helena in *All's well,*'

---

* See above, ch. i. p. 75. .

&c., both the critic just named, and Mr. Henley, have observed that in the words ' great floods have flown from simple sources,' there is an allusion to Moses smiting the rock in Horeb, Exod. xvii. 6 ; but they differ about the allusion in the verse that follows : the former considers that by ' the greatest' we are to understand Pharaoh, who ' denied,' or would *not hearken to* the miracles of Moses in Egypt; the latter, that the elders of Israel are meant, who, notwithstanding the miracles wrought for their preservation, refused that compliance which they ought to have yielded. Both critics suppose that the preceding half line refers to the drying up of the Red Sea.

Another example of the same kind is the poetical expansion which Shakspeare gives to the Scriptural notion, that it is the duty of men, in the moral, no less than in the natural world, to ' discern the signs of the times.' See Matt. xvi. 1-3, and elsewhere. I allude to the dialogue in *King Richard III.* between certain citizens of London, when they received news of the death of King Edward IV.

> *1st Cit.* Come, come, we fear the worst; all will be well.
> *3rd Cit.* When clouds are seen, wise men put on their cloaks;
> When great leaves fall, then winter is at hand ;
> When the sun sets, who does not look for night ?
> Untimely storms make men expect a dearth :
> All may be well ; but, if God sort it so,
> 'Tis more than we deserve, or I expect.
> *2nd Cit.* Truly the hearts of men are full of fear ;

You cannot reason * almost with a man
That looks not heavily, and full of dread. .
    3rd Cit. Before the days of change, still is it so ;
By a divine instinct, men's minds mistrust
Ensuing danger ; as, by proof, we see
The water swell before a boisterous storm.   Act ii. Sc. 3.

Take, again, the following argument from the
Gospel :—

> What king [said our Lord] going to make war against another
> king, sitteth not down first and consulteth whether he be able
> with ten thousand to meet him that cometh against him with
> twenty thousand ? or else, while the other is yet a great way off,
> he sendeth an ambassage, and desireth conditions of peace.
>   Luke xiv. 31, 32.

With what force and beauty is this argument—
this illustration of the duty of counting the cost
when we enter upon our Christian warfare—applied
by our poet to an individual case, in the *Second Part
of King Henry IV.*, where Morton expostulates with
the Duke of Northumberland, who, upon hearing
of the death of his son, Harry Percy, gave way to
overwhelming passion at a moment when there was
most need for instant and effectual counsel :—

> You cast the event of war, my noble lord,
> And summed the account of chance, before you said—
> Let us make head.   It was your presurmise,
> That in the dole of blows, your son might drop :
> You knew he walk'd o'er perils, on an edge,
> More likely to fall in, than to get o'er :
> You were advis'd his flesh was capable
> Of wounds and scars ; and that his forward spirit
> Would lift him where most trade of danger ranged ;

---

* Converse, talk.   .

Yet did you say — Go forth ; and none of this,
Though strongly apprehended, could restrain
The stiff-born action : What hath then befallen,
Or what hath this bold enterprise brought forth,
More than that * being which was like to be?

                                        Act i. Sc. 1.

But there was another illustration to the same
effect, in that discourse of Christ :—

Which of you intending to build a tower, sitteth not down
first, and counteth the cost, whether he have sufficient to finish
it ? Lest, haply, after he hath laid the foundation, and is not
able to finish it, all that behold it begin to mock him, saying :
This man began to build and was not able to finish.

                                        Luke xiv. 28, 29.

And this, too, our poet has appropriated, and at the
same time, luxuriates, rather too much, perhaps, in
the amplification he has given it, in a subsequent
scene of the same play. Lord Bardolph is speaking
in consultation with the Archbishop of York, Lords
Mowbray and Hastings, all enemies of the King,
and in discouragement of their enterprise :—

The question, then, Lord Hastings, standeth thus ;—
Whether our present five-and twenty thousand
May hold up head, without Northumberland ?

And his ' judgment,' that in the mean time, at
all events, they ' should not step too far ' into open
rebellion, is thus maintained :—   •

When we mean to build,
We first survey the plot, then draw the model ;
And when we see the figure of the house,
Then must we *rate the cost of the erection* :

•   * State of things, result, consequence.

Which if we find outweighs ability,
What do we then but draw anew the model
In fewer offices ; or, at least, desist
To build at all ?   Much more in this great work
(Which is almost to pluck a kingdom down,
And set another up) should we survey
The plot of situation and the model ;
Consent upon a sure foundation ;
Question surveyors ; know our own estate,
How *able such a work to undergo,*
To weigh against his opposite : or else,
We fortify in paper and in figures,
Using the names of men instead of men ;
Like one that draws the model of a house
Beyond his power to build it ; who, half through,
Gives o'er, and leaves his part-created cost
A naked subject to the weeping clouds,
And waste for churlish winter's tyranny.

Act i. Sc. 3.

16. The well-known apologue of Menenius Agrippa in our poet's play of *Coriolanus*, Act i. Sc. 1, is not to be traced to S. Paul's Epistle to the Corinthians, i. c. xii., but rather to the common source in Roman history, from which they both, we may suppose, adopted it ; except that S. Paul probably read it in Livy, and Shakspeare in North's translation of Plutarch.   But when, in the *Third Part of King Henry VI.*, the Earl of Warwick says to Richard Plantagenet—

Victorious Prince of York,
Before I see thee seated in that throne,
Which now the house of Lancaster usurps,
I vow by heaven *these eyes shall never close* ;—

Act i. Sc. 1.

and when, again, in *First Part of King Henry IV.*, Prince Henry says to Falstaff—

> Wisdom cries out in the streets, and no man regards it ;—
> Act i. Sc. 2.

we need not, doubt that our poet had in view a resolution of King David, Ps. cxxxii. 4, in the former case, and a complaint of King Solomon, Prov. l. 20, in the latter. The notion of expressing silence by laying the finger on the lips, or hand upon the mouth, which we find in *Othello*, ii. 1, and in *Troilus and Cressida* iii. 3, is also, probably, of Scriptural origin; see Judges xviii. 19, and the references given there in the margin. The same may be said of the adoption, by Shakspeare, of the true prophetical style, whereby that which is foretold is said to be actually brought to pass and accomplished by him who predicts it. Thus Macbeth, speaking of the prophecy of the Witches in his favour, complains :—

> Upon my head they *placed a fruitless crown,*
> And *put a barren sceptre in my gripe.*   Act iii. Sc. 1.

Just as the chief butler of Pharaoh, in telling how Joseph had interpreted his dream, and the dream of the chief baker, describes it in these words :—

> Me he *restored unto my office,* and him he *hanged.*
> Genesis xli. 13.

See also Jerem. l. 10, Ezek. xliii. 3, and elsewhere.

I will only notice further, that a figure of speech of which S. Paul is fond, is also to be met with very frequently in Shakspeare ; I mean the figure which grammarians have called *Oxymoron*. Of Scriptural examples it may suffice to refer to that sublime passage in the 2nd Epistle to the Corinthians, which ends thus—' as having nothing and [yet] possessing all things,' vi. 10. Of instances in our poet the reader probably will not desire to see more than the following sample :—

> Fairest Cordelia, thou art most rich, being poor ;
> Most choice, forsaken ; and most loved, despised.
> > *K. Lear,* Act i. Sc. 1.

> My long sickness
> Of health and living now begins to mend,
> And *nothing* brings me *all things.*
> > *Timon of Athens,* Act v. Sc. 2.

So, too, we have 'noble misery,' in *Cymbeline,* v. 3 ; and in the same play, iv. 3 :—

> Wherein I am false, I am honest ;

with which we may compare S. Paul, in the passage last referred to, ' as deceivers and [yet] true.'

When Touchstone, in *As you like it,* says—

> I do now remember a saying, *The fool doth think he is wise, but the wise man knows he is a fool ;*—

is the saying he thus quotes derived from 1 Cor. iii. 18 ?

INTERIOR OF GRAMMAR SCHOOL.

CONCLUSION.

I HAVE now gone through the interesting and instructive task which I proposed to myself; and the conclusion at which I have arrived is this:—Take the entire range of English literature; put together our best authors, who have written upon subjects not professedly religious or theological, and we shall not find, I believe, in them *all united*, so much evidence of the Bible having been read and used, as we have found in Shakspeare *alone.* This is a *phenomenon* which admits of being looked at from several points of view; but I shall be content to regard it solely in connection with the undoubted fact, that of all our authors, Shakspeare is also, by general confession, the greatest and the best. According to the testimony of Charles Lamb, a most competent judge in regard to all the literary elements of the question, our poet, 'in his divine mind and manners, surpassed not only the great men his contem-

poraries, but all mankind.' *   And looking at this
superiority from my own point of view, I cannot
but remark that, while most of the great laymen
of that great Elizabethan age—Lord Bacon, Sir
Walter Raleigh, the poet Spenser, Sir Philip Sidney,
Lord Burleigh, Ben Jonson—have paid homage to
Christianity, if not always in their practice, yet in
the convictions of their understanding, and in the
profession of their faith, none of them has done
this so fully or so effectually as Shakspeare.

But I may go further.   Not a little remarkable
is it that those only have disputed the superior
merit and excellency of our poet who have also
denied the value and authority of Holy Scripture.
The disparagement of such judges—I allude especially to Voltaire and David Hume—is an additional confirmation of the otherwise unanimous
panegyric with which he has been honoured.   It
will appear scarcely credible at the present day
that the accepted *Historian of England*, in speaking
of England's greatest poet, should have given vent
to criticisms such as these :—

A striking peculiarity of sentiment . . . Shakspeare
frequently hits ; *a reasonable propriety of thought he cannot for any
time uphold.* . . . It is in vain we look [in him] for either
purity or simplicity of diction. . . . Both he and Ben Jonson
were equally deficient in taste and elegance, in harmony and
correctness. . . . The English theatre has ever since taken a
strong tincture of Shakspeare ; and *thence it has proceeded that the*

---

* *Specimens of Dramatic Poets*, Preface, vol. i. p. 7.

nation has undergone from all its neighbours THE REPROACH OF BARBARISM, from which its valuable productions in some other parts of learning would otherwise have exempted it.*

The author of these remarks upon Shakspeare has himself informed us that the volume which contained them, when first published, so far from being popular, was received 'with one cry of reproach, disapprobation, and even detestation,' on account of its political views: nor, if the rest of its contents had been equally erroneous with the passage which I have quoted, would it have deserved any better reception. And how did Hume console himself under the disappointment? He proceeded to write his *Natural History of Religion,* in which he gave the world to understand that, as he had looked in vain, in Shakspeare, for *purity or simplicity of diction,* for *taste or elegance,* for *harmony or correctness,* so he had been unable to derive anything but 'doubt, uncertainty, and suspense of judgment,' from the written Word of God! The concluding remark of the passage quoted above, in which Shakspeare and Ben Jonson are accused of having brought upon us 'as a nation the reproach of barbarism from *all* our neighbours,' is evidently founded upon the strictures of Voltaire,† who, not long before, had characterised our poet as 'a writer of monstrous Farces, called by him Tragedies,' had

---

* Hume's *Hist. of England,* Appendix to Reign of James I.

† All that can be said in *excuse* for Voltaire's criticism has been fairly stated by Mr. C. Knight, in his *Studies of Shakspeare,* p. 540, *sq.*

pronounced *Hamlet* to be 'the work of a drunken savage,' * and had attributed 'barbarism and ignorance' to the nation by which he was admired! What the same French author also thought and wrote of divine Revelation, and of the profession of Christianity, need not be told.

The best answer to this latter critic has been given by another foreigner—not a Frenchman, but a German—Augustus William Schlegel, who has shown an admirable appreciation of the genius and characteristic excellences of our great poet in his masterly *Lectures on Dramatic Literature* :—

> Shakspeare is the pride of his nation. . . . He was the idol of his contemporaries; and after the interval of Puritanical fanaticism . . . his fame began to revive with more than its original brightness towards the beginning of the last century, and since that period it has increased with the progress of time : and for centuries to come, I speak with the greatest confidence, it will continue to gather strength like an alpine avalanche, at every period of its descent. . . . In general, Shakspeare's style yet remains the very best model both in the vigorous and sublime, and in the pleasing and tender.—Vol. ii. p. 102, *sq.* and p. 146.

To the criticism of Hume, which first appeared in 1764—exactly *a century* ago—the best reply will be the *Tercentenary* Festival in honour of the poet's birth, which our 'barbarous nation' is preparing to celebrate in the present year. Or, if we desire to

---

* Such criticism is not even yet quite extinct. An American writer has recently discovered that 'Shakspeare . . . and Walter Scott were remarkably morbid men; while Spenser, Milton, Wordsworth . . . were undoubtedly insane!'—See *Quart. Rev.* Jan. 1864, p. 56.

.see the very different opinion of another historian
of England, and man of letters—a writer, moreover, who was no enthusiast, but cool and cautious
in his judgments—it is Mr. Hallam who pronounces that 'the name of Shakspeare is the
greatest in our literature; it is THE GREATEST IN
ALL LITERATURE.'*

Dr. Farmer, in his celebrated essay *Upon the Learning of Shakspeare*, arrived at the conclusion that our
poet's 'studies were demonstratively confined to
nature and his own language.' To this conclusion
(while I partly demur, as I have before intimated,
to the narrow limits which it assigns to Shakspeare's reading) I would presume to add that, of
all the books which he studied in his own language,
there was none with which he was more familiar
than with the English Bible. That in every instance the characters in his plays have treated Holy
Scripture with the nice and exact reverence which we
should feel to be desirable at the present day, is
not to be maintained; but still less is the charge
which has been brought against him, of frequent
irreverence and profaneness in his use of God's
word, to be justified, or received. The mass of
reference and allusion to Scripture which his works
contain, must be looked at as a whole, in order to
discover its true *animus*. This would be only just

---

* *Hist. of Literature*, vol. iii. p. 547.

and fair to an author under any circumstances ;·
but how much more necessary and indispensable is
it in our poet's case, when we know that his plays,
for the most part, were not published by himself,
nor till some years after his death ; and when we
also know that into many of his scenes low jokes,
for which he is not responsible, were foisted by the
players in order to ' please the million.'   For instance, Dr. Farmer considered it ' extremely pro-
bable ' that the French ribaldry* in the last scene of
King Henry V. was at first inserted by a different
hand ; as ' the many additions in that same play
most certainly were, after he had left the stage.'
In like manner the wretched jest (which we learn
from other quarters to have been *current* in our
poet's days), by which the name of the *Ten Commandments* was given to the fingers and thumbs of
the two hands, has found its way into the *Second
Part of King Henry VI.*; where Eleanor, Duchess of
Gloucester, says to Queen Margaret, in language as
coarse as it is profane—but language, be it remembered, addressed to an adulteress by one whom she
had grievously insulted by reflexions upon her
husband, and, moreover, grossly insulted by *boxing
her on the ear* :—

---

* We have only to compare the *names* of Shakspeare's plays with
the *names* of those of the principal dramatists who were his contemporaries—Ford, Massinger, Marlowe, Beaumont and Fletcher,
Rowley, Shirley, and even Ben Jonson—in order to perceive the
superior *delicacy* of our poet's mind for one living in that age.

Could I come near your beauty with my nails,
I'd set *my ten commandments* in your face.

Act i. Sc. 3.

The authenticity of this play has been called in
question by good judges; for instance, by Dr.
Farmer: though, for my own part, I must confess
I agree with Schlegel, if not in accepting the whole
as unquestionably Shakspeare's, yet in maintaining
that some parts of it, especially the death scene of
Cardinal Beaufort, could have been written by no
other hand. It is in the same play that another
instance occurs of Scriptural reference, which certainly falls short of what we now feel to be due,
in speaking upon so sacred and solemn a subject. Richard, son of the Duke of York, says to
young Lord Clifford, who had called the Yorkists
' rebels,'

Fye! charity, for shame! speak not in spite,
For you shall *sup with Jesus Christ to-night* ;—

Act v. Sc. I.

in ironical allusion, evidently, to the promise which
our Lord made to the Penitent Thief upon the
Cross. However, I must repeat, that before we
censure Shakspeare for verses such as these, justice
requires us to have certain evidence that he actually
wrote them; which evidence cannot now be obtained: and I must add, that before we determine
to withhold from him the high praise given to the
poet Thomson by his friend and patron, Lord

Lyttelton, viz. that in all his works there was not
to be discovered

One line which dying he would wish to blot,

charity would suggest to us to make the fullest
allowance for the influence of causes* which have
unquestionably led, in many instances, to the injury
and adulteration of our poet's text.

I am the more jealous of any misconception upon
this point, because I have endeavoured in one, and
that the most considerable portion of the foregoing
pages, to exhibit Shakspeare as something more,
something higher and better, than an incomparable
dramatist. 'We are apt,' says Mrs. Montagu, in
her celebrated essay, 'to consider Shakspeare only
as a poet; but he is certainly one of the greatest
moral philosophers that ever lived.' And whence
did he become such? I answer without hesitation,
because, while he possessed the keenest natural
powers of observation, together with an unfailing
spirit of gentleness and love and universal sympathy,
he drew his philosophy from the highest and purest
source of moral truth. In like manner, Johnson
has observed, that from the writings of Shakspeare,
who *looked through* life in all its relations public and
private, 'a system of social duty may be selected.'
Would it be too much to add, that from the same

---

* For a full account of these causes, see, in the Variorum edition,
vol. i. Pope's Preface, p. 12; Theobald's do. p. 32; Sir T. Hanmer's do. p. 44; Warburton's do. p. 46; Johnson's do. pp. 91, 196.

writings may be gathered also no inconsiderable contribution towards a full and accurate system of religious doctrine ? He himself, in his modesty, would doubtless have been content to say of himself, with the Soothsayer in *Antony and Cleopatra*,

> In Nature's infinite book of secrecy
> A little I can read.

Others, I trust, will not hesitate for the future to declare in his behalf, that God's own ' infinite Book ' of Grace and Truth had not been revealed to him in vain.

Before I drop altogether the subject upon which we have been engaged, I may mention a somewhat curious coincidence, of which the reader perhaps is not aware, between the outward form of the Holy Scriptures and of the plays of Shakspeare. I allude to the fact, that originally the former were not divided into chapters and verses, nor the latter into acts and scenes. Our poet's plays were written, and at first printed, in one unbroken continuity (*Othello* being, it is said, the only exception), until Mr. Rowe, in 1709, by introducing the present divisions and subdivisions, did for them what had been done by Hugo Cardinalis, in the thirteenth century, and by Rabbi Nathan, in the fifteenth, for the Books of the Old Testament (with the exception of the Book of Psalms, which had been originally divided as we now have it), and by Robert and Henry Stephens, in the sixteenth century, for the

Books of the New Testament, by dividing them into chapters, and by prefixing to the verses the numbers which they now bear. And as the complaint has been frequently made, not without reason in some instances, that this division of the Bible, into chapters especially, while it has great advantages, is attended also with frequent inconvenience, and leads to misunderstanding and misinterpretation of God's word; so it has been remarked by Shakspeare's greatest critic, that his plays, instead of being broken up in the representation, as they now are, 'ought to be exhibited with short pauses interposed as often as the scene is changed, or any considerable time is allowed to pass;' and he adds, 'this method would at once quell a thousand absurdities.' Whether this observation is a just one, I cannot tell: only, as editions of the Bible have been called for, and published, which represent the Sacred Text printed continuously in its original form, so it would, perhaps, be desirable that the lovers of Shakspeare might have the option, if not of seeing upon the stage his plays acted in the way which Dr. Johnson has.pointed out, yet of reading them in a popular edition * arranged upon that plan. But be this also as it may; yet one opinion, at all events, I am prepared to maintain. In whatever shape the genuine plays of Shakspeare may be pre-

---

* The recent *fac simile* reprint of the first folio is a valuable movement in this direction.

sented to us, there is nothing—nothing of a literary kind—for which we have greater reason to thank the GIVER OF ALL GOOD, than for a large proportion of those works—excepting only the *Book of Common Prayer*,* and THAT, which has imparted alike to it and to them no small share of the surpassing excellence, which, though in very different ways, they both possess—HIS OWN INCOMPARABLE, MOST HOLY, EVERLASTING WORD.

---

* In confirmation of this high estimate of the *Prayer Book*, I may be allowed to quote two authorities—one clerical and the other lay— not inferior, perhaps, upon a literary question, to any who have written in the English tongue :—

'As to the greatest part of our Liturgy, there seem to be in it as great strains of true sublime eloquence as are anywhere to be found in our language.'—DEAN SWIFT, *Works*, vol. ix. p. 152.

'That great model of chaste, lofty, and pathetic eloquence, the *Book of Common Prayer*.'—LORD MACAULAY, *History*, vol. iii. p. 355.

To these testimonies it may not be out of place to add here, what I have somewhere read, that the greatest *tragedian* of the age, when asked what was the noblest composition in the English language, replied, ' The Burial Service of the Church of England.'

SUPPLEMENTARY NOTES.

PAGE 2. *Note.*

Mr. Singer perhaps alluded to the remark of Mr. Capel Lloft, in his *Aphorisms from Shakspeare,* published in 1812 :—'He (Shakspeare) had *deeply imbibed* the Scriptures.' *Introd.* p. xii.

PAGE 75.

In defence of the somewhat questionable allusion to *Nebuchad-nezzar's punishment,* it is only fair to point out that our English Theophrastus, Bishop Earle, the author of MICROCOSMOGRAPHY, has the following passage in his character of *A plain Country Fellow :—*

'He seems to have the punishment of *Nebuchadnezzar*; for his conversation* is among beasts, and his talons none of the shortest; only he eats not *grass,*† because he loves not *sallets,*' p. 64.

Before our poet is condemned for the allusion in question, let it be remembered that the author of the work from which the above (precisely parallel) passage is quoted was, in 1642, elected one of the Westminster Assembly (but refused to act); and, at the Restoration, was made Dean of Westminster, and afterwards

---

* See above, p. 32.
† 'Grass' was formerly used for 'salad.'

Bishop of Salisbury. Add to this, there was no one of that generation more universally esteemed. We have the highest character of him given by men, his contemporaries, who differed from one another so widely, as Lord Clarendon, Richard Baxter, and Isaac Walton. Walton, in his *Life of Hooker*, speaks of him in these terms:—Having had occasion to mention 'the happy pen of Dr. Earle, now Lord Bishop of Salisbury,' he adds; 'of whom I may justly say—that since Mr. Hooker died, none have lived whom God hath blessed with more innocent wisdom, more sanctified learning, or a more pious, peaceable, primitive temper; so that this excellent person seems to be only like himself, and our venerable Richard Hooker.'

PAGE 98.

I am glad to find myself supported in my opposition to the disparaging remark of Dr. Johnson by the high authority of Schlegel, who, in his notice of *King Lear*, observes that Shakspeare 'lays particular stress on the circumstance that *the Britons of that day were still heathens.*' And again : ' The persons of this drama have only such a faint belief in Providence as heathens may be supposed to have.'—*Lectures on Dramat. Literature*, vol. ii. p. 207, *sq.*

PAGE 104.

I might have added in that place, that Shakspeare has introduced the notion of Guardian Angels in *K. Henry IV. 2nd Part*, Act ii. Sc. 2.

> For the *Boy*—there is *a good Angel* about him ;—

according to the teaching of the New Testament, more particularly with reference to the young; see S. Matt. xviii. 10, and Bishop Bull's *Works*, vol. i. p. 301. But where, in the same play, Act i. Sc. 2, the Chief Justice says to Falstaff, ' You follow the young prince up and down like his *ill angel*,' our poet was either drawing merely upon his own imagination, or from what he had read· respecting the belief of the heathen in genii, or dæmons, · evil as well as good; – a belief, of which he has made use in *Antony and Cleopatra*, Act ii. Sc. 3; and again in. *Macbeth*, Act iii. Sc. 1.

PAGE 163.

I was under the impression that the notes which bear the name of HENLEY in the Variorum edition of Shakspeare were from the pen of *Dr.* Samuel Henley, who was principal of Hail-ybury College, and died about fifty years ago. Accordingly he is so designated above, in p. 90, and elsewhere. But having since observed that Mr. James Boswell, the editor of that edition, styles him ' *Mr.* Henley,' I have thought it better (not being certain of his identity) in the page here referred to, and subsequently, where his name occurs, to do the same.

PAGE 194. *Note* †.

Since that note was written I have observed among the miscellaneous poems of Sir Philip Sidney, which doubtless Shakspeare had read, the same epigram of Catullus ' Englished ' to his hand. See his *Miscellaneous Works*, p. 173. I must therefore surrender what looked to me like an evidence of the original Latin having been in the mind of our poet. An image very similar to Catullus', with the difference only between 'writing on *water* ' and ' writing on *ice*,' is to be found in some verses—called St. Bernard's verses—Latin and English, subjoined to Tusser's *Five hundred points of good husbandry*, with which, we may suppose, Shakspeare was acquainted, the first (complete) edition having been published in 1580.

Plus crede literis *scriptis in glacie*,
Quàm mundi fragilis vanæ fallaciæ.

More credit see thou give to letters *wrote in ice*,
Than unto vain deceits, of brittle world's device.

X

PAGE 222.

I have ascertained, through the kindness of the present vicar of Stratford-on-Avon, that the falsified copy of Shakspeare's will, though still in existence, is no longer exhibited among the 'relics,' which are now very properly taken under public superintendence, and committed to a responsible guardian. The forged or spurious will of which I am speaking as noticed above, in p. 222, is not to be confounded with (though it may have owed its origin to) the will of *John* Shakspeare, which purported to be that of our poet's father, though not discovered till ' about the year 1770,' and which is still more plainly upon the face of it a Romanist document. The history of its discovery, real or pretended, is curious. See Dr. Drake's *Shakspeare and his Times*, vol. i. pp. 8–16, and Mr. Malone's *Life of Shakspeare*, p. 516, *sq.* The latter concludes that the document in question, if genuine, was the will of *another* John Shakspeare—not the father, nor any relation of our poet.

PAGE 224.

That I was justified in suspecting a design, on our poet's part, to impute infidelity to the character of a Transalpine friar, may appear from a passage in Lord Burghley's *Advices to his Son* Robert Cecil, afterwards Earl of Salisbury : ' Suffer not thy sons to pass the Alps, for they shall learn nothing there but pride, blasphemy, and *Atheism*.'—See Nares' *Life of Lord Burghley*, vol. iii. p. 513 ; Peck's *Desiderata Curiosa*, p. 47.

INDEX.